CANADIAN AGRICULTURAL POLICY

Vernon C. Fowke

Canadian Agricultural Policy
The Historical Pattern

UNIVERSITY OF TORONTO PRESS
Toronto Buffalo London

Copyright Canada 1946
Reprinted in paperback 1978
Toronto Buffalo London
Printed in Canada
ISBN 0-8020-6352-7

*The publication of the first printing was assisted by a grant
from the Canadian Social Science Research Council.*

To
the memory of
FRANK NESBIT FOWKE
Canadian pioneer

PREFACE

CANADIANS are familiar with the idea that agriculture is Canada's basic industry. A statement to this effect is commonly assumed sufficient to explain the position of agriculture within the Canadian economy. In particular, such a statement is assumed sufficient to explain the agricultural policy of Canadian government. The underlying assumption is that agriculture, because of its exceptional importance within the Canadian economy, can—and always has been able to—expect exceptional consideration. An historical analysis of Canadian agricultural policy indicates the inadequacy of the prevailing concept of agriculture. Argument concerning the degree of truth in the description of agriculture as "Canada's basic industry" conceals the fact that the expression has through prolonged repetition become a *cliché*, devoid of content. Its continued ritualistic use offers no assistance towards the interpretation of Canadian agricultural policy or of the place of agriculture within the framework of the economic and political life of Canada.

In this study the hypothesis is advanced that agricultural policy can best be explained by an historical consideration of agricultural functions. Essential to an understanding of governmental treatment of the agricultural community, it is argued, is an historical knowledge of the uses to which agriculture has been put from time to time and from place to place. If we can learn why agricultural development was wanted at a particular time and place there arises the possibility of knowing why agriculture was encouraged or neglected, what groups were interested in its development, and the political pressures under which agricultural assistance was extended. In support of this contention the present volume seeks to portray the role or roles of agriculture within territories which now form the Dominion of Canada, and to relate these roles to the formation of the agricultural policies of the respective governments.

The central analysis of this volume was prepared originally as a doctoral dissertation for the University of Washington. Since its acceptance in that form by the University of Washington in 1942 the materials have been re-worked and extended. The research was carried on chiefly in Ottawa, in the Public Archives of Canada, the Parliamentary Library, and the Main Library of the Department of Agriculture; and in Toronto, in the Library of the University of Toronto, and in the Reference Department of the Toronto Public Library. The author gratefully acknowledges his indebtedness to the officials and staffs of these libraries for generous and unfailing courtesy in making their services available to him. He also acknowledges his indebtedness to the members of his advisory committee at the University of Washington for approving a research project of particular interest to a Canadian student; to the officials of the University of Toronto who made possible for the author a year's appointment at that institution under conditions which permitted very considerable research opportunities; and to the officials of the University of Saskatchewan who allowed the author leaves of absence and who assisted towards the productive utilization of those leaves.

Among the many individuals who have contributed to this study the author is particularly indebted to the following: to Dr. W. W. Swanson, former Head of the Department of Economics of the University of Saskatchewan, and to Dr. H. H. Preston, Dean of the College of Economics and Business of the University of Washington, whose continued and co-operative interest in the progress of the author's research served to untangle many a knotty problem; to Dr. H. A. Innis for the opportunity of spending a year at the University of Toronto where frequent consultations with him and other members of the staff and access to suitable library facilities gave direction and meaning to the author's researches; to Professors M. M. Skinner, Henry A. Burd, Joseph Demmery, and Vernon Mund of the University of Washington for careful reading and helpful criticism of the thesis manuscript; to Professor V. W. Bladen for editorial advice and for assistance in the conduct of arrangements for publication; and to Mrs. Hewitt and her staff for meticulous editorial assistance.

The author gratefully acknowedges his debt to the Canadian Social Science Research Council for the generous financial assistance which contributed to the completion of the research involved in this study and which now renders its publication possible. The comments and careful criticisms of the Council's panel of readers provided most helpful guidance in the re-working of the materials of the original dissertation into the form of the present study.

VERNON C. FOWKE.

University of Saskatchewan,
October, 1945.

TABLE OF CONTENTS

PART ONE

THE PRE-CONFEDERATION PERIOD

CHAPTER I

THE HISTORICAL ROLE OF CANADIAN AGRICULTURE*

THE significant features of Canadian agricultural policy become apparent only as the historical functions of Canadian agriculture are understood. The common impression that the colonies of the British North American mainland were, from their beginning and until comparatively recent times, basically self-sufficient agricultural economies, is incorrect and renders impossible an understanding of the purposes of governmental assistance to Canadian agriculture. Assistance to agriculture has been consistently recognized as a function of government at all times in areas which now form part of the Dominion of Canada. Had colonial agriculture approached self-sufficiency, neither buying nor selling, it would not have attracted governmental assistance. Agriculture was aided, not because it was the chief colonial activity, but in order that it might more fully contribute towards the chief colonial activities.

The clearest and most significant uniformity regarding Canadian agriculture for more than three hundred years has been its deliberate and consistent use as a basis for economic and political empire.[1] Towards this end it has been fostered, moulded, and supported by legislation and public moneys. It has served as an instrument of empire in different ways according to the requirements of place and time. Simplest and most obvious has been its use as a defence device, where settlement has been encouraged for the protection of territory

---

*The substance of this chapter formed part of a paper read at the joint session of the Canadian Historical Association and the Canadian Political Science Association at their annual meeting at Kingston, May 22, 1941, and published in the *Canadian Journal of Economics and Political Science,* February, 1942, under the title "An Introduction to the History of Canadian Agriculture." It is here adapted with editorial permission.

[1] We might add ecclesiastical empire to the economic and political, at least for the duration of the French régime. Agriculture was as important for the establishment and expansion of Church domain in the New World as it was for that of commerce and temporal authority. Church leaders were active in the formulation of agricultural policies. When the young men of the colony took to the life of the woods instead of settling on farms and raising large families, they thereby robbed the community of some of the benefits anticipated from a flourishing local agriculture. No group was more vigorous in the condemnation of the *coureur de bois* than was the Church.

and trade routes. Equally widespread has been its use as the provisioner of the great staple trades, whether of fish, fur, sugar, or timber, or of the carrying trade itself. Provisioning, of course, has been partly a defence function, since in the economic conflict of competitive empires, notably the English and the French, survival necessitated a degree of commercial vitality possible only on a strong agricultural base. A significant change occurred, probably within the past hundred years, when Canadian agriculture finally achieved direct commercial importance as the provider of a staple product, wheat. With this development there came to be a Canadian agricultural frontier in the sense that agriculture now offered to commerce, finance, and industry the vitality which can derive only from an ever-expanding circumference of economic activity and the investment opportunities associated therewith. It is suggested, therefore, that Canadian agriculture over the centuries has been an instrument of commercial and political empire in three ways:[2] first, as a means for the defence of territory and trade routes; second, as a provisioner of the great staple trades; and third, as the provider of investment opportunities on the agricultural frontier.

The relationship between agriculture and empire was sharply projected, from the earliest days of North American settlement, in the light of the long and bitter struggle between the French and the English for New World dominance. Codfish, fur, sugar, slaves, provisions, and shipping occupied similar positions in the commercial plans of the French and the English, and trade in these goods and services in turn required provisioning. In the intensely competitive staple markets the relative cheapness and abundance of the salable staple were largely determined by the relative abundance of contributory agricultural supplies. More than that, territory and trade routes needed defence, for military conflict was inseparable from economic conflict.

Settlement of the St. Lawrence, and the introduction of the seigniorial system, were imperative in the vain hope that French

---

[2]Significance may also attach to the role of Canadian agriculture as a reservoir of surplus labour for industry, commerce, and the professions. This approach offers interesting possibilities for historical analysis, beginning with the earliest days of North American settlement. From the very beginnings the colonists on the St. Lawrence forsook their grants and meagre clearings to take part in the fur trade; later to go to the timber bush, and later still to the factories.

fur-trade routes might be adequately garrisoned against the constant harassing of Iroquois-European alliances. Until 1713 French hopes for an agricultural basis of empire rested on the possibilities of Acadia as well as of the St. Lawrence; and with some justification, for the diked marshes of the Bay of Fundy gave somewhat the same grudging tolerance to primitive animal husbandry as the St. Lawrence region did to cereal husbandry. The Treaty of Utrecht, however, was proof of the relative ineffectiveness of French agriculture in the two areas; and by its terms the balance was shifted still further in favour of the English with the transference to English control of the Acadian agricultural regions. Establishment of Halifax and colonization of Lunenburg were English defence moves effective in countering French aggressiveness at the middle of the eighteenth century; but of more fundamental importance in the final French withdrawal from the St. Lawrence and Cape Breton was the agricultural backwardness of New France as compared with New England. The New England colonies early developed agricultural resources more than sufficient to provision the British staple trades. France could scarcely withstand an opponent upon whom she continuously relied for foodstuffs.

The functional relationship between New World agriculture and commercial and territorial empire is clear throughout the French régime. After 1763, and particularly after 1783, however, inter-relationships of agricultural and other interests in British North America appear more complex. The predominant economic phenomenon associated with the conquest was the commercial revitalization of the St. Lawrence by Anglo-American traders; but agriculture too was improved, and this enough to establish the self-sufficiency of the St. Lawrence settlements which the French had sought in vain. Thereafter, despite the persistent efforts of Montreal commercial interests further to improve habitant agriculture, French settlements remained at the level of self-sufficiency, not called on to provision the fur trade or the timber trade, and failing even to provision Montreal. Population growth was largely cared for by movement into the fur and timber trades of Canada, the timber trade of Michigan, and finally the textile industry of the New England states.

Turning attention back to 1783, the influx of settlement tended to diversify New World agriculture. The impetus given by Loyalists and post-Loyalists was a divisive as well as a creative force. New

Brunswick was set apart from Nova Scotia, and Upper Canada from Lower Canada. Timber preferences introduced by Britain after 1800 created farmer-lumberman economies in the St. John and Ottawa River valleys which differed from each other and from agricultural economies in other areas. The establishment of the Selkirk settlement in the western territories added a final element of agricultural diversity. At this point there is ready agreement with the statement that ". . . the history of British North America before 1867 must resolve itself into histories of the various regions, if not of the separate provinces."[3]

If, however, there is need for detailed studies of agricultural development after 1783, related to particular places and times, there is also need to search for the underlying unity of the problem. Viewed in relation to commercial empire, the varied agriculture of the British North American colonies retained the unity which characterized it in the French period. At least until 1825 its essential functions were the defence of territory and trade routes, and the provisioning of the staple trades. Settlement of Loyalists and of disbanded soldiers, first at the upper posts and later along the upper St. Lawrence, was clearly a joint provisioning and defensive move,[4] carefully fostered to feed the garrisons and to form a barrier of loyal British subjects against the subversive influences of enemies of the Empire. The "strategic motive" was evident in plans for settlement after 1812.[5] Though timber replaced fur as the staple of the St. Lawrence after 1800, and was added to cod as a staple for the Maritimes, the need for defence and provisions remained. The timber trade made additional use of immigration and settlement as a means of providing cargoes for west-bound timber ships. As settlement and agricultural production gathered momentum in Upper Canada, particularly after the War of 1812, traders in Montreal gradually built up *entrepôt* facilities and established agencies to handle the trickle of inward and outward traffic, a trickle which grew in volume as Upper Canadian agriculture became less and less self-sufficient and finally forced its recognition as a fully-grown export economy.

[3]Lower, *The North American Assault on the Canadian Forest*, p. 64.

[4]Innis and Lower (eds.), *Select Documents, 1783-1885*, pp. 10-11, 18-20; Burt, *The Old Province of Quebec*, chap. xv.

[5]Lower, "Immigration and Settlement in Canada, 1812-20" (*Canadian Historical Review*, March, 1922), pp. 37-47.

In the Maritime colonies from 1783 to 1850, the provisioning function of agriculture was more in evidence than that of territorial defence. The prime economic interest of Nova Scotia remained centred in the cod fisheries, trade, and ship-building; and the intense commercial competition with Newfoundland and New England could be maintained only on the basis of cheap provisions for the fisheries and cheap, assorted trade cargoes requiring agricultural produce— grains and meats, horses, and cattle. New Brunswick timber camps required provisions, and here appeared the anomaly of "farmers" buying farm produce with which to carry on timbering and ship-building operations. Boston readily offered cheap provisions, but mercantile groups in New Brunswick distrusted such lack of independence and attributed the recurring crises which characterized the timber trade to the persistent specie drain associated with food imports. Prince Edward Island became a genuine agricultural colony, partially provisioning Nova Scotia and New Brunswick, supplying horses and hay for lumber camps and cattle for the Newfoundland trade. No aspect of Canadian agricultural policy in the period 1783-1850 is more interesting than that of the attempts of Maritime commercial interests to encourage domestic agriculture, attempts which included example, cajolery, evangelical persuasiveness, warnings, threats, and all varieties of petty cash assistance.

Considering Canadian agriculture as auxiliary to commerce, the period 1850-1930 forms a unit. It is uncertain when exports of Canadian wheat first reached the proportions of a staple trade, but the commercial character of the annexation movement of 1849, following the removal of colonial wheat preferences, indicates that such proportions had been reached by 1850. Having come to be recognized as the originator of a new staple trade, Canadian agriculture assumed an additional and more direct relationship to commercial activity. Provisioning and defence functions survived; but with the ability to provide a staple for commerce, the agriculture of the St. Lawrence came increasingly to fill the gap left by the decline of fur and later of timber, in contributing to commerce the dynamic of the frontier. Fur had ceased to vitalize the St. Lawrence even before 1821, for the fur frontier had halted at the Arctic and the Pacific. Timber had similarly failed by 1850, with the shrinkage of timber preferences, though this failure was disguised for some time by the profitable nature of the associated commerce in great droves of immigrants. With the collapse of immigration after 1847 the reliance of St. Lawrence commerce and finance on the agricultural frontier became evident. The suggestion here is that from 1850 to 1930 the commercial, financial, and later the industrial groups on the St. Lawrence pinned their first hopes for prosperity on the possibility of continued expansion of staple-producing agriculture.

To corroborate this suggestion there may be cited the efforts of St. Lawrence interests to tap the American frontier by means of canals and railways, to create a Canadian agricultural frontier in the Ottawa-Huron tract, and finally to assure, by the instrument of Confederation, that the western territories be prevented from falling prey to the commerce of the eastern United States. The Canadian Bureau of Agriculture, created in 1852, was charged specifically with the encouragement of immigration from other countries. In the ten years preceding Confederation thirteen committees reported to the Assembly of the Province of Canada on various aspects of immigration and colonization, but only when they mentioned the agricultural possibilities of the West does one sense a glimmer of hope in their deliberations. The groundwork for the eventual fulfilment of these hopes was laid gradually over the decades: by investigation and exploration—the investigation of the Hudson's Bay Company's administration by the British House of Commons, and the exploration of the western territories by Palliser, Dawson, and Hind; by the consummation of Confederation, the constitutional medium for the empire-colony relationship contemplated within British North America; by Canadian acquisition of the western territories, and by the placing of western lands in federal custody for the so-called "purposes of the Dominion"; by the construction of a transcontinental, all-Canadian railroad; by the institution of the "National Policy" of tariff protection, to canalize the flow of economic benefits from the western plains, up and over the natural barrier north of Lake Superior, and into the central Canadian regions; and finally by the establishment of the experimental farm system to hasten the migration northward of American techniques for the agricultural conquest of the prairie. By 1890 all these steps had been taken, and only the long-anticipated results were lacking. Not till after 1900 were the pre-Confederation hopes for an abundant export-agriculture in the West fully realized. From 1900 till 1930 western agriculture expanded within the Canadian economy, absolutely and relatively, providing in the accompanying investment opportunities the chief basis of Canadian prosperity; but with the rise of newsprint and minerals, western agriculture had by 1930 relinquished the frontier role to these newer staple industries.

This is the essential background for a study of the agricultural policy of Canadian government. There is little justification for the general impression that down through the generations the embattled Canadian farmer has won grudging concessions from the entrenched interests of commerce, finance, and industry, either by the pressure of endless complaint or by an appeal to reason and justice. The Canadian farmer has had political power, but this power has varied in proportion to the contribution which agriculture could make, at any given time, to the cause of commerce, finance, and industry, rather than in proportion to farmers' numbers or their state of organization.

CHAPTER II

THE FRENCH RÉGIME: DEFENCE AND PROVISIONS

THE functional analysis put forward in Chapter I makes possible an interpretation of the agricultural policy of government throughout the various periods of Canadian history. This interpretation must be elaborated in relation to the circumstances of time and place. A brief analysis of the French régime goes far to substantiate the interpretation of the role of Canadian agriculture which is suggested in Chapter I and to indicate the significance of that role in the analysis of state benefactions to early Canadian rural economy.

1. Mercantilism in the New World

Earliest settlements in the New World developed under the sponsorship of competitive imperial European powers. As colonies, or potential colonies, these settlements were necessarily shaped in the mould of the prevailing mercantilistic doctrine and practice of the day. Colonies were designed to serve the interests of their respective mother countries, and local development was to be tolerated or encouraged in proportion as it served these interests. As their name suggests, the mercantilists stressed the mercantile pursuits, identifying the prosperity of the merchant class with national strength, prosperity, and general economic health. Their doctrine of the favourable balance of trade made sense in a situation where commercial rivalry between empires lapsed naturally and persistently into military and naval rivalry, and where—an effective degree of patriotism being non-existent—it was necessary to pay soldiers and sailors a competitive wage in "hard" money. Specie imports under such conditions spelled greater national strength, and specie exports, unless compensated for by conquest or production, spelled national peril. To the extent that agricultural products entered only slightly into international trade, thus apparently contributing but little toward the balance of trade, the mercantilists considered agriculture to be of negligible economic importance, and as occupying a position roughly at the bottom of the hierarchy of economic usefulness.

The discovery of the Americas, and early indications of their potential riches, gave added impetus to mercantile principles and their application to colonial situations. Spanish contacts with the New World by way of the West Indies and Central America started a flow of precious metals eastward toward Spain and, indirectly, toward the Old World in general. With these new sources of specie, Spain was enabled to expand military and naval establishments on a basis so lavish as to threaten increasingly to displace the precarious balance of power among the leading nations of western Europe. Britain, France, and Holland, individually and competitively, were hard put to meet the situation. Obviously some means were needed whereby to match the specie wealth of Spain. Britain, France, and Holland were as promptly interested in the New World as was Spain, but their contacts were with northern areas where sources of precious metals were not unearthed, despite considerable search and the occasional stirring of false hopes. Indications were that the surest way in which England, for instance, could match the growing flood of Spanish gold and silver was to divert that flood, or as large a proportion of it as possible, into her own national coffers. Piracy, preying upon the Spanish treasure convoys, offered one means to this end. Mercantilistic practices offered another. Spanish gold might be acquired through the processes of trade provided the country in question, England, for example, could export more goods and services to Spain than she imported from Spain. Spain would be required to balance the account with gold. From such reasoning, and under circumstances altered by New World discoveries, the mercantilists found their policies increasingly acceptable to the statesmen of England, France, and Holland; and even of Spain, for the natural defence against mercantilism has always been more mercantilism. Colonial policy, accordingly, came to be an important segment of mercantilistic policy. Colonies were held useful and desirable to the extent that they contributed to the trade and commerce of the mother country, but more particularly, to the extent that they contributed to trade with Spain. Colonies were particularly desirable which offered a product or products urgently needed in Spain, or a product which would replace imports formerly obtained from Spain.

Though yielding no precious metals, the northern areas of America fitted well into the prospects of the merchants of England, France, and Holland. Cabot's voyages of discovery revealed the potential wealth in fisheries surrounding Newfoundland, for dried cod had long been important in Catholic Europe, deficient in protein agriculture and in storage and preservative facilities for perishable foodstuffs. Cartier's voyages in 1534 and 1535 established the knowledge of the St. Lawrence as a gateway to the continent, and revealed the natives already well acquainted with trade in furs. Codfish and furs offered possibilities for profitable trade, and the former commodity had the added appeal of a particular entrée to the Spanish market. By the end of the sixteenth century the trade in fancy furs had given way to the much more substantial trade in staple fur, with the establishment in Paris of the fashion for beaver hats. Also, with the development of the dry-fishery, with its exacting shore requirements, the French had increasingly sought the mainland fisheries and coincidentally had developed the trade in furs on a more and more significant scale.

Where, in this unfolding of opportunity for merchants and carriers, for mercantilistic statesmen and empire builders, is there scope or function for colonial agriculture? Cartier found agricultural Indians on the St. Lawrence when he travelled inland as far as Hochelaga. Three-quarters of a century later, when Champlain traced out Cartier's steps, no agricultural Indians were left on the St. Lawrence. The Huron-Iroquois groups were scattered westward beyond Lake Simcoe and to the south of Lake Ontario. The few agricultural products cultivated by these Indians—maize, beans, squash, and tobacco—had no direct interest for European merchants with an infinitely greater range of domestic plants and animals cultivated throughout their native lands. European merchants were interested in the cod of the western Atlantic; the tobacco, sugar, and indigo of the West Indies and southern mainland; and, as for the northern mainland, the prize lay in the apparently limitless fur trade. Except for the production of semi-tropical products such as tobacco and sugar, which should probably be classed as agricultural products, colonial agriculture in the New World developed as a subordinate enterprise, tolerated only where it contributed to the major commercial interests. Where, however, potential contributions were obvious, encouragement of considerable proportions was lavished upon it. Territory which is now Canada was, in early colonial days, most closely connected with the fur trade and the fisheries, and early agriculture in these areas was accordingly related primarily to these pursuits. An analysis of this relationship is fundamental; but there were also important interrelationships between the agriculture of the St. Lawrence and Acadian regions, on the one hand, and the semi-tropical trades, such as sugar and tobacco, on the other, and these, too, require analysis.

By the end of the sixteenth century official France was persuaded that Cartier's explorations of the New World mainland were worth exploitation. It would be presumptuous to suggest that this persuasion was solely on economic grounds. French interests in the New World were complex, relating to desires for territorial and ecclesiastical expansion, as well as for commercial advantage. That individuals sought new scope for personal advancement as well does not detract from their oft-times sincere determination that the French territorial empire, with its secular and clerical institutions, with its political and economic opportunities, should be greatly expanded. The relative weight to be assigned to these elements of French imperialism, or to the corresponding elements of English and other imperialism, as touching on northern North America, cannot be stated or even guessed at here. Empire may be territorial and political; economic, or commercial; and even ecclesiastical. Agriculture in the colonies was auxiliary to empire in all its facets. It was prerequisite to lasting empire, whether territorial, ecclesiastical, or commercial.

2. *Agricultural Development in New France, 1598-1659*

Whatever the other elements involved, the revival of French interest in America at the end of the sixteenth century coincided with the development of the fur trade to a position of substantial importance.[1] In 1598 a Brittany nobleman, the Marquis de la Roche, was appointed "lieutenant-general and governor of the countries of Canada, Hochelaga, Newfoundland, Labrador, the River of the Great Bay, Norembega, and of the countries adjacent to the said territories and rivers."[2] La Roche was given powers to match the sweep of the territories involved. Among these powers was permission to grant land in the form of seigniories "to be held in such manner as he shall deem in keeping with their services, and on such terms and conditions as shall conduce to the defence of the said countries. . . ."[3] In return for the powers and privileges of the

1Innis, *The Fur Trade in Canada*, pp. 20 ff.
2As cited by Munro, *Seigniorial System in Canada*, p. 18.
3*Ibid.*, p. 19.

grant, La Roche was obligated to transport settlers to the designated territories at his own expense. In a desperate attempt to satisfy this obligation he resorted to the Rouen jails, embarked some scores of "settlers" only to leave sixty of them stranded on Sable Island where five years later less than a dozen survived.

Certain features of this incident are significant from the standpoint of agriculture and agricultural policy. Munro states specifically that La Roche was attracted to the St. Lawrence "as a favorable field for the exploitation of the fur trade,"[4] and that he was simply the first of a long list of those who came forward in the first quarter of the seventeenth century, "all professing eagerness to try their hands at the establishment of settlements in Canada in return for a monopoly of the fur trade."[5] Concerning these individuals Munro adds: "To one after another the desired opportunity was given; but in each case it took but a few years to show that the real aim was to exploit the fur trade for personal enrichment, and that there was little or no sincere desire to undertake the much less lucrative work of serious colonization. In vain the king revoked one monopoly and granted another."[6] The primacy of the fur trade, of the commercial interest in the New World, is obvious. Almost equally clear is the official French conception of agriculture and settlement as instruments of empire, or, more concisely, as a mechanism of defence for colonial enterprise. La Roche, for example, was permitted to exercise wide discretion regarding the terms to be imposed on those to whom he granted seigniories, waiving these terms in certain circumstances "excepting always the duty of service in time of war."[7]

A paradox appears. The fur trade required defence, and such defence rested on agricultural settlement on the St. Lawrence. But fur traders did not aid settlement, nor even favour it. Part of the failure of New France lay in the fact that the fur trade could not live without strong agricultural settlement, and could not—or would not—live with it. Fur trade and agriculture have had a long history of such incompatibility. Settlers killed beaver and destroyed their habitat, partly for profit and partly to preserve their hay meadows. Moreover, they persisted in trading in pelts as a side line, thus constantly undermining monopoly grants. The transportation of settlers and settlers' effects, and of the provisions necessary to sustain

[4] *Ibid.*, p. 18.   [5] *Ibid.*, p. 19.   [6] *Ibid.*, pp. 19-20.   [7] *Ibid.*, p. 19.

them in the early years, further intensified the natural one-sidedness of the ocean traffic associated with the fur trade. Nevertheless, fur-trade routes could not be held without an agricultural basis for garrisons, provisions, and arms-bearers. After the destruction of the Huron middlemen, the French were forced inland to perform their own middleman functions. *Coureurs de bois* became prevalent and formed the core of the labour force in the fur trade. Farm families were an obvious source of this necessary labour.

Settlement on the St. Lawrence was almost negligible until the sixteen-sixties, despite repeated monopoly grants of the fur trade conditioned by settlement obligations. By 1627 only three seigniorial grants had been made. The Company of One Hundred Associates, during its tenure of privilege between 1633 and 1663, made only sixty such grants, of which two-thirds were never occupied.[8] Individuals and companies promised settlement only as a means of obtaining trade monopoly, and none was willing or able to fulfil the settlement pledge. Nevertheless, settlement was a prerequisite to safe commerce in furs and to the establishment and maintenance of new territorial and ecclesiastical outposts. The question was one of securing the trade route of the St. Lawrence against the inroads of the Iroquois-Dutch (and after 1664, of the Iroquois-English) alliance. True, the fur trade could be conducted at Tadoussac, without dependence on the St. Lawrence, but this involved reliance upon the tedious head-water route through the interior and down the Saguenay. Development of a satisfactory trade, even while the Hurons survived to act as middlemen, required safe conduct of the St. Lawrence and the Ottawa rivers. Settlements at Three Rivers and Montreal followed the one at Quebec, but agricultural bases were inadequate. The dispersion of the Huron tribes (the middlemen of the French fur trade) by the Iroquois in 1648 and 1649 threw the issue into sharp relief. Defence projects had failed. Drastic steps were necessary to secure the St. Lawrence if the trade were not to be abandoned. Salutary action came only after 1663 when intensified military action was coupled with intensified settlement measures.

Official language indicates clearly the defence function attaching to French settlement and agriculture in America from the earliest times. We have noted the emphasis on the defence aspects of La

8*Ibid.*, p. 25.

Roche's grant of 1598. Monopoly privileges were awarded the Company of One Hundred Associates in 1627 in return for settlement promises, "Having in view," said the preamble to the charter, "the establishment of a powerful colony in order that New France with all its dependencies may, once for all, become a dependency of the crown without any danger of its being seized by the king's enemies—as might be the case if precautionary measures are not taken against such a contingency—and wishing, likewise, to remedy the faults of the past, since under the management of individuals who possessed the whole of its trade the country has been left uncultivated and almost wholly void of population."[9] In view of these considerations, and in return for a monopoly of the fur trade, the company agreed to transport to New France two or three hundred men of all trades during the first year, and four thousand within fifteen years; to provide these men with shelter and subsistence for three years (or enough cleared land to live on), corn for the first seeding, and subsistence until the first harvest.[10] The failure of this company to provide settlement and defence made the French authorities eager to accept the surrender of its charter in 1663, reasoning that, "Instead of finding that this country is settled as it ought to be after so long an occupation thereof by our subjects, we have learned with regret not only that the number of its inhabitants is very limited, but that even these are every day in danger of annihilation by the Iroquois."[11]

3. The Seigniorial System

Agriculture and agricultural settlement were not sufficient in themselves for the defence of the St. Lawrence pathway of empire. Agricultural organization played its part. Munro states that "Seigniorialism was transplanted to Canada simply because it existed almost everywhere at home."[12] The same author, however, hastens to point out that the significant features of the system as transplanted to Canada were those relating to defence and military strength.[13] French seigniorialism by the sixteenth century was well on the way to uselessness, and by the beginning of the seventeenth century it

9*Ibid.*, p. 22.
10Salone, *La Colonisation de la Nouvelle-France*, pp. 39 ff.
11The King's edict as cited by Munro, *Seigniorial System in Canada*, p. 27.
12*Documents relating to Seigniorial Tenure in Canada*, p. xix.
13*Ibid.*, p. xxi.

had developed abuses, such as absenteeism, which later rendered the whole edifice intolerable. The natural European product of the absence of strong central authority, providing as it did an organization readily convertible into a military instrument, the seigniorial system found in New France an environment of perpetual alarm which rendered its defensive capabilities of particular importance. The various aspects of feudalism in New France—its military nature, its new simplicity, the fact that the seignior lived on his domain and with his people—these, says Munro, "serve to give to Canadian seigniorialism a form and spirit very much like that of pristine feudalism shorn of the excrescences which in France barnacled its later days."[14] The fact that the obligation to render military service is not specified in seigniorial grants made by the French crown is not proof that such an obligation was either non-existent or ineffective. Correspondence between the homeland and the colony indicates clearly that the French government relied on the military service of all colonists, whether landholders or not.[15] In taking the oath of fealty, seigniors pledged their service in arms whenever required, and disbanded soldiers were settled on the land on seigniorial terms, the unchallenged assumption being that they would be available there at all times to resist attack. Indeed, Munro adds: "During the greater part of the French régime the seigniors were forced by the stern logic of facts to be in constant readiness to defend their seigniories,"[16] and in the absence of strong central forces, the defence of the colony, of its population, territories, trade routes, and missions rested largely on the defence of the seigniories by the seigniors and their dependents. Seigniors built manor houses designed to serve as fortresses, and favoured retired soldiers as grantees of their lands, for with their experience in warfare and the possession of muskets the latter might instruct and even lead the other inhabitants of the seigniory in times of danger.

The dispersion of the Huron tribes by the Iroquois in the mid-seventeenth century, with the accompanying complete disruption of the French fur trade, made clear the most urgent requirement of the French commercial, political, and ecclesiastical empire on the St. Lawrence. Grant after grant of settlement-conditioned fur-trade

[14]Ibid.
[15]Munro, Seigniorial System in Canada, pp. 65-6.
[16]Ibid., p. 66.

monopoly had failed to ensure the St. Lawrence trade route, and unless adequate protection could be promptly established the hopes of empire in all its aspects would have to be abandoned.

4. *Settlement on the St. Lawrence, 1659-73*

Not till 1663 were Louis XIV and Colbert able to persuade the Company of One Hundred Associates to yield its charter rights, but for several years prior to this surrender the King and his ministers had concerned themselves directly and actively in the affairs of the colony, and had set in operation the first system of agricultural assistance to make any appreciable impression on the urgent problem of colonial defence. In 1659 Louis XIV pledged himself to send to the colony three hundred persons per year for ten years.[17] For six years, till 1664, when New France was handed over to the West Indies Company, this pledge was kept, at least three hundred persons being transported to New France yearly; though the colonists were not well chosen and, packed as they were into unsanitary ships, smallpox wasted as many as one-third of the numbers in particular years. Louis XIV and his minister, Colbert, thought of colonization in terms of families capable of agricultural settlement. Talon and the Council at Quebec favoured the system of indentured labour. The two schemes went on side by side, indentured labourers going to New France at this period to a total of one hundred per year.[18] When the West Indies Company assumed the charter rights to trade in New France in 1664, the French King turned over to the Company the selection and transportation of the colonists, but continued to pay costs on the basis of 100 *livres* per person.[19] The period of substantial and subsidized agricultural colonization in New France, inaugurated by the French crown in 1659, came to an end in 1673 with the transportation of a group of seventy women, which brought to a total of 4,000 the number of new inhabitants received by the colony during the fifteen-year period.[20] From the bare beginnings of a colony of from two to three hundred in 1640, New France increased in population to 2,500 in 1663, 3,215 in 1665, and 6,705 in 1673.[21]

[17]Salone, *La Colonisation de la Nouvelle-France*, p. 143.
[18]*Ibid.*, pp. 156-8.
[19]*Ibid.*, pp. 156 ff.   For two years, 1666 and 1673, the Company bore this cost.
[20]*Ibid.*, p. 169.
[21]*Ibid.*, pp. 63, 109; Munro, *Seigniorial System in Canada*, p. 72.

Costs of this colonization were considerable. The basic outlay of 100 *livres* per person provided for the following: recruitment, 10 *livres*; provision of wearing apparel, 30 *livres*; and transportation, 60 *livres*.[22] Selection and transportation completed, the settlers had to be established on the land. They were provided with clothing, tools for cultivation, and subsistence for one, two, or even more years as need existed.[23] In some cases lands were cleared and even planted. Some were paid for clearing and sowing two arpents of land at 40 *livres* per arpent. To some settlers, houses were presented, as to the members of the last six companies of the Carignan regiment. Not only the indigent, but even army officers, were encouraged by means of direct cash subsidies to go to the colony.

Military settlement during this period greatly strengthened New France, and its incidents exemplify the defence aspects of agriculture in the colony. Following the near-annihilation of the Huron tribes the Iroquois group had gathered such predatory strength that gradual settlement could not be counted on to check them. Military action was imperative on a scale hitherto unknown in the colony. A few soldiers had been sent out, forty in 1642 and sixty in 1644.[24] In 1648, the year of the Huron massacre, the effective garrison of New France comprised twelve soldiers at Quebec, ten at Montreal, six at Three Rivers, and a *camp volant* of forty men—sixty-eight in all.[25] In 1651, 105 soldiers were sent out.[26] Following repeated requests from the colonists over the succeeding years substantial military action was finally taken in 1665 in the dispatch to the colony of the Carignan-Salières regiment of 1,200 men.[27] After a few years of military operations conducted by the newly arrived forces, the Iroquois were persuaded to make a peace satisfactory to the French, and the question was, what to do with the regiment, its mission fulfilled. Talon cited Roman experience in military colonization and urged upon the French officials an elaborate plan for the settlement of the soldiers and officers of the regiment in the colony to swell its numbers and assure its continued defence.[28] French officials favoured the plan and Talon arranged to grant seigniories to the officers who in turn should sub-grant lands to the soldiers. Strategic considera-

22Salone, *La Colonisation de la Nouvelle-France*, p. 159.

23*Ibid.*, pp. 174-5.   24*Ibid.*, p. 93.   25*Ibid.*   26*Ibid.*, p. 94.

27Munro, *Seigniorial System in Canada*, p. 67.

28*Ibid.*, pp. 69-71, and *Documents relating to Seigniorial Tenure in Canada*, pp. xxxiii ff.

tions led to the location of the grants along the Richelieu River, a constant threat from southern enemies. Between 1668 and 1672 seigniories were granted to twenty-five or thirty officers, and lands to over four hundred non-commissioned officers and soldiers. Cash grants facilitated development, 1,200 *livres* being divided among the officers. The grants contained no mention of military service, though the preamble to each title deed stated the royal expectation that the settlement of the officers would strengthen the colony's defence.[29]

5. *Problems of Procreation*

Military settlement, however, and even the agricultural settlement of general immigration, offered but a partial solution to the strengthening of the colony on an agricultural base. Population increase should progressively come from within. But New France suffered from the typical frontier shortage of women, and officials both locally and at home recognized the need to adjust the balance. Talon sought to have groups of women sent out particularly in connection with the programme of military settlement, "strong and vigorous peasant girls for the soldiers and fifteen demoiselles, or ladies of gentle birth, for the unmarried officers who had now become seigniors of New France."[30] The King sent out numbers of women from year to year: for example, 100 in 1665, 200 in 1666, 150 in 1669,[31] and 500 between 1669 and 1673 inclusive.[32] In 1667 Talon complained of the old men and infants sent out, and secured Colbert's promise to send in future only men between the ages of sixteen and forty, and women healthy, strong, not unattractive, "à l'âge de la génération," and, except for those from religious orphanages, accompanied by testimony of good character.[33] Salone states that nothing but the prospect of getting a husband would have sufficed to persuade any considerable numbers of women to go to New France.[34] As proof of the success of female transportation, however, Munro cites Laval's report of 1,100 baptisms in the colony in 1672.[35] Female immigrants were looked to also as a means towards internal order in New

[29]Munro, *Seigniorial System in Canada*, p. 70.
[30]*Ibid.*, p. 71.
[31]Innis (ed.), *Select Documents, 1497–1783*, pp. 291-3.
[32]Munro, *Seigniorial System in Canada*, p. 72.
[33]Salone, *La Colonisation de la Nouvelle-France*, p. 163.
[34]*Ibid.*, p. 160.
[35]*Seigniorial System in Canada*, p. 72.

France, since they would "marry a number of persons who cannot find any wives here, and who create a thousand disorders in the settlements of their neighbors, and especially in the more distant places, where the women are very glad to have several husbands when the men cannot get even one wife."[36]

Regulations of the period suggest that the provision of potential wives was insufficient at times to ensure marriage, and, further, to ensure that marriage would be fruitful even when undertaken. Regular soldiers needed no urging to marry, but volunteers caused concern.[37] Looking forward to a life in the woods when their years of service might be completed, marriage and agicultural settlement held few attractions for them. Talon ordered that a volunteer whose three years of service were ended, and who was not married within fifteen days of the arrival of a boat bearing women, would lose the rights to trade and hunt. The King ordered financial penalties for parents in the colony who failed to marry their sons before the age of twenty and their daughters before the age of sixteen, and the Council required, in 1670, a biennial report from such parents, stating reasons for their tardiness, on pain of fine. Men of twenty years or under who married were to receive the "King's Gift" of 20 *livres*.[38] Inhabitants with ten legitimate living children, not priests or nuns, were to receive 300 *livres* per year, and those with twelve, 400 *livres* per year. In 1670 the King of France spent 6,000 *livres* in these bounties and in *cadeux de noces*.[39] The Sovereign Council was asked to show preference to the heads of the largest households in apportioning parish and village administration posts.[40]

6. Agricultural Experiment and Demonstration

Vigorous agricultural development, however, required more than population, dwelling houses, and cleared land. Newcomers needed to learn of the agricultural peculiarities of the country, and to stock their clearings with domestic plants and animals adaptable to the new conditions. Talon gave the first official recognition in New France to the idea involved in model, demonstration, or experimental farms. In 1666, in the villages and hamlets which he prepared for

---

[36]Innis (ed.), *Select Documents, 1497-1783*, p. 294.
[37]Salone, *La Colonisation de la Nouvelle-France*, pp. 169 ff.
[38]*Ibid.*, See also Innis (ed.), *Select Documents, 1497-1783*, pp. 293-4.
[39]Salone, *La Colonisation de la Nouvelle-France*, p. 170.
[40]Innis (ed.), *Select Documents, 1497-1783*, p. 294.

settlers in the suburbs of Quebec, he reserved lots for "old-timers" capable of teaching newcomers how best to till the soil.[41] In 1667 he dispersed new soldier settlers among former settlers and announced this as considered policy for the future. By 1671 on his own property on the St. Charles River he maintained horses and a fine herd of horned cattle. He had a great nursery where he raised all sorts of poultry—turkey cocks, ducks, geese, pigeons, and bustards —for distribution among the inhabitants.[42] He was interested in introducing new cultures in plant life as well. He planted hops on his farm, and, constructing a brewery, made beer, twice enough for the colony in 1671.[43] In 1666 he planted hemp and distributed hemp seed. He seized all yarn in the colony and gave it only to those who promised to repay in hemp.[44] When some had been persuaded to grow hemp, he hastily bought their crops in order to induce others, too, to produce it.

The decade more or less of intensive French efforts to colonize New France, which ended in 1673, saw equally intensive efforts to establish in the colony the foundation of an abundant livestock. Champlain had imported cattle in the early years of the century, as well as having planted grains and vegetables to test the productive qualities of the soil.[45] In 1665 there was one horse in the colony. The census of 1666 indicated that a population of 3,215 possessed 3,107 head of oxen and cows, with a few pigs, donkeys, sheep, and dogs.[46] Attempts to domesticate the moose and beaver failed. Colbert and Talon undertook to increase the total numbers of livestock. As with settlers, similarly with animals, the Company of West Indies procured them—i.e., bought and shipped—the King paid the bill, and Talon supervised their arrival and disposal.[47] Starting with a shipment of 14 horses in 1665, 55 were sent before 1670. By 1679 there were 145 horses in the colony; by 1692, 400; and by 1706, 1,812. Twelve donkeys sent out in 1679 had no posterity. Forty-five sheep were sent out in 1667 and 44 in 1668. The 1679 census indicated 719 sheep in the colony. Though there were many hogs in New France by 1671, the first census listing came only in

[41]Salone, La Colonisation de la Nouvelle-France, p. 175.
[42]Ibid., p. 200.   [43]Ibid.   [44]Ibid., p. 201.
[45]Burton, "Wheat Supply of New France" (Royal Society of Canada, Transactions, 1936, sec. II), pp. 137-50, espec. p. 138.
[46]Salone, La Colonisation de la Nouvelle-France, pp. 122-3.
[47]Ibid., pp. 198 ff. The succeeding data are from the same place.

1688, when their numbers were put at 3,701. Talon saw no need for sending more hogs, and it became rather a matter of preventing those already there from destroying crops. By 1673 the Council was establishing regulations towards this end.

Between 1673 and 1713 official colonization and settlement efforts were slack, and there was a constant drain on the agricultural section of the population resulting from the comparative attractiveness of the life of the *coureur de bois*. Nevertheless, population increased markedly from within, with substantial surpluses of births over deaths, and to a lesser extent due to the colonization efforts of a few of the seigniors.[48] By 1713 the population of New France was around 18,000;[49] cultivated land exceeded 50,000 arpents;[50] and in 1719 the wheat crop totalled 234,566 bushels.[51] In 1706 livestock was listed as follows: cattle, 14,191; horses, 1,872; sheep, 1,820; and hogs over 5,000. By 1700 the local authorities were discouraging horse-raising.[52] This is interesting evidence of the role of agriculture. The habitants preferred horses to oxen for the cultivation of their land and for hauling wood and grain, but the authorities feared the habitants might lose the ability to walk, so necessary for defence activities. For this and other vague reasons, frontier people have commonly been urged to use oxen instead of horses.

7. The Treaty of Utrecht and After

The major French withdrawal signalized by the Treaty of Utrecht in 1713, indicated clearly that the French empire in the New World was lagging far behind that of England, and agricultural shortcomings were instrumental to the lag. In some years crops were abundant, only to be accompanied by unremunerative prices for agricultural produce. Other years saw crop failures which left New France dependent on the mother country for wheat and seed and pork.[53] In 1690 Frontenac complained of being reduced to drinking nothing but water.[54]

After 1713 the French government picked up the threads of its former policy of providing an agricultural population for New France.[55] They restored earlier rules requiring ship captains to carry

48*Ibid.*, p. 228.   49*Ibid.*, p. 306.   50*Ibid.*, p. 328.   51*Ibid.*, p. 374.
52Innis (ed.), *Select Documents, 1497-1783*, p. 300.
53*Ibid.*, p. 298.
54*Ibid.*, p. 297.
55Salone, *La Colonisation de la Nouvelle-France*, pp. 342 ff.

three to six indentured labourers each trip, according to the size of their vessels. They attempted further soldier settlement, but secured few soldiers, perhaps 1,500 between 1713 and 1763. In 1723 they reluctantly sent their first batch of prisoners, 138 in number, and from then till 1749 and the start of the war they sent out 1,000. A few English settled in the colony. But the real increase came from within, from the inherent fertility of the pioneer population. To capitalize on this fertility it was necessary to provide and care for illegitimate as well as legitimate children, the former being particularly numerous in a situation where many men—soldiers, sailors, foreign merchants, and particularly many prisoners—were unmarried.[56] In 1722 there was revived an early French law prescribing death for abortion. Live-born illegitimate children were declared to be wards of the state and foster parents were provided for them. This policy was successful to the extent that in 1736, for example, of 390 illegitimate children, only twelve or thirteen died.[57] By 1752 the cost to the colony for illegitimate children was 12,153 *livres* representing the support of one hundred such children.

8. *The Importance of Provisions*

The implication of the analysis so far is that the French encouraged agriculture and agricultural settlement on the St. Lawrence chiefly for the defence of territorial, commercial, and ecclesiastical empire. But the defensive functions of New World agriculture went farther than the provision of man-power, and concerned the defence of more than the St. Lawrence fur-trade route. In times of crisis, of Iroquois or British attack, the presence of sturdy arms-bearers was the important consideration; but the defence of empire went deeper than that. Military and commercial stamina could not be maintained without adequate provisions, foodstuffs, and supplies, not only for immediate military activities, but also for the various commercial activities upon which the empire depended. In answer to the suggestion that commercial pursuits might be provisioned from abroad, without reliance on a reluctant local agriculture, there must be recalled the prevailing mercantile dread of importation, as well as the more reasonable factors of uncertain and inadequate transportation, the danger of British blockade, and the usually precarious nature of the colony's public finances. To grasp the full significance

56*Ibid.*, p. 355.   57*Ibid.*, p. 356.

of French agriculture in North America, it is necessary to relate this agriculture to the various aspects of the French New World empire, and to the conflict between this empire and that of England.

From the earliest days of the exploitation of America, French and English plans for economic expansion were so similar as to clash inevitably. For both France and England, codfish offered a key to Spanish gold; fur trading followed naturally; tobacco and sugar helped in securing Spanish gold, by replacing corresponding imports from Spain; sugar and tobacco plantations offered a commerce in slaves; all these trades, including that in slaves, offered an outlet for shipping and an opportunity to build a strong merchant marine; all trades as well as shipping required provisioning. The obvious interdependence of the economic interests of each country went still further. Sugar produced rum for the fur and slave trades; low-grade cod offered the basic foodstuff for slave-operated plantations. The fur trade was least of all dependent on agriculture for provisioning, for to a considerable extent it "lived off the country," though even the fur trade relied on Indian corn and whatever agriculture could be established around the trading posts. The other activities, particularly the cod fisheries and the sugar plantations, required a considerable variety of agricultural produce—grains, flour, cattle, horses, meats, and dairy produce—and required such produce in abundance to assure cheapness of the final product. Since French producers of the products mentioned above, codfish, furs, sugar, and tobacco, were constantly competing against the British in the markets of the Old World, it is easy to grasp the significance, for empire strength, of an agriculture capable of supplying an abundance of provision products. Carrying and agricultural interests in England railed against the New England colonies, because these colonies, particularly New York and Pennsylvania, early developed an agriculture more than adequate to the needs of the British Empire in America,[58] thus cutting off the lucrative trade in provisions from home. Nevertheless, this same abundant local agriculture enabled the English to conquer and dismember the French economy in the New World. New France and Acadia never supplied the French adequately with flour and salt beef.

[58]Burton, "Wheat Supply of New France" (Royal Society of Canada, *Transactions*, 1936, sec. ii), pp. 137-50, espec. p. 137.

The agricultural strategy of France for her New World empire, therefore, involved not only the design to secure the trade route for furs, to assure the very existence of New France, but also to provide a sound agricultural base on which all the empire pursuits might rest, on which French territorial, commercial, and religious interests might be held in the face of constant English pressure. French hopes for this agricultural base of empire had a dual and complementary foundation. Settlement in New France was accompanied by settlement in Acadia where soil and climate combined to favour animal husbandry on an easy-going, extensive scale. The severity of the continental winters about Quebec made fodder and housing problems acute for the care of animals, but cereals for the most part grew comparatively well. There was, accordingly, reasonable expectation that Quebec and Acadia might together serve the needs of the new French empire. But the English were as fully aware as the French of the significance of agricultural strength to the purposes of empire. The Acadian agricultural area was among the first objects of English attack whenever commercial rivalry had progressed beyond the bounds of non-military adjustment.[59] The Treaty of Utrecht ended a phase in the long history of French failure to establish an agricultural base sufficiently sound for survival in the struggle against the English, and the same treaty rendered certain the French failure throughout the next half-century, for it transferred the Acadian agricultural region from French to English possession.

The Treaty of Utrecht curtailed French economic activities but left substantial prospects along the various general lines formerly pursued. Despite the loss of trading posts, fishing and agricultural territories, there was still, for France, the fur trade, the fisheries, sugar plantations and slaves, and the possibility of interdependent trade and provisioning among these staple industries. France proceeded to attempt the consolidation of the remnants of empire. Withdrawing from Acadia, as required by the treaty, she established herself in Cape Breton Island and fortified Louisburg as a military and naval base. Economically, the question of co-ordination rested as before on the prospects of agriculture, on the possibility of securing a local source of provisions and man-power for fortification, fisheries, fur trade, and sugar plantations. And, as before, the French

[59]Brebner, *New England's Outpost: Acadia before the Conquest, passim.*

attempted to build up St. Lawrence agriculture by fostering colonization and settlement, by encouraging the raising of cattle and sheep and discouraging the raising of horses,[60] by urging the cultivation of hemp, flax, tobacco, and potatoes,[61] and by taking steps to assure the quality of what flour there was available for export. The musty flour shipped out in green wood barrels had somehow to give way to fresh, sweet flour in barrels made from carefully seasoned wood.[62] Hocquart introduced ten cylindrical cribbles, 1722-30, and gave them to millers; habitants were forbidden to sell uncribbled grain.[63] In view of the continuing uncertainty of St. Lawrence agriculture, and of the long annual season during which the St. Lawrence was icebound, the French attempted to develop agriculture in the maritime region, near Louisburg, to offset the loss of the Fundy area. They envisaged Prince Edward Island (*Isle St. Jean*) as a place to which the Acadians might be moved and where a French maritime agriculture might be recreated.[64] But Prince Edward Island held few attractions for the long-settled Acadians, as comfortable now under British as under their former French rulers. Louisburg came to rely for provisioning partly on cattle from the Bay of Fundy, now English territory. The French were thus reduced to smuggling provisions from their enemy in order to maintain their military stronghold.

9. *Summary*

French efforts to establish territorial, economic, and even ecclesiastical empire in the New World relied heavily upon the prospects for local agricultural development. Territory and trade routes had to be secured against the encroachment of economic and military rivals, particularly the British. The fur trade constituted the prime lucrative opportunity on the St. Lawrence, and this river could be made effective as a basis for the fur trade only if it could be adequately garrisoned with arms-bearers. An abundant agricultural settlement offered the only feasible instrument towards this end. In addition to the fur trade, French imperial prospects in the New World relied on the cod fisheries and the codfish trade, upon

---

[60] Innis (ed.), *Select Documents, 1497-1783*, pp. 352 ff.
[61] Salone, *La Colonisation de la Nouvelle-France*, pp. 374-8.
[62] Innis (ed.), *Select Documents, 1497-1783*, pp. 367 ff.
[63] Salone, *La Colonisation de la Nouvelle-France*, p. 377.
[64] Harvey, *French Régime in Prince Edward Island*, passim.

sugar plantations and the sugar trade, and upon the defence and provisioning of all these varied activities. Agriculture was essential for both defence and provisioning, and French encouragement to New World agriculture is understandable in the light of this fact.

In order to establish and encourage agriculture in New France, the government of France subsidized the migration and settlement of thousands of selected persons; it subsidized military settlement; it attempted to correct the typical frontier shortage of females; it subsidized marriage and rewarded the demonstration of procreative willingness and capacity. The seigniorial system of land tenure was transplanted from the motherland, at least partly because of its defensive possibilities. Local administrative officers established model gardens and farmyards, and attempted to determine and demonstrate the adaptability of various species of plants and animals.

Although the French struggle to develop local agriculture in New France was persistent, it was comparatively ineffective. Before the fall of the colony to the British there were many years when crops, particularly wheat crops, were bountiful enough to permit exports to Louisburg and the West Indies.[65] But the difficulty concerning wheat was its uncertainty,[66] and there was persistent inadequacy of other cereals and of cattle. Drought and insect pests devastated cereal crops, which led in turn to the destruction of herds. Far from abundantly provisioning the staple trades of the French in America, New France repeatedly was forced to rely on the mother country for her own sustenance. The final fall of Quebec, and the Treaty of Paris in 1763, may be taken as proof of the failure of French agriculture in the New World to fulfil its defence and provisioning functions, despite persistent governmental aid and encouragement towards that end.

[65]Salone, *La Colonisation de la Nouvelle-France,* pp. 376-8: Burton, "Wheat Supply of New France" (Royal Society of Canada, *Transactions,* 1936, sec. ii), pp. 137-50, espec. p. 138.

[66]The years 1737, 1738, 1741, 1742, 1743, 1748, 1751, 1756, 1757, 1758, for example, were years of crop failure and great distress in the colony. See Innis (ed.), *Select Documents, 1497-1783,* pp. 360-7; Lunn, "Agriculture and War in Canada" (*Canadian Historical Review,* June, 1935), pp. 123-36.

CHAPTER III

THE MARITIMES BEFORE CONFEDERATION

MARITIME agriculture and agricultural policy before Confederation are most readily intelligible when related functionally to particular aspects of empire, notably the commercial aspects. Settlement in the Maritime colonies was a long and arduous process, and in over a century of efforts towards this end the French had failed to develop in Acadia any great abundance of agricultural produce, and had failed to secure what exports there were from this region for their own purposes in the face of the proximity of the attractive Boston market. Withdrawing from Acadia in 1713, the French retired to Cape Breton and Prince Edward Island, but accomplished little of an agricultural nature there in the fifty years preceding their final withdrawal from the Maritimes and the St. Lawrence.

1. *British Efforts in the Maritimes, 1713-83*

In the same fifty years, 1713-63, English mercantile policy contributed to a considerable expansion of settlement and agricultural production in the Maritime region. Nova Scotia offered strategic possibilities as an outpost against French fortifications at Louisburg, and as a check to French trade and fisheries. To fulfil its possibilities in the British plan Nova Scotia would have to develop military and naval strength, adequate bases for fisheries, provisions for both military and commercial activities, and, if possible, a range of commodities for the West Indies trade. Great Britain, financing group migrations from Europe to Nova Scotia, founded Halifax in 1749 as a military and naval specific against French aggressiveness from Louisburg, and colonized Lunenburg as a measure of support to military and commercial strength, to offer provisions and to render labour abundant in the colony.[1] Settlers at Halifax were

[1]Innis (ed.), *Select Documents, 1497-1783*, pp. 167 ff., 202-3; Hansen and Brebner, *Mingling of the Canadian and American Peoples*, pp. 24-6. Migrants were given passage, land, subsistence, and equipment. Lunenburg was established in 1853 by about fifteen hundred Germans and Swiss who found agricultural prospects in and around Halifax impossible. Even in Lunenburg the settlers were supported from the public stores for nine years before they could provide for themselves (*ibid.*, p. 26).

offered a bounty of twenty shillings an acre for clearing and fencing their land.[2] One of the earliest acts of the Nova Scotian Assembly provided bounties for erecting stone fences around Halifax lots and for raising English hay thereon.[3] British authorities, with mercantile interests in mind, long held that no gain in empire strength could result from peopling Nova Scotia from the motherland, for artisans going to the colony would certainly spread their skill among the colonists and endanger the position of producers and merchants at home.[4] Continentals and New Englanders, however, were desirable acquisitions to the colony. The time came, indeed, when empire commercial interests *required* the migration of New Englanders to Nova Scotia, for the New England colonies were becoming so well populated that newcomers and old residents were tempted into manufacturing for local demand, thus threatening to encroach upon British trade.[5] Empire mercantile interests, therefore, saw in Nova Scotian waste lands a great opportunity. If settlers in other colonies were offered these lands free of charge, and were assisted to migrate to them, they would not be left in idleness or drawn into local manufacturing. Instead, they would produce in Nova Scotia, hemp for the navy and for the merchant marine, and provisions for the West Indies trade. In the process of establishing themselves and clearing new lands they would require great quantities of tools and supplies, which requirements would stimulate British trade.[6]

The Acadian French, left in possession of their farm lands on the Bay of Fundy when the region was transferred to British control in 1713, eventually lay athwart British commercial hopes in Nova Scotia. Whatever their loyalty or disloyalty to their new political masters, the British, they were distressingly disloyal to British commercial interests, because they persisted in supplying agricultural produce, particularly cattle, to French military and commercial outposts on Cape Breton. British colonial officials came to see in proposals for the removal of the Acadians the possibility of a political and, more particularly, an economic blow at France, for, the Acadians dispersed, their long-established farm lands would lie ready-tilled for settlers from the continent or from New England, who would, supposedly, cultivate them more vigorously than the Acadians and would supply produce for British, rather than French,

²Innis (ed.), *Select Documents, 1497-1783*, p. 241.
³*Ibid.*   ⁴*Ibid.*, pp. 176-7, 179.   ⁵*Ibid.*, p. 178.   ⁶*Ibid.*, pp. 178-9.

troops and trade.[7] In line with such reasoning the Acadians were dispossessed and dispersed. Their livestock was largely liquidated to provision British troops, and the region was thus seriously retarded. The verdict that the Acadians were slovenly and ignorant of sound farming practices had soon to be revised, for the British were forced to bring back Acadians to instruct them in the techniques of marshland farming.[8]

The preceding analysis of the role of agriculture in Nova Scotia around the middle of the eighteenth century, and after, makes it obvious that the bonusing of Loyalist settlement in 1783 was no new departure in policy. Vigorous attempts were made after 1755 to settle the Acadian lands with New Englanders. Proclamations issued by Governor Lawrence in 1758 and 1759 promised New Englanders free land and provisions, and in 1760 large grants of land were made with settlement obligations imposed upon the "proprietors," the grantees.[9] From that time onward British officials increasingly urged that migration from New England to Nova Scotia be encouraged,[10] and the assistance granted to Loyalists was but a part of the continuing attack upon military and commercial agricultural needs.[11] The new element in the situation was that, with New England lost to the British Empire, those who traded with the British West Indies would have to look elsewhere for the provisions for well-rounded cargoes. As early as 1775 Dartmouth wrote from Whitehall ordering that land-sale regulations of 1774 be cancelled,

[7]Ibid., pp. 188-9. In 1755, Governor Charles Lawrence wrote to the Lords Commissioners of Trade and Plantations, in part: "As soon as the French are gone, I shall use my best Endeavours to encourage people to come from the Continent to settle their Lands, and if I succeed in this point, we shall soon be in a condition of supplying ourselves with Provisions, and I hope in time to be able to strike off the great Expence of Victualling the troops; This was one of the happy effects I proposed to myself, from driving the French off the Isthmus, and the additional circumstance of the inhabitants evacuating the country, will I flatter myself, greatly hasten this event, as it furnishes us with a large quantity of good land ready for immediate Cultivation, renders it difficult for the Indians, who cannot as formerly be supply'd with Provisions and Intelligence, to make incursions upon our settlers" (ibid., p. 191).

[8]Ibid., pp. 192-5.

[9]Hansen and Brebner, Mingling of the Canadian and American Peoples, pp. 29-33; Innis (ed.), Select Documents, 1497-1783, pp. 240-8.

[10]Ibid., pp. 177-9.

[11]Ibid., pp. 179-87, 204-5; Hansen and Brebner, Mingling of the Canadian and American Peoples, chap. III.

that grants be made "gratuitous" and "exempt from Quit Rent for Ten Years," and that indigents be victualled at public expense.[12] His reasoning was that "His Majesty considers that His Province of Nova Scotia may become a happy Assylum to many unfortunate families and may also under proper Encouragement afford those supplies to the West India Islands which they can no longer receive from other Colonies." Thirty thousand Loyalists entered the colony of whom twelve thousand went to the St. John River valley.[13] In line with long-established policies of settlement aids, Loyalists were granted free lands and privileges of wood-cutting, while the destitute were given provisions for one year, clothing, farm implements, medicine, window glass, nails, and other building supplies, along with arms and ammunition.[14] So far as the Loyalists comprised disbanded troops, the settlement aid extended to them had purposes similar to the aid extended to soldier settlers by the French on the St. Lawrence just over a hundred years before.[15]

After the first great influx of Loyalists to Nova Scotia in 1783, immigration maintained a steady flow. Emphasis on the agricultural problem shifted from the attempt to increase settlement[16] to the more intensive use of agricultural resources. Government continued to aid and encourage agriculture, and, as before, the welfare of the farming community was only a potential by-product of governmental aid, though such aid was nominally agricultural. The basic and profitable activities of Nova Scotia and New Brunswick, and of the British Empire in America in general, were non-agricultural, and aid to agriculture was designed as further aid to the basic activities, not at all as a means of making agriculture the leading colonial pursuit. Agriculture was basic to the Maritime economies only in the sense that commercial pursuits in the colonies required provisioning, in the sense that fishermen, lumbermen, sailors, and slaves had to eat, and that some of the things they ate might be produced on Maritime farms. Mercantile mentality thought that foreign produce was dear produce, and that home products were cheap. Prince Edward Island

[12]Innis (ed.), *Select Documents, 1497-1783*, pp. 180-1.

[13]*Ibid.*, p. 186; Hannay, *History of New Brunswick*, vol. I, pp. 135-6.

[14]Innis, *Economic History of Canada*, pp. 83-4; Hannay, *History of New Brunswick*.

[15]See above, pp. 19-20.

[16]Except in New Brunswick where the need continued to be interpreted largely as one of securing more and more labour by continuous immigration.

early became an agricultural colony with little governmental encouragement, because alternative opportunities were early exhausted. Nova Scotia and New Brunswick strove long and arduously to "correct" their persistent inadequacy of "bread corns" and of livestock, of cereal husbandry and of animal husbandry. For both colonies the bread-corn shortage was the more acute, and received first attention, for climate and topography in both were less suited to cereal than to animal husbandry.[17] Both colonies were less self-sufficient in agricultural produce at Confederation than they were a quarter of a century before.

2. *"Bread-Corn" Policy in Nova Scotia*

For agricultural policy in Nova Scotia before Confederation the significant relationships are between agriculture on the one hand, and the cod fisheries, the codfish trade, and the general trade in provisions with the West Indies, on the other.[18] The lucrative provisions trade with the West Indies sugar colonies required low-grade dried cod for slaves and a considerable range of agricultural produce— flour, salted meats, beef and pork, butter, lard, cheese, potatoes, apples, and livestock—for the white population.[19] Horses were needed for the mills and grains with which to feed the horses. By the time of the Revolutionary War, New England had long since displaced the motherland as the source of these supplies. By their successful prosecution of this war, however, the Thirteen Colonies had at one and the same time freed themselves from the restraints of the British mercantile system and excluded themselves from its benefits, the substantial advantage of this system having been an assured entry to the West Indies trade. After the close of the war there developed in Halifax a group of commercial interests shrewd enough to see the opportunity thus presented, and eventually powerful and energetic enough to seize it.[20] New England had but to be forced

[17] Innis (ed.), *Select Documents, 1497-1783*, pp. 57-60.

[18] Before agricultural committees had evolved in the Nova Scotian Legislature, committees of the House commonly dealt with these as one problem. In 1807 the Nova Scotian Council and the Assembly each appointed committees to meet jointly and consult "on the subject of the Fisheries and Agriculture of the Province." In 1814 a single joint committee examined the "Agriculture, Commerce, and Fisheries of the Province." See Nova Scotia Assembly, *Journal and Proceedings*, 1807-8, p. 8; 1814, pp. 39-40, 79-81.

[19] Innis, *Cod Fisheries*, p. 343 n.

[20] For a full treatment of this point see *ibid.*, chaps. IX, X.

to abide by her decision and Nova Scotian traders, backed by a greatly expanded agricultural population, would be the obvious heirs to a profitable commerce.

Agricultural development and agricultural policy in Nova Scotia after 1783 are understandable in relation to the efforts of the commercial interests in the colony to dominate, first, the West Indies trade (an intra-empire trade); and later, extra-empire trade, such as trade with Europe and South America. Their attempts to secure statutory and administrative exclusion of New England traders from the West Indies, and to curtail the New England fisheries, do not directly concern agriculture, but their efforts to expand Nova Scotian fisheries and to develop sources of agricultural produce, do. Cheap and abundant cod could only be secured if agricultural products were also cheap and plentiful. Agricultural produce might, of course, be obtained from Boston or from the St. Lawrence, and Nova Scotian merchants had some success in developing an *entrepôt* traffic; but New England produce was long excluded, and later subject to duty, and supplies from Canada were unreliable and burdened with heavy transport charges. Besides, merchants could scarcely bear to import what might be produced at home. All factors combined to suggest to the merchant class that local agriculture should be improved.

Deficiency of bread corns first attracted attention.[21] Climate and topography in Acadia had always been less kind to cereal than to animal husbandry. The Acadians on the Fundy marshlands could raise cattle but little grain, and the uplands repelled them because these areas were heavily wooded. Settlement in Nova Scotia after 1760, and particularly after 1783, crowded on to the uplands, where cereals could more readily be grown, but where the heavily timbered land had to be cleared painfully. The possible progression from bush lot to chopping, to *brûlé*, to stump farm, to cultivable land required a minimum of five or six years. In the absence of stump pullers or dynamite, stumps were left to rot, and land chopped and burned over permitted no real cultivation, only the broadcast sowing

[21]The Nova Scotian government, as did that of practically all New World colonies, attempted to encourage the raising of hemp. Land grants specified that a certain acreage should be seeded to hemp, and the government distributed hemp seed. See Nova Scotia Assembly, *Journal and Proceedings,* 1802, ff.; Mackintosh, "Economic Factors in Canadian History" (*Canadian Historical Review,* March, 1923), pp. 12-25.

of wheat or rye, or perhaps the hoeing-in of potatoes or Indian corn. With the cereals, grass seed was sown, and after the first cereal crop the stump land produced hay which might be pastured or cut, in either case contributing to the support of cattle. Even the uplands, therefore, though climatically suited to cereal husbandry, favoured livestock-raising so long as the clearing process continued, for each successive clearing produced one crop of cereals, followed by four or five hay crops. Pushing back the agricultural margins on the uplands was a costly business. In 1774 cutting and burning could be hired done for 20s. an acre.[22] About 1830 "cutting, heaping, burning, and fencing" cost £3 per acre.[23]

By 1800 bounties were the accepted means of directly aiding the cod fisheries and in 1805 Nova Scotia extended the device to the bread-corn[24] situation as an indirect aid to commerce, though nominally as an aid to agriculture. The act of 1805 (Nova Scotia: 46 Geo. III, c. 9) provided "for granting Two Thousand Pounds for the encouragement of the Agriculture of this Province," and offered a bounty of 15s. per acre "for clearing, fencing and sowing" new lands. Additional votes raised the grant under this act to £2,845. Bushels rather than acres, however, were the important consideration, and an act of 1806-7 (Nova Scotia: 47 Geo. III, c. 3) designed as the previous one "to encourage the raising of Bread Corn on New Lands," placed the bounty on a bushel basis. With minor revisions this act was annually renewed till 1815. Sketchy information concerning the operation of these acts includes the following: that at 15s. per acre the grants under the 1805 act covered claims for 3,800 acres cleared and sown over a period of several years; that in 1808 the terms of bounty were 10d. per bushel for wheat, and 7½d. for rye, and that by 1812 the rate on wheat had been raised to 1s. per bushel;[25] that the annual bread-corn vote varied from £1,500 to £2,000;[26]

---

[22]Innis (ed.), *Select Documents, 1497-1783*, p. 195.

[23]Haliburton, *Historical and Statistical Account of Nova Scotia*, vol. II, p. 364. In 1832 John MacGregor reported clearing costs in New Brunswick of £3.10s. to £4 per acre (*British America*, 2nd edn.: Edinburgh, 1833, vol. II, pp. 91-2).

[24]Bread corns were bread-making cereals, and the list ordinarily included wheat, oats, barley, rye, buckwheat, and Indian corn.

[25]See Nova Scotia Assembly, *Journal and Proceedings*, 1809, p. 63; 1814, p. 30.

[26]In 1807-8 the Nova Scotia House voted bounties as follows: fisheries £2,000, bread corn £2,000, and salt £1,000. Total expenditures of the colony

that appropriations under the 1806-7 act and its revisions may have totalled £12,000 though claims over the decade were probably for much less. The bounty applied only to the first cereal crop grown on new clearings, and probably covered less than a quarter of the costs of clearing, seeding, and harvesting.

The end of the Nova Scotian bread-corn bounty policy coincided, in 1815, with the end of the European and American wars, with the end of local farm prosperity induced by military contracts for beef, pork, and hay, and with crop failures and an influx of field mice in 1815 and 1816.[27] Relief rather than bounty was required and the government imported and distributed quantities of grain and seed. In the ensuing years of acute rural distress the agrarian Assembly urged re-enactment of bounty legislation as a source of cash farm income, however small. Bounty bills were repeatedly passed by the Assembly and rejected by the Council as late as 1831, for the Council had become convinced that bread-corn bounties constituted no solution to the commercial interests in agriculture.

Few episodes in the history of Canadian agriculture and agricultural policy have received such favourable publicity as that involving Agricola and the Central Board of Agriculture of Nova Scotia. The episode had special concern with the character traits of an individual, Agricola; but in its broadest aspects it clearly underlines the functional relationship between agriculture and the commerce of the pre-Confederation colonies, as well as the willingness of government at times to contribute generously so that agriculture might better perform its commercial functions.

The situation developed some years after the conclusion of the Napoleonic wars. Governmental relief in seed and grains had tided

---

that year were £18,175 including £5,000 for roads. In 1812 corresponding votes were: fisheries £6,000, encouragement of agriculture (bread corns) £1,500; out of total expenditures of £34,000, including £11,000 for roads and bridges. See Nova Scotia Assembly, *Journal and Proceedings*, 1807-8, p. 30; 1812, p. 62.

[27]Martell and Harvey, "Achievements of Agricola and the Agricultural Societies" (Public Archives of Nova Scotia, *Bulletin*: Halifax, 1940), p. 1. The year 1816 was widely known throughout British American colonies as "the year without a summer." During the Napoleonic war, hay had sold in Nova Scotia for £10-£15 per ton, beef and mutton for 8d.-10d. per pound, and other agricultural produce in proportion. See Young, *Letters of Agricola*, Introduction.

Nova Scotian agriculture over the most acute reactions in 1815 and 1816, but the outlook for farmers remained gloomy, particularly in contrast to previous easy prosperity. The commercial outlook too was gloomy. Conditions were ripe for recovery or for revival. Revival came late in 1818, with something approaching camp-meeting enthusiasm, following the publication in the *Acadian Recorder* of the first few in a series of anonymous letters by Agricola, and enthusiasm grew with the correspondence and meetings which followed. By mid-December official patronage was extended to the movement when Governor Dalhousie presided over a meeting in Halifax which organized the Central Board of Agriculture, advanced 120 subscriptions of 20*s.* each, contributed £350 including £100 from the Governor, and made Agricola, still anonymous, secretary to the new board. Dalhousie's prediction to the meeting that the Legislature would generously support the society was justified, for early in the ensuing session there was passed "An Act for the encouragement of Agriculture, and Rural Economy, in this Province" (Nova Scotia: 59 Geo. III, c. 13), which incorporated the central board (or society), granted a seven-year charter, and appropriated £1,500 "to enable them to import Horses, Neat Cattle, and Sheep, and other animals of the best description, and most suitable for this Province; and also Seeds of various kinds, and implements of Husbandry, for the benefit of the Province . . . and generally to enable them to encourage Rural Economy and Agricultural Improvement throughout the Province."[28]

The nature and location of the organization meeting, its official patronage, and the number and size of the subscriptions advanced towards the "cause," clearly indicate the paternalistic, non-agrarian nature of the project. Not one in twenty of the 120 one-pound subscribers could have been a dirt farmer. Some weeks later Agricola revealed himself as John Young, a Halifax merchant who had fallen between medicine and theology at Glasgow University, had then taken a liberal education, worked for a time with Sir John Sinclair, first president of the British Board of Agriculture, and had eventually settled reluctantly to business.[29] In his letters he pointed

[28]Nova Scotia Assembly, *Journal and Proceedings*, 1819, p. 102.
[29]Martell and Harvey, "Achievements of Agricola," p. 9.

to the absence of agricultural societies in Nova Scotia[30] as "a decisive proof of the low and degraded state, which the profession [agriculture] occupies,"[31] and mentioned as examples of salutary institutions the Dublin Society in Ireland, the Highland Society of Scotland, the British Board of Agriculture, and agricultural societies in Germany, France, Italy, and the United States.[32] The whole venture of a new agricultural board in Nova Scotia was an attempt to apply British, or more particularly Scottish, "high" culture and intensive techniques to the frontier agriculture of the colony, and much of the outcome is understandable in the light of this fact. The Council, which since 1815 had refused to renew bread-corn bounties, permitted, even actively sponsored, the generous governmental support accorded the new society, basically because they desired an abundant provisioning agriculture,[33] but specifically because of their prejudice for British institutions and British methods. Agriculturists accepted the bounteous gesture, but were concerned that so little of the actual grants sifted into their pockets through the fingers of intervening officialdom.

[30]Neither agricultural societies nor central agricultural boards were new to Nova Scotia at this time. The province had four central boards before Confederation, commencing respectively in 1789, 1819, 1841, and 1864, and agricultural societies waxed and waned roughly in inverse proportion to the degree of agricultural and commercial prosperity in the province. On November 5, 1789, a "society for Promoting Agriculture in Nova Scotia" was formed in Halifax under the patronage of Governor Parr, Bishop Inglis, and others. It was conceived as a central board, for its forty-eight directors came from various parts of the province and each was expected to form a branch society in his own district. Records do not indicate whether any societies were thus formed, though two others were set up in Nova Scotia about the same time. The Kings County Society was established at Horton, December 10, 1789, for "the better improvement of Husbandry, encouragement of Manufactories, cultivation of social Virtue, acquirement of useful Knowledge, and to promote the good Order and well being of the Community to which we belong." The Hants County Society was organized July 10, 1790. The Kings County Society celebrated its one hundred and fiftieth anniversary in 1939. Both the Kings and the Hants societies were in operation at the time when Agricola was writing, as was the West River Pictou Agricultural Society, organized in 1817 (*ibid.*, pp. 6-7).

[31]*Letters of Agricola*, Letter I.   [32]*Ibid.*, Letter II.

[33]In announcing the 1821 scheme for the disposition of the board's funds, John Young said, "the Central Board is limiting its attention primarily to the rising [*sic*] of bread-corn for the supply of our internal consumption . . . all the premiums, though scattered and diffused over many objects . . . verge to this one great point" (Martell and Harvey, "Achievements of Agricola," p. 30).

When the central board's charter came up for reconsideration in 1826, its renewal was refused by the Assembly by a vote of nineteen to twelve. The government had voted a total of £7,300 to the board,[34] an average of nearly £1,200 per year until 1825 when only £200 towards the secretary's salary was voted. The board's private funds, chiefly derived from subscriptions, totalled £1,400, so that the board had disposal of £8,700 over a seven-year period. These funds went for secretary's salary and travelling expenses; for premiums for clearing land, summer-fallowing, fertilizing, growing cereals and root crops, taking produce to Halifax, and oatmill construction; for the importation of implements, seeds, and livestock; and for cattle shows and ploughing matches. The bulk of the expenditures were made in the first two or three years. Seeds were imported only the first year, when £1,500 went for clover, turnips, barley, beans, and peas from London, Glasgow, Aberdeen, New York, and Boston, and such a storm of farmers' protests arose over their late arrival and trashy condition that the experience was not repeated.[35] No livestock was imported after 1821, nor were any further cattle shows held, such was the discontent over the board's judging.[36] The only expense which went on unabated from year to year was that for John Young's salary, as secretary to the board. This amounted to £250 per year plus a substantial travelling allowance from the legislative grants, while the board added up to £50 each year with additional travelling allowances from its private funds. Of the total funds at the disposition of the board, John Young drew 30 per cent for salary and travelling allowance, while on his farm he used the board's demonstration implements and livestock.

Agricola's letters and the organization of the central board inspired widespread interest in agricultural improvement. Within a year from the appearance of the first letters, fourteen new local agricultural societies had been formed, and by 1824 there were thirty in the province.[37] The oatmill bounties offered by the central board facilitated the construction of several mills throughout the province and set the pattern for similar grants later offered by the Nova Scotian and New Brunswick governments. In 1823 Nova Scotian cattle, sheep, and other farm produce were exported to New Brunswick, constituting, as the board reported, "a new feature in Nova Scotian Agriculture." In 1821 local flour and produce appeared in

34*Ibid., passim.*   35*Ibid.,* p. 23.   36*Ibid.,* p. 4.   37*Ibid.,* p. 18.

Halifax so abundantly as seriously to depress farm prices. Yet the bounty of nature helped toward these situations. In 1826 the Legislature voted no funds to the board except £200 for Young's salary. The board's subscription list had declined steadily from 235 in 1819 to 79 in 1824. The board outlived its usefulness and Young outlived the farmers' confidence in him as an agricultural adviser. The stimulus given by the board toward agricultural improvement was ephemeral. By 1841 when a new central board was formed, only three of the thirty societies existing during Young's career survived.

Of the reasons for the transitory nature of the central board's influence, some were associated with the personality and character of John Young. Pioneer farmers laboriously existing on rocky stump farms understandably criticized Young's salary of £300 per year plus travelling expenses. Settlers from New England, and the descendants of such settlers, were not impressed by the fact that Young was a Halifax merchant, but more particularly they could not tolerate his boorish arrogance,[38] nor could they be convinced of any inherent sinfulness in using "Superfine" American flour, particularly when Young's proposed alternative was a diet of oatmeal. Furthermore, pioneer settlers undoubtedly recognized that much of the board's advice was thoroughly bad advice. Young had no understanding of the relativity of "good" cultural practices. He took it for granted that a good system of cultivation in old Scotland would also be a good system for New Scotland; he urged a system of intensive cultivation with the use of the "best" implements, with fertilizers and green crops, and with a summer-fallow method involving three or four ploughings and a minimum of three harrowings in the process.[39] That John Young's influence on Nova Scotian agriculture

[38]Young's letters, and undoubtedly his speech, abounded with such expressions as "the degradation of local agriculture," the "agricultural debasement" of the province, "foolish and ignorant neighbours." The following typify his statements: "In fact, a most profound ignorance of all the better practices which have exalted modern agriculture, maintained here an unlimited dominion over the intellectual faculties." "The Dutch plough—a clumsy and awkward machine—disgraces our Agriculture in more than one district, and would not be tolerated a moment by the most illiterate boor in England." And on asking Nova Scotian farmers if they had read certain agricultural works, "the only answer I received was the broad and vacant stare of inanity" (Letters of Agricola, passim).

[39]Martell and Harvey, "Achievements of Agricola," p. 19.

was so slight suggests the hypothesis that farmers do grope, by trial and error processes, towards ways of agriculture which have significance in relation to their environment.

Apart from minor assistance to be mentioned later, Nova Scotian agriculture was neglected by government for fifteen years after the central board expired in 1826. Farmers agitated for help; but the facts were that farmers could not secure aid unless supported or led in their appeals by the merchant class, and for the time being the merchants' interests were better served in other ways. The merchants' essential need was for cheap provisions for assorted trading cargoes, and local production offered but one possible source of supply. In times of depression the fundamental mercantilistic conscience regarding the evil of loss of specie came to the fore and made domestic provisions especially attractive. But in times of reasonable prosperity, foreign supplies—from New England, Prince Edward Island, or Canada—could be tolerated, and offered much greater prospect of adequacy.

The problem was to get a breach in the British colonial system which would permit non-Empire produce into the colonies directly, or, specifically, that would permit New England produce into Nova Scotian ports for re-export in Nova Scotian vessels. The agitation for free ports was an attack upon this problem, and beginning with the earliest proposal in 1790,[40] progress in this direction became real with a British free-port act in 1818,[41] and with the extension of warehousing privileges in 1823 and 1826. These measures contributed greatly to the possibilities for assorted commercial cargoes and were so encouraging as to stifle, temporarily, mercantile interest in Nova Scotian agriculture. The effectiveness of the free-port movement is evident from the farmers' opposition to it. Farmers sought not lighter, but heavier duties on American produce, but with little success, for mercantile interests dominated the Council. In 1820 the Union Agricultural Society of Kings County deplored the whole tendency toward easy entry of American farm produce, arguing that high wages and poor harvests had long made it impossible for domestic produce to bear foreign competition, and now "scarcely had Providence smiled on the labours of our husbandmen . . . than the free port act, 'like the genius of despair,' blasted our expectations."[42]

[40]Innis, *Cod Fisheries*, p. 243 n.   [41]*Ibid.*, pp. 250 ff.
[42]Cited in Martell and Harvey, "Achievements of Agricola," p. 29.

Agricultural agitation for governmental assistance was not sufficient to secure such assistance unless the major economic interests in the colony, those of trade and the fisheries, wanted agriculture to be helped for their own purposes.

Institutional aid to Nova Scotian agriculture was not resumed after 1826 until 1841 when a new central board was chartered and provided with funds. By the eighteen-forties Nova Scotia, as well as New Brunswick and Prince Edward Island, turned more realistically to develop the latent domestic possibilities for animal husbandry, instead of cereal husbandry. But before such efforts were put forward on any substantial scale there were recurrent efforts made, particularly following the onset of commercial depressions, to cope with the local inadequacy of bread corns. Farmers grazed cattle and bought "Superfine" American flour for their tables. Wheat was admittedly the most difficult of the cereals to be grown locally, but coarse grains could be raised, and the mercantile argument was that the farmer should be content with coarser fare if by so doing he, and the province, could be made independent of the foreigner.[43] Why, for instance, it was argued, should the farmer not eat oatmeal, and thus avoid the drain of funds for foreign flour.[44] Taste stood in the way, but also the lack of mechanical facilities

[43]Haliburton voiced the typical mercantile morality on the question of bread corns in 1829: "It will hardly be credited," he said, "that in a Country where the prevalence of grazing rendered the importation of flour necessary for the support of its inhabitants, the best quality of foreign manufacture, was not only required but in general use even among the laborious part of the population, and that the cheaper and more humble fare of the rye and Indian meal, was rejected as coarse and unpalatable." By 1829, however, he thought that "the folly and extravagance of these habits have given place to a more rational and more economical system" (*Historical and Statistical Account of Nova Scotia,* vol. II, p. 368).

[44]In 1848 the Nova Scotian Committee on Agricultural Matters said in part: "Considering the severe loss of the Wheat and Potato Crops for the past three years, every encouragement should be afforded to the people to induce them to manufacture and use a cheaper, and at the same time more wholesome description of food; the example of the people of the New England States in this particular affords a useful lesson to us. . . . It would be indeed desirable if the Farmers of many parts of Nova Scotia would imitate their example, and be content to raise and cultivate in more abundance the inferior description of Corn and Grain: and thereby save the constant drain upon their pockets arising from . . . using the best description of American Flour" (Nova Scotia Assembly, *Journal and Proceedings,* 1848, App. no. 86).

for making oatmeal. To remedy this condition, oatmill bounties were offered. Instituted apparently by John Young in 1819, they were sporadically offered over the years: one £20 grant in 1823 to John Gutridge "to aid him in completing his mill, at Horton, for the manufacturing of Oat Meal";[45] in 1826 ten votes of £20 each; in 1834 eleven grants of £20 each; in 1838 and succeeding years general votes were made of £20 to £30 per county. Twenty pounds were considered adequate to provide the metal parts for a mill and kiln.[46] Crop failures and commercial insecurity in the middle eighteen-forties induced regularity of oatmill bounties at £30 per county per year from 1847 to 1854.[47] After 1848 the grants were graduated according to the size of the mill: £15 each where the kiln was at least 14 feet in diameter; £10 where it was 11-14 feet; and no grant when it was less than 11 feet.[48] With gradual installation of mills, with the returning prosperity of the eighteen-fifties, and with the swing over to an interest in livestock prospects, the Nova Scotian oatmill bounty policy lapsed after 1854.

The formation of a new central agricultural board in 1841 gave a certain permanence to Nova Scotian attempts at agricultural improvement. In 1840 the agricultural committee of the provincial Assembly traced the sorry plight of Nova Scotian agriculture, when compared with that of Scotland, New York, Massachusetts, and Prince Edward Island, to the absence of a central board of agriculture.[49] In 1841 their recommendations for the re-establishment of such an institution were effected by legislation (Nova Scotia: 4 Vic., c. 2), and with slight lapses and modifications the hierarchy of board and local societies lasted until 1885 when the board was abolished and a member of the Executive Council was made "Secretary for Agriculture."[50] The board of eleven men, appointed by the Governor in Council in 1841, and situated in Halifax, was designed chiefly as supervisor of local societies. It was required to aid them, to audit their accounts, and to import implements, seed, and livestock as directed by the societies. The board was granted £500 for salaries

45*Ibid.*, 1823, p. 261.
46*Ibid.*, 1830-31, App. no. 4.
47See *ibid.*, 1847 ff.
48*Ibid.*, 1848, App. no. 86.
49*Ibid.*, 1840, App. no. 23.
50Martell and Harvey, "From Central Board to Secretary of Agriculture" (Public Archives of Nova Scotia, *Bulletin:* Halifax, 1940), p. 25.

and activities, and local agricultural societies might draw up to £75 per county per year. In 1841 three locals survived of Agricola's thirty; by the middle eighteen-fifties there were upwards of fifty locals. After a lapse of a few years, a new board created in 1864 was entitled by act[51] to draw $2,000 for its own uses and up to $240 for the societies of each county, the latter grants, however, to be issued only in the ratio of two dollars to one of local subscriptions. From 1845 to 1857 payments to locals averaged £950 to £1,000 per year.[52] In 1852 out of total provincial expenditures of £126,000, "agriculture" drew £1,071, plus £201 for oatmills, "fisheries" drew £5,000, and "statistics" drew £1,562.[53] In 1862 expenditures totalled $1,000,000, of which "agriculture" drew $2,360; railway interest was $244,000 and railway expenses $102,000.[54] On the average, in the years immediately preceding Confederation, the Nova Scotian government was spending $5,000 per year on agricultural encouragement, on the central board and societies, with an occasional special grant for livestock, as, for example, the $10,000 grant in 1865. The agricultural hierarchy of institutions was drawing one-half of one per cent of the provincial budget.

The structure and activities of Nova Scotian agricultural organizations after 1841 were so typical of those gradually evolved in other pre-Confederation provinces that they bear brief analysis. Central boards and agricultural societies constituted European techniques for the improvement of agriculture, immediate models being the Highland Agricultural Society of Scotland and the British Board of Agriculture. They were paternalistic and could be used by any group which wished that agriculture be improved, or which desired farmers to think that efforts were being made in their behalf. The "dirt-farmer" interest in them was incidental. Appointed by the Governor, the Nova Scotian board, as those of other colonies, was made up of interests centring in the capital city, generally representing the executive, professional, and commercial sections of the provincial economy. Among these groups it was easy to find individuals who owned farms, or who had amateur interests in the

51Revised Statutes of Nova Scotia, Title XXVI, c. 96 (1864).

52Nova Scotia Assembly, Journal and Proceedings, Public Accounts, 1845-57.

53Ibid., 1853, App. no. 12, pp. 220-1.

54Nova Scotia Assembly, Journal and Proceedings, 1863, App. no. 3.

farming community. Local societies were constituted according to provincial statute, reported and accounted to the board, and received annual grants conditioned on, and later proportional to, local subscription. Standard activities for the societies included the holding of "shows" and the granting of premiums for a wide range of performance: for the showing of superior stock, cereals, and implements; for ploughing matches; and for the importation of livestock, seeds, and farm equipment. More of their efforts concerned animal than cereal husbandry, but in both fields they were of some use in transferring techniques from older economies to the frontier. Till the days of the western Canadian range development late in the nineteenth century, farm animals and techniques of animal husbandry came for the most part from Europe and especially from Britain,[55] but for implements and cereals, more satisfaction resulted from reliance on American sources. Much of the funds and energies of colonial agricultural societies and boards was wasted in attempting to transplant British and European methods and implements of cultivation to the new environment, following blindly in the John Young tradition. Particularly when officered by New Englanders or their descendants, however, agricultural societies came more and more to import implements and cultural practices from New England. The rough products of the workshops of ingenious Yankees were commonly better adapted to parallel frontier conditions in the British colonies than was the most elaborate and up-to-date Scottish "drill" machinery.[56] Items imported served as models for local

[55]The Loyalists brought American stock to Upper Canada.

[56]Accounts of thirty-odd local agricultural societies tabled in the Legislature in 1846 indicate that they were importing the following tools and implements from the United States: ploughs, beet and turnip drills, forks, manure forks, horse rakes, fanner mountings, a winnowing machine, horse powers, a corn sheller, and one or two threshing machines. Notably absent in this list is any harvesting device. The age-old "bottle-neck" of cereal production, that of the harvesting process, was relatively more acute by 1850 than ever before. Apart from the cradle, introduced from the United States well before 1800, no device as yet attacked the urgent need for careful harvesting at the critical time. See Nova Scotia Assembly, *Journal and Proceedings*, 1846, App. no. 77. Some of the implements imported were contraptions paying equal tribute to Yankee ingenuity and Yankee persuasiveness. In 1850 the Nova Scotia Central Board of Agriculture imported "a very superior horse-power threshing machine with a circular saw attached, together with rotary churns on the most

artisans.[57] Societies subscribed for American farm papers for free
distribution among their membership, and new methods of cultivation were thus introduced.

3. Bread Corns in New Brunswick

The significant elements of agricultural policy in New Brunswick are similar to those in Nova Scotia. Just as Nova Scotian
agricultural development and agricultural policy are unintelligible
apart from the fisheries and the West Indies trade, so in New
Brunswick, agricultural phenomena are meaningless apart from
lumbering (or timber-making) and ship-building. In no Canadian
province, with the possible exception of British Columbia, did early
agriculture meet such an indifferent environment as in New Brunswick; but in few provinces was there such an active and persistent
belief that agriculture should take root and thrive. In no province
in the pre-Confederation period was there such insistence on the
fertility of the soil and the "salubrity" of the climate.

New Brunswick was created a separate province as a result of
the first great scheme of governmental aid to agricultural settlement
in the British Maritime region, the assisted settlement of 12,000
Loyalists in the St. John River valley in 1783. On the formation of
the new province in 1784, it may have contained 16,000 people
including 2,500 "old timers" and 1,500 French.[58] Though lumbering
was a major enterprise from the earliest days of the province,[59] the
early settlers also had some agriculture; they grew hay and fed
cattle.[60] At the turn of the century considerable winter wheat was
grown in the colony, but not enough for local consumption.[61]

The first great impetus towards the development of an export
staple in New Brunswick came following the establishment of
Napoleon's Continental System with its sharp menacing of Britain's
Baltic timber supplies, so necessary for British naval and mercantile

---

approved principles." This cost £56 plus charges. The Agricultural Committee peremptorily advised the Board to dispose of it at once (ibid., 1850,
App. nos. 45, 93).

[57]Ibid., 1847, App. no. 39.

[58]Hannay, History of New Brunswick, vol. I, p. 142. Hansen and Brebner,
Mingling of the Canadian and American Peoples, pp. 55-6.

[59]Innis and Lower (eds.), Select Documents, 1783-1885, p. 267.

[60]Hannay, History of New Brunswick, vol. I, pp. 289, 292.

[61]Ibid., p. 292. Kings County sold 200 to 300 barrels of flour a year besides
supplying its own population. Other counties did nearly as well.

strength. Britain turned to the development of colonial possibilities, establishing preferences on colonial timber in 1809, and increasing them to a peak of 65*s*. per load (50 cubic feet) in 1813. These preferences were revised downward in 1821 and from time to time thereafter till their virtual removal by 1851. In the meantime, however, the superb white pine forests of the St. John and other watersheds, easily accessible by water transportation and attractive to capital and labour even without market preference, were overnight transformed into a resource the exploitation of which offered exceptional returns. Even with relatively stable preference in the British market, the timber trade was subject to the greatest extremes of prosperity and depression; it might be described as a manic-depressive industry. Reduction and eventual abandonment of the British preference, coupled with the depletion of the pine resources[62] and the swing over from wooden to iron ships, brought the industry to an exceedingly low ebb by the middle of the century. Nevertheless, while the New Brunswick pine stands lasted, and while even a degree of British preference survived, timber-making and ship-building ranked far in the lead of the alternative economic opportunities in New Brunswick. If there existed any reason why agriculture should take root in the province, it would be up to its advocates to show cause, and it would be necessary to put forward financial or other persuasion to achieve any marked results.

As in Nova Scotia, so in New Brunswick, the mercantile group were the most frequent agitators for aid to agriculture. In general, timber and ship-building interests needed abundant provisions—flour and salt pork, as well as horses, hay, and oats—and on occasion they professed to believe such abundance to be locally attainable. The first onset of commercial depression, the first signs of collapse in the market for timber and ships, provided the cue for an outburst of exhortation directed towards the improvement of agriculture. However, timber and ship-building "interests" require definition. Much New Brunswick timber, and indeed many of the ships, were produced by settlers, nominally farmers.[63] Well-timbered ridges bounded

62Lower and Innis, *Settlement and the Forest and Mining Frontiers*, p. 37. Lower states that by 1850 good timber was scarce in New Brunswick, and that by 1860 the pine was nearly done.

63See *ibid.*, pp. 31-7 for an account of the intimate farmer-lumberman relationship in New Brunswick.

fertile valleys where farming was possible, so that geographic as well as seasonal relationships tempted settlers to take out timber, to avail themselves of the "cash crop" provided ready to harvest. The "farmer" went to the woods in winter with a gang of men, with horses, with provisions for men, and feed for horses—altogether comprising a camp.[64] Paradoxically, New Brunswick farmers bought farm produce from merchants with which to carry on these timber operations.

If individual New Brunswick farmers were not self-sufficient in provisions and horses, no more was the province as a whole. Ordinary and reliable sources for these requirements were Prince Edward Island and New England. When the timber trade prospered neither farmer-lumbermen nor timber merchants cared much what the source, so long as the supply was abundant and cheap. When the timber market collapsed, both groups crusaded for aid to domestic agriculture, the former group because it was for the time being necessary for them to revert to genuine farming, and the latter group, the lugubrious merchants, because they immediately traced the existing depression back to the specie drain associated with the importation of American flour and salt pork, and Prince Edward Island horses and hay. At such times the breast-beating of the self-appointed leaders in the province was unbelievable. The bread-corn question and the farmer-lumberman relationship took on moral, even spiritual, significance. What hope was there, they protested, for a province which persisted in importing foodstuffs, which preferred timber-making to tilling of the soil? Who could escape condemnation in a community which exposed its sturdy yeomanry to the debauchery of the lumber camp and of the spring drive? Such were the appeals. Agriculture must be encouraged. Moralists thus readily took up the case for agricultural assistance. The Baltic timber

---

[64]The Rev. W. Christopher Atkinson described the activity in part: "The male population . . . go in the winter into the woods for the purpose of lumbering, without which many would not be able to raise their numerous families. The plan of these winter campaigns is as follows:—An enterprising farmer enters into an engagement with a timber merchant, whereby the person with whom the farmer makes his engagement, furnishes him and his gang or gangs, of twelve or more men each, with provisions and other necessaries, taking for the same the timber and saw logs of the farmer, and in spring pays him the balance due for whatever quantity of timber he has furnished him with." See his *Historical and Statistical Account of New Brunswick*, pp. 50-1.

merchants in Britain were another interested group. It is impossible to learn what influence they had, but they were convinced of the viciousness of the New Brunswick timber trade and favoured any measures to keep New Brunswick farmers busy on their farms and away from the timber camps.

Particular aids to New Brunswick agriculture can be related to cereal husbandry and to animal husbandry respectively, the former receiving earliest attention. As in Nova Scotia, so too in New Brunswick, bread-corn and oatmill bounties, and agricultural societies, were the chief instruments used for the attack on foreign dependence for daily bread. The New Brunswick economy was not disorganized by the ending of the Napoleonic wars as was the Nova Scotian,[65] for while the Nova Scotian provisions trade collapsed with the ending of army contracts, the New Brunswick timber trade went ahead by leaps and bounds on the basis of recently acquired preferences and on the reversion of timber carriers from naval to commercial purposes. The first substantial faltering of the timber trade came after 1820, coinciding with a downward adjustment of colonial timber preferences, and acting as a great stimulus to agricultural assistance. The earliest difficulties of sufficient severity to induce legislative intervention in New Brunswick agriculture, however, arose out of the crop failure in 1816, which threatened famine and necessitated direct farm relief in the form of food and seed, grains and potatoes, and occasioned an embargo on the exportation of corn, meal, flour, and potatoes for a period of four months.[66]

Of greater significance arising from this condition of distress was the institution in New Brunswick of a system of bread-corn bounties which lasted till the eighteen-thirties. The New Brunswick act of 1817 (57 Geo. III, c. 5), "An Act to Encourage the raising of Bread Corn on New Land," was modelled after Nova Scotian legislation which had expired in 1815, and provided bounties of 1s. per bushel for wheat, rye, Indian corn, and buckwheat, 8d. per bushel for barley, and 4d. per bushel for oats, "which shall be raised

---

[65]Hannay states, "The peace which came in 1815, was nowhere more heartily welcomed than it was in the Province of New Brunswick" (*History of New Brunswick*, vol. 1, p. 333). The first indication of provincial prosperity was a phenomenal increase in public revenues: those of 1815 were four times as large as those of 1811; those of 1816, five times those of 1815; and those of 1818 greater still (*ibid.*).

[66]*Ibid.*, vol. I, p. 342.

on any new Land in this Province, within two years from the time when the wood growing thereon shall have been cut down, burned or cleared off and the said Land be laid down with grass seed or prepared for a second crop. . . ." The two-year rule, of course, permitted payments for only one grain crop since only one could be raised in that time.[67] An act of 1820 (New Brunswick: 60 Geo. III, c. 12) provided for "bounties on grain raised in this province," without limiting such bounties to the first crop. This act soon expired, and throughout the period till 1833 the first-crop bounty act was in effect. Over the period during which this policy was in force, bounty payments on bread corns approximated £41,500.[68] Their contribution towards a solution of the bread-corn problem cannot be determined. In 1824 in the middle of the bounty period, and at the peak of a timber boom, New Brunswick imported 38,000 barrels of flour for its 70,000 inhabitants.[69] In 1832 towards the close of the bounty period, MacGregor complained: "and, to the disgrace of the inhabitants of the province, who might be independent of others for bread stuffs by more industrious attention to the cultivation of the soil, from 50,000 to 60,000 barrels of flour and meal, and from 3,000 to 4,000 quintals of bread, besides Indian corn, have been for some years annually imported from the United States, for which scarcely any thing but Spanish dollars is paid."[70] Excepting times when the timber trade was in a state of collapse, even reasonable bounties for first crops were inadequate to attract labour and capital into agricultural pursuits. With the timber depression of 1837-43 came an unsuccessful attempt to revive the grain-bounty system.

In further imitation of Nova Scotian methods of agricultural assistance, the New Brunswick government instituted and long pursued a policy of oatmill bounties. Scattered grants preceded 1830, but by 1831 the grant was formalized to permit payments of £25

67See Haliburton, *Historical and Statistical Account of Nova Scotia*, vol. II, pp. 363 ff.

68New Brunswick Assembly, *Journal*, 1828-9, pp. 115-16; and New Brunswick Public Accounts, *ibid.*, Annually, Appendices. This figure compares with perhaps £12,000 paid in bread-corn bounties by Nova Scotia, 1805-15. New Brunswick further emulated Nova Scotia by paralleling bread-corn bounties with fisheries bounties, paying £30,000 toward the latter over the period of bread-corn payments.

69*Montreal Gazette*, May 21, 1825, as cited in Lower, *Forest Frontier*, p. 35.
70*British America*, vol. II, p. 78.

for any mill certified by the Court of General Sessions of the Peace, to be in operation in a convenient location and equipped suitably for the manufacture of oatmeal.[71] The general policy of granting oatmill bounties persisted in New Brunswick for decades. Each year the agricultural committee of the Assembly dealt with petitions for bounties and recommended payments wherever they found conformity with the legislative bounty terms. During the eighteen-thirties grants of £25 each went to from one to ten mills per year.[72] In 1841 the grant was £275, for nine mills.

Activities of New Brunswick agricultural societies for the most part so closely followed the Nova Scotian pattern that little comment is necessary. One special feature is noteworthy: the extent to which New Brunswick agricultural societies were involved in the province's attempts to encourage immigration and agricultural settlement. Labour shortage was one facet of the early problems of all British North American colonies. Much of the agricultural assistance extended in New France was, as outlined previously, assistance towards immigration and settlement to cope with labour scarcity. Assistance given to United Empire Loyalists was partially directed at the same condition. After the Loyalists were established, however, New Brunswick was the only Maritime province which attempted especially to secure immigration.[73] More than any other province, New Brunswick interpreted domestic ills as due to shortage of population. Cheap labour was as essential for timber-making as were cheap provisions, and neither cheap labour nor cheap provisions were obtainable while population remained scanty.

Earliest agricultural societies in New Brunswick organized in 1790, in 1819, and in 1820,[74] were not specifically interested in immigration. Others were specifically "agricultural and emigrant"

[71] New Brunswick Assembly, *Journal,* 1831, pp. 115-16.

[72] *Ibid.,* Annual Public Accounts.

[73] Whitelaw, *Maritimes and Canada before Confederation,* p. 26.

[74] Governor Carleton sponsored an agricultural society in New Brunswick in 1790 in line with similar activity in Halifax and Quebec. The Charlotte Agricultural Society, formed in 1819, survived into the present century. In 1820 there was formed in Fredericton the Central Society for promoting the Rural Economy of the Province, with a grant of £300 in 1820, and one of £500 in 1821 with which to import two horses. In 1825 the Agricultural and Emigrant Society formed at Fredericton took over the funds and duties of the preceding society. See Trueman, *Early Agriculture in the Maritime Provinces,* p. 25, *passim.*

societies. In 1816 the New Brunswick government voted £1,000 to encourage immigration, and that year 111 persons arrived from Greenock, without means.[75] New Brunswick received a considerable proportion of the British emigration after 1815, and by 1820 "Emigrant societies for the purpose of relieving the distress of new arrivals had already been formed and were doing good work."[76] Such was the distress among the newcomers that around 1820 "Emigrant Aid and Agricultural Societies were formed all over the province with the double object of improving agriculture and assisting the poor emigrants to settle on their forest farms."[77] An act of 1820 (New Brunswick: 60 Geo. III, c. 22) providing for the settlement of immigrants was continued at least until 1827 (3 Geo. IV, c. 10). The two roles, encouragement of agriculture and of immigration, were combined in rural New Brunswick societies for decades.

New Brunswick agricultural organization passed through a phase of revivalism approaching that of the Agricola period in Nova Scotia. On the eve of the collapse of the timber trade in 1825-6 Governor Douglas voiced uneasiness over provincial prospects. In opening the 1825 session of the Legislature he noted that "The main branch of our manufacturing industry [ship-building] has increased prodigiously."[78] But, he cautioned, were not adventitious and external circumstances partly responsible? Should the fisheries not be encouraged? Finally he voiced the New Brunswick theme song: "Vast sums are sent from this Province, in specie, for the purchase of foreign agricultural produce. . . . Agricultural, Emigrant, and other Societies, should be encouraged . . . to augment the production of subsistence." As in Nova Scotia in 1818, the Governor took the initiative, and summoned legislators and other provincial leaders to meet at Fredericton in February, 1825. Expounding the doctrine that specie drain could be stopped if New Brunswick would but cultivate her fertile lands, he urged the establishment of agricultural and emigrant societies, with a savings bank for good measure. The New Brunswick Agricultural and Emigrant Society was promptly formed, succeeding the Central Society of 1820, and supported by a £700 grant from the Legislature "for the promotion of Agriculture

75Hannay, *History of New Brunswick,* vol. I, p. 344.
76*Ibid.,* pp. 374 ff.
77*Ibid.*
78New Brunswick Assembly, *Journal,* 1825, p. 3.

throughout the Province."[79] In the temporary enthusiasm engendered for agricultural encouragement, agricultural and emigrant societies sprang up all over the province. Governmental grants to the central society lasted five years and totalled £3,100.[80] While the fervour lasted there was much talk of improvement and considerable claims that improvement had been accomplished.

The basic problems, involving shortage of labour and dependence on foreign sources for bread stuffs, persisted unabated. As in Nova Scotia, little was done to encourage agriculture in New Brunswick in the eighteen-thirties. By 1839, however, the timber economy was so depressed that agricultural aids again came to the fore. The Governor suggested an experimental farm; the agricultural committee was not impressed, urging instead restoration of bread-corn bounties.[81] After a quarrel over this measure, grants were voted to agricultural societies in 1839 and the system has persisted since. In 1840 the grants were put on a standard basis, maximum sums being available for county societies in the ratio of two dollars for each dollar of local subscription. In 1849 an act (New Brunswick: 12 Vic., c. 35) put the grants on an automatic annual basis. No central society was set up till 1859. New Brunswick support to agricultural societies before Confederation was more generous than that of Nova Scotia. In the years immediately preceding Confederation, New Brunswick was granting nearly $10,000 per year to agricultural societies and central board, while the Nova Scotian figure was closer to $5,000. Individual societies in New Brunswick received an average grant of £70 yearly as compared with £25 in Nova Scotia. New Brunswick societies were more interested in livestock improvement than were those of Nova Scotia. These activities will later be analysed.

4. Encouragement of Animal Husbandry Before 1850

Since Prince Edward Island before Confederation was little troubled over bread-corn, or cereal matters, we may turn immediately to consider the Maritime problems relating to animal husbandry, and the attempts made to improve domestic livestock. Though

[79]Trueman, *Early Agriculture in the Maritime Provinces;* MacGregor, *British America,* vol. II, p. 88; New Brunswick Assembly, *Journal,* 1825, p. 78.
[80]*Ibid.,* Annual Public Accounts.
[81]*Ibid.,* 1839, Speech of Lieutenant Governor, p. 251; also pp. 294-5.

conditions in the Maritimes were naturally more favourable to livestock than to cereal culture, the expanding commercial economies of Nova Scotia and New Brunswick made demands for livestock and livestock products beyond the agricultural capacity of either province. Commerce militated against livestock expansion by diverting economic energies, labour, and capital into the more profitable pursuits. In addition to the general provisioning requirements for salt beef and pork, butter and cheese, the Newfoundland trade called for black cattle, the West Indies trade required cattle and horses, and the New Brunswick timber camps, particularly, required horses. The need for cereals was also a need for animals for draught purposes. The relationship of livestock to general mercantile philosophy need not be elaborated; it was identical with the relationship of cereals to this philosophy.

The Maritime Provinces turned towards the improvement of domestic livestock more particularly in the decade or two preceding Confederation. The policies directed towards this end were more realistic than were the bread-corn policies, simply because the livestock case was less hopeless. However, cereal inadequacies did not cease distressing them, and assistance was extended to both animal and cereal husbandry. Sporadic governmental aids towards the improvement of livestock from 1819 onward illustrate the methods involved, even before such activities occurred on any large scale.

Livestock improvement relied heavily on importations of breeding stock, and less strikingly but more persistently on the stimulation of local rivalry and emulation by the holding of "shows" and the offering of premiums for competitive excellence. A considerable share of both types of encouragement was conducted by agricultural societies, for the most part out of their general funds, though the quantity and yield of such efforts is indeterminate. Maritime governments made many specific grants towards the improvement of their livestock, practically all to enable animals to be imported. Such grants were made to the government itself, to agricultural boards, or to agricultural societies. The livestock so imported was either sold at public auction or retained by the importing agency; the services of male animals retained were available typically to the farming community on a fee basis. Isolated instances before 1850 illustrate the various methods.

The Nova Scotian government made several gestures before 1850 specifically directed towards the improvement of provincial livestock. The first grant made to the newly-formed central agricultural board in 1819 was for £1,500 "to enable them to import Horses, Neat Cattle, and Sheep, and other animals of the best description, and most suitable for this Province,"[82] as well as for the encouragement of the rural economy generally. For a year or two the board was most energetic in introducing livestock and altogether imported five stallions, nine bulls, and three cows.[83] Hogs and sheep were given to the board as gifts. Male animals were stationed in various parts of the province for service on a fee basis. In 1825 and 1826 the Legislature voiced at one and the same time its continuing belief in livestock improvement and its lack of confidence in the central board, by voting £450 to the Lieutenant-Governor to enable "the best kinds of the Dishly Breed of Sheep to be imported from England for the use of the Thirty Agricultural Societies; equally to be divided."[84] In 1826 Nova Scotia established a provincial stud. A vote of £1,000 to permit the importation of "two or more thoroughbred Seed Horses" purchased not only three horses but three mares as well, "all thoroughbred . . . of the purest blood and finest character."[85] A special legislative committee appointed to decide the disposition of the animals recommended their maintenance by the government so that the horses might be kept in condition and the mares protected from inferior sires. With a fourth horse obtained in Halifax for £200, there was one for "each of the four sections of the Province."[86] They were wintered in Halifax and dispatched to stations in the spring, there to serve a maximum of one hundred mares at a fee of 30s. The stud was maintained by the government for four seasons. The animals were disposed of in 1831 to private individuals and bonds were taken "that said Horses should be continually retained and used as Stallions in this Province."[87] The net annual cost to the province was between £200 and £300. Two stallions imported by the Nova Scotian government in the eighteen-forties were kept for nine years under similar arrangements, with

[82]Nova Scotia Assembly, *Journal and Proceedings,* 1819, p. 102.
[83]Martell and Harvey, "Achievements of Agricola," p. 3.
[84]Nova Scotia Appropriation Act, 6 Geo. IV, c. 1 (1825).
[85]*Ibid.,* 7 Geo. IV, c. 1 (1826); *Journal and Proceedings,* 1827, pp. 75-6.
[86]*Ibid.*
[87]*Ibid.,* 1836, App. no. 35.

regular annual deficits on maintenance accounts.[88] A Nova Scotian
act of 1832 (c. 44) "to encourage the importation of improved
Breeds of Cattle," provided up to £300 yearly towards aiding
individuals to import cattle of British or Irish breeds. The act was
renewed till 1842[89] but evidence of its uses is lacking.

Earliest public importations of livestock into New Brunswick
followed quickly those into Nova Scotia. In 1821 the Legislature
voted, "To the Central Agricultural Society of New Brunswick, a
sum not exceeding £500, for the purpose of importing for the use of
this Province, two entire horses, the one to be of the English hunter,
the other of the Irish hunter breed."[90] Whether or not these horses
were imported, the agricultural and emigrant society at Fredericton
reported in 1827 that they had imported "from England, in the
course of last summer a strong and beautiful horse, and sixteen
Dishly or Leicestershire sheep."[91] The animals were auctioned. The
society also imported Shorthorn cattle.[92] In 1837, £960 were granted
to William Crane "to repay him the amount advanced for the
purchase of stock in England, and the freight and other charges."[93]
More typical of New Brunswick methods was the vote in 1845 to
obtain four stallions for the province "in aid of individual subscription."[94] Though the conditional offer was renewed in 1846, no
evidence indicates that it was employed. In each of the years 1847
and 1848 the government voted £700 as premiums to encourage the
private importation of improved stallions, £200 each to go for the
best thoroughbred and the best Irish hunter, and £150 to go for the
second best of each kind. Importers were to give bonds of £1,000
per horse that the aminal should remain in the province as a stallion
for five years. Mr. McMonagle availed himself of the offer in 1847
and bought three horses in England at a cost of £757 sterling, not
counting incidental expenses. The horses were lost when the vessel
carrying them struck a ledge and sank. The Legislature voted a

[88]*Ibid.,* 1850, pp. 606-7, and App. no. 62.
[89]Martell and Harvey, "From Central Board to Secretary of Agriculture,"
p. 3.
[90]New Brunswick Assembly, *Journal,* 1821, p. 358.
[91]MacGregor, *British America* (1st edn., Edinburgh, 1832), vol. II, p. 325.
[92]*Ibid.,* p. 314. These were apparently the first Shorthorns introduced to
territory now Canadian.
[93]New Brunswick Appropriation Act, 1837.
[94]New Brunswick Assembly, *Journal,* 1845, pp. 269, 301.

special premium of £550 provided McMonagle import three more horses, and he later claimed and received this sum.[95]

As for Prince Edward Island, the Royal (or Central) Agricultural Society administered whatever funds were made available for agricultural improvement on the Island, from the inception of the Society in 1827 to the middle eighteen-sixties when the government established a stock farm. Scattered and trifling special grants for livestock importation, made to this society before the middle eighteen-fifties, were couched in resolutions of the minutest detail, requiring the animals to be auctioned, the object being to apportion the benefits equally among the three Island counties. The first special livestock grant of £150 made in 1838 enabled the Central Agricultural Society to import one stallion, two bulls, and two heifers for £345 currency, while the auction proceeds were £243.[96] In 1835 a grant of £150 permitted the importation of a horse, Saladin, for £273, while his sale yielded £220.[97] In 1848, £200 were provided for the importation of animals, chiefly sheep, with the proviso that "on arrival, the number shall be divided into three equal portions, as near as may be, to the same value," and one portion sold in each county.[98]

5. Encouragement of Animal Husbandry After 1850

Early in the eighteen-forties the belief in the Maritimes as a potential grazing country began to crowd out the hope that they might be developed into a "wheat country," as John Young and many others had assured the people was possible. Notable first activities of the agricultural societies, newly created or restored from dormancy after 1840, were those concerning livestock improvement. The new central board in Nova Scotia, organized in 1841, stated that "one of the principal objects of the Board was the Importation of improved Breeds of Stock, and several of the Societies expressed a desire to have their funds, in whole, or in part expended in that way."[99] The board imported cattle, sheep, and swine from England

[95]Ibid., 1848, p. 246.
[96]Prince Edward Island Assembly, Journal, 1838, p. 76; 1840, App. I.
[97]Ibid., 1846. App. I.   [98]Ibid., 1848, p. 150.
[99]Nova Scotia Assembly, Journal and Proceedings, 1842, App. no. 35. Martell says, speaking of Nova Scotia in the years 1840-4, "Nearly every [agricultural] society imported livestock from somewhere, Great Britain, the United States, Canada, the other Maritime provinces, or even another district in Nova Scotia" ("From Central Board to Secretary of Agriculture," p. 7).

costing £955 sterling, delivered; a stallion from Canada costing £100; as well as hogs from Boston, the pigs and boars "far from prepossessing in appearance."[100] Societies in New Brunswick acted similarly. Commencing in 1845, however, and continuing for seven or eight years, crop conditions were so serious, with blight, wheat-fly, and drought ruining potato, wheat, and hay crops,[101] that livestock had to be sacrificed and all efforts turned towards securing immediate relief. The need for developing substitutes for wheat flour gave special point to the policy of oatmill bounties. All in all, it was not till the middle eighteen-fifties, with some restoration of grain and hay crops and of prices in provisions markets, that the interest in livestock improvement in the Maritimes came to the fore with any degree of permanency.

In Nova Scotia in the eighteen-fifties the central board wound up a tenuous existence with few funds, and without benefit of legislation from 1852 to 1858, when it expired. The government had not sufficient confidence in it to entrust it with any substantial grants, and experience with governmental maintenance of livestock indicated clearly the advantages of auction disposal. The new Governor, however, Le Marchant (1852-8), was a livestock enthusiast. His reputation as a judge of farm animals had much to do with influencing the Legislature to undertake substantial imports, and Le Marchant acted as purchasing agent.[102] The programme was unprecedented in scope. In 1853 a vote of £400 to the Governor enabled the importation from England of five Shorthorns, three Guernsey cattle, and four Berkshire hogs.[103] A £2,000 vote in 1854 went to procure nine stallions from Canada and the United States. These were allotted by "ballot" on arrival, one to each pair of counties, then auctioned.[104] With this transaction the agricultural committee of the Legislature, always carrying a majority of country members, felt that the bars were down, and in 1855 they recom-

[100]Nova Scotia Assembly, *Journal and Proceedings*, 1842, App. no. 35.

[101]In 1851 the Nova Scotian Central Agricultural Board spoke of the period of "adversity unparalled [*sic*] in the Annals of Agricultural History." As cited in Martell and Harvey, "From Central Board to Secretary of Agriculture."

[102]*Ibid.*, pp. 12 ff.

[103]Nova Scotia Assembly, *Journal and Proceedings*, 1853, p. 368; 1854, App. no. 59.

[104]*Ibid.*, App. no. 59, and p. 501; 1854-5, App. no. 49.

mended three substantial grants: £2,000 for nine more stallions, £750 for brood mares, and £1,000 for sheep.[105] The Legislature voted only the last-mentioned grant, £1,000 for sheep, and in 1856 they voted an equal additional sum for more sheep.[106] The resulting importations were large and included other animals as well as sheep. Governmental imports in 1855 from Canada and Prince Edward Island comprised 122 sheep and lambs, two bulls, one Durham heifer, and three stallions.[107] In 1856 from England there came six Guernsey heifers, two Guernsey bulls, fifteen rams and ewes, and five hogs; and from Canada, sixty-eight Leicester rams and lambs.[108] The financial results of these importations, as auctioned, were consistently disappointing.[109] The livestock interest, however, did not falter. A new agricultural board, formed in 1864, under a constitution which finally decentralized control into the hands of country members, had substantial funds at its disposal and made livestock improvement its main objective.[110] In 1865 a $10,000 grant went for horses and sheep in England. In 1866 Nova Scotia passed a stock farm act,[111] which provided for a farm where the government might keep imported stock in order to prevent auction losses. A fund of $8,000 was set

[105]*Ibid.*

[106]*Ibid.*, Committee of Supply, p. 721; Nova Scotia Appropriation Act, c. 38 (1856).

[107]Nova Scotia Assembly, *Journal and Proceedings*, 1857, App. no. 76.

[108]*Ibid.*

[109]Auction proceeds of Nova Scotian importations during the middle eighteen-fifties ranged from 8-37 per cent of the delivered cost of the various consignments (calculations made from annual reports of Agricultural Committee, Nova Scotia Assembly, *Journal and Proceedings*).

[110]Martell says that "In its first four years the Board imported 'not fewer than 22 thorough-bred bulls, 9 thorough-bred cows and heifers, upwards of 100 thoroughbred rams, and 20 thorough-bred pigs' and sold them at public auction where they were frequently picked up by purchasing agents of the societies" ("From Central Board to Secretary of Agriculture," p. 17). By Confederation the societies too had come to consider their chief function to be that of procuring good breeds of imported stock. In the eighteen-fifties an increasing number of Nova Scotian agricultural societies were little more than co-operative livestock-buying clubs, their activities waxing and waning in direct proportion to the Board's prospect for new livestock funds. As the better-off members came to own breeding stock, and to offer the animals for service, the functions of agricultural societies dwindled (*ibid.*, pp. 18, 21).

[111]*Nova Scotia Statutes*, 29 Vic., c. 22, An Act to Authorize the establishment of a Provincial Stock Farm.

aside, but the farm was not established and the fund was used in elaborate importations for auction after 1872.[112]

New Brunswick increased the scale of encouragement to live-stock about 1850, though not as generously as Nova Scotia. The results were negligible. The premium plan of 1847 and 1848[113] was followed by offers in 1853 and 1854 partially to reimburse agricultural societies for importing horses, cattle, sheep, and swine.[114] The government required proof of importation and bond that the stock should be kept in the county for three years for breeding purposes. Seven societies qualified for aid for the importation of horses, their grants ranging from £50 to £125, and two or three societies qualified for grants for other importations.[115] An unconditional grant of £2,000 was made in 1853 to obtain six stallions from England, "inasmuch as a large amount is annually drained out of this Province and paid for Horses imported from the neighboring Colony of Prince Edward Island."[116] By 1860 New Brunswick had a central board of agriculture with a grant for the first year of £2,000 with which to import stock for auction.[117] Four horses were purchased in New England, and a few sheep and swine in England, but the bulk of the grant which had been allotted to the purchase of cattle, was not used because of the prevalence of pleuro-pneumonia in foreign herds. The New Brunswick Central Agricultural Board was in continuous conflict with the Assembly, though supported by the Legislative Council.[118] It did little more regarding stock, but continued to urge a stock, or breeding, farm as advised by the 1856 Commission.[119] In contrast to the inactivity of the board, however,

112Martell and Harvey, "From Central Board to Secretary of Agriculture," p. 19.

113See above, pp. 56-7.

114New Brunswick Assembly, *Journal*, 1853, pp. 335-6, 342; 1854 (first session), pp. 391, 424-5.

115*Ibid.*, 1854 (first session), pp. 261-2; 1856, App. cxxxiii-cxliv.

116*Ibid.*, 1853, pp. 224-5, 285.

117*Ibid.*, 1861, App. no. 4, "First Annual Report of the Board of Agriculture of the Province of New Brunswick," pp. 64 ff.

118*Ibid.*, 1866, App. no. VI, "Sixth Annual Report of the Board of Agriculture of the Province of New Brunswick."

119*Ibid.*, 1857-8, App. no. dcii, "Report of the Commission appointed under Address of the House of Assembly relating to the public encouragement of Agriculture."

the agricultural societies were notably active in promoting livestock improvement.

Prince Edward Island also greatly increased the scale of encouragement to livestock in the eighteen-fifties, especially paralleling Nova Scotia in emphasizing improvement in horses. Substantial grants were issued in contemplation of the importation of several horses at one time. In 1853 a joint address from the Assembly and the Council led to a grant of £1,000 to enable the Royal Agricultural Society to import "six Stud draught Horses, and one full bred horse," to be apportioned by lot among the counties and auctioned at specified places.[120] In 1854 the Royal Agricultural Society petitioned for a further £1,000 grant for stallions, setting forth that it had purchased seven entire horses in England in accord with the intentions of the House, "but that in consequence of the loss on the voyage of three Clydesdale horses, a large portion of the grant so appropriated was sunk and great disappointment and inconvenience in consequence experienced by the Farmers of the Island."[121] Though the desired grant was offered in 1854, and again in 1855, it was not used. Meanwhile the Royal Agricultural Society had secured a modification of its charter to permit it to retain ownership of imported livestock, the intention being to replace the costly auction method of disposal by means of a stock farm. In 1856 the Legislature voted £1,000 to the society "to be disposed of as they may direct," and the sum went towards the establishment of a breeding farm, the first governmentally aided one in the Maritimes.[122] This venture collapsed in a year or so,[123] and in 1865 the government organized a stock farm directly under its own management.[124]

6. Results of Agricultural Policy in the Maritimes

What can be said of the results of governmental encouragement to Maritime agriculture prior to Confederation? At the time of Confederation the governments of the Maritimes were financing encouragement of agriculture on a variable but generally undiminished scale. The preceding ten or fifteen years had been characterized

120Prince Edward Island Assembly, *Journal*, 1853, pp. 13-14, 18, 20, 21, and App. I.
121*Ibid.*, 1854, p. 25.
122*Ibid.*, 1856, pp. 41-2, 103; 1857, pp. 20, 43-4.
123*Ibid.*, 1858, pp. 16, 18.
124*Ibid.*, 1865, p. 38.

by a relative lessening of emphasis on bread-corn, or cereal, problems, and a greater emphasis on the improvement of livestock. This same period was marked by conditions of Maritime prosperity —contributed to by the Reciprocity Treaty and trade with the United States, and by a conjuncture of external circumstances,[125] which pulled the Maritimes out of the extreme economic depths of the late eighteen-forties and provided them with greater opulence than they have known since. This contrasted with the eighteen-forties when crop failures and general economic distress had driven the inhabitants of New Brunswick and Nova Scotia to growing and eating buckwheat, oatmeal, and maize.[126] Fundamentally as late as Confederation there was little change; the most serious interest in agriculture was shown in periods of commercial distress. At no time were the advocates of agricultural aid in Nova Scotia and New Brunswick sincerely anxious to make these provinces agricultural provinces.

Of the three colonies, Prince Edward Island was the only one to be considered an agricultural colony before Confederation. Prince Edward Island long before Confederation was famous for a variety of agricultural produce. New Brunswick relied heavily on the Island for horses, oats, and hay for lumbering; Nova Scotia and Newfoundland relied on her cattle, sheep, beef, pork, and bacon for provisioning the fisheries and fishing trade. Nova Scotia and New Brunswick bought a great deal of breeding stock from Prince Edward Island.[127] Prince Edward Island oats sold in Boston at

[125]S. A. Saunders has demonstrated that the Reciprocity Treaty was among the least of the forces working toward Maritime prosperity in this period. He attaches much greater significance to "external forces which greatly stimulated the ship-building industry and the carrying trade; railway construction in Nova Scotia and New Brunswick; and last, but not least, the American Civil War." See "Maritime Provinces and the Reciprocity Treaty" (*Dalhousie Review*, vol. XIV, 1934-5), p. 355.

[126]Johnston, *Notes on North America*, vol. I, pp. 41, 44, 100 and *passim*.

[127]In 1842 the Wallace agricultural society of Nova Scotia imported from Prince Edward Island two boars, twenty-one lambs, and three bulls "of good breeds" (Nova Scotia Assembly, *Journal and Proceedings*, 1843, App. no. 32). In 1846 the Nova Scotia Central Board reported: "The improved breeds of cattle, sheep and swine are now in great demand, and large numbers have been imported by the Eastern Counties, from Prince Edward Island" (*ibid*, 1846, App. no. 77). In 1847 the same Board reported that the River John society had imported eight Leicester lambs from the Island, as their sheep had been so much improved by previous importations from there (*ibid.*, 1847, App. no.

prices higher than were paid for domestic oats.[128] By 1855 it was estimated that one-quarter of the total land acreage of the Island was cleared for cultivation.[129] It was, of course, a question of alternative opportunities, and the Island's forests were so far stripped that the cultivation of fertile land was an increasingly attractive alternative employment for labour and capital. This was the case because, as Monro said, "Repeated fires, as well as the operations of the lumberman, and shipbuilder, have made great havoc among the woods. . . ."[130] In 1867, Prince Edward Island exported 4,600 sheep, 950 cattle, 400 horses, and 470 hogs—"being more than seven times the number of those exported in the year 1855."[131]

Nova Scotia and New Brunswick were repeatedly reforming, but were never reformed, for there was no sincere and lasting desire to be reformed. Self-appointed advisers to the agricultural community constantly professed to see these provinces on the point of entry to a new era, but the new era never came. The "reforms" advocated over the years could have been imposed by a powerful and determind central body, but they would have made for markedly inefficient uses for labour and capital. In 1850 New Brunswick's exports were nearly all timber shipped to Great Britain, and 40 per cent of her imports were agricultural products—flour, grain, meal, livestock, meats, and vegetables, largely from the United States.[132] Of Nova Scotian imports for 1854 valued at £1,790,000 currency, wheat and rye flour accounted for £320,000, cornmeal and oatmeal for £52,000, and all agricultural produce for about £450,000; of her exports of £1,250,000 currency, £150,000 were of agricultural produce.[133] In

---

39). In 1853 a committee of the New Brunswick Assembly recommended a vote of £2,000 for six English stallions to cut short the annual drain of money to Prince Edward Island (New Brunswick Assembly, *Journal*, 1853, pp. 224-5).

[128]Andrews, *On the Trade and Commerce of the British North American Colonies* (House Executive Document, 32nd Congress, 2nd session, no. 136, 1853), p. 551.

[129]Monro, *New Brunswick*, p. 365.

[130]*Ibid.*, p. 359.

[131]Prince Edward Island Assembly, *Journal*, 1868, App. J, Report of the Stock Farm Committee.

[132]New Brunswick Assembly, *Journal*, 1851, Customs Returns, App. no. ccxx ff.

[133]Nova Scotia Assembly, *Journal and Proceedings*, 1854-5, App. no. 86.

1856 on the verge of the commercial crisis, the agricultural committee of the New Brunswick Legislature gave the opinion that the
whole matter of governmental assistance to agriculture should be
reconsidered.[134] The Agricultural Commission appointed pursuant
to that recommendation reported that New Brunswick was importing
"provisions and farm produce, more particularly wheaten flour, to a
great extent," and estimated that farm produce imports ran at
£600,000 yearly, or £3 per head of the population, and one-third of
the total provincial demand.[135] Even more significant was their statement that the domestic deficiency of foodstuffs was not diminishing,
but rather increasing. In 1861 the New Brunswick Board of
Agriculture noted steady improvement in livestock, in "rotation and
cropping. . . . Turnips are now thoroughly established in New
Brunswick. . . . The establishment of this crop marks an era in the
history of practical agriculture in this province."[136] However, their
main thesis was the old, old one: "It seems hardly right that New
Brunswick should be paying an annual tribute of more than £50,000
to Nova Scotia, and more than £20,000 to Prince Edward Island, for
such articles as New Brunswick itself ought to produce."[137]

Even for Nova Scotia and New Brunswick, however, there had
been agricultural development before Confederation, and particularly
a tendency towards specialization in livestock. Nova Scotia and New
Brunswick had certain agricultural exports during this period—
potatoes and hay from New Brunswick and Nova Scotia;[138] and
cattle, pork, and some horses from Nova Scotia to Newfoundland
and the West Indies.[139] Significant was the increasing emphasis in
Nova Scotia on "green" crops instead of "white" crops; that is,
broadly speaking, on roots such as turnips, carrots, and mangel
wurtzel instead of on cereals. Nova Scotian agricultural reports
through the eighteen-fifties stressed "esculent" foods for cattle. In

---

[134]New Brunswick Assembly, *Journal,* 1856, p. 283.

[135]*Ibid.,* 1857-8, App. no. dcii, Report of the Commission appointed under
Address of the House of Assembly relating to the public encouragement of
Agriculture.

[136]*Ibid.,* 1861, App. no. 4, Preface.

[137]*Ibid.,* p. 12.

[138]Andrews, *On the Trade and Commerce of the British North American
Colonies.*

[139]Nova Scotia Assembly, *Journal and Proceedings,* 1847, App. no. 39;
1854, App. no. 59.

the change of cultural practices the failure of potato crops gave a considerable impetus, but it was basically a change of technique quite suitable to frontier conditions and contributory to the increased emphasis on animal husbandry after mid-century. Governmental funds dispersed by agricultural boards and societies did facilitate the transfer of techniques concerning livestock, implements, and methods of cultivation, some of which had no lasting significance because they were irrelevant to frontier conditions, but some of which were helpful. Generally, "high" cultivation practices had better not have been advocated; summer-fallowing and fertilization would have been thoroughly bad practice throughout most of the Maritime regions in the pre-Confederation period. But agricultural societies facilitated the introduction of livestock and the culture of root crops for their better care. By mid-century the care of livestock was coming to have a place among the opportunities attractive to Maritime labour and capital. Agricultural societies also contributed to the introduction of sensible techniques in implements, chiefly from the New England colonies, and models thus introduced were copied by local artisans. Machinery which was designed for local conditions was of considerable significance because of the scarcity of labour in the frontier areas.

7. Summary

Agriculture did not develop naturally or easily in the Maritime colonies except in Prince Edward Island and in the Acadian region of Nova Scotia. Yet local agricultural development was thought to be essential to the Maritime economies. So long as the French maintained their hold on the St. Lawrence and in Maritime areas, defence was the chief British concern. Thus Halifax was founded, with attempts at surrounding agricultural settlement; thus also the Acadians were dispersed and encouragement given towards the settlement of New Englanders upon their lands. The defence problem was an important consideration in the extension of aid to Loyalist settlement after the Revolution.

With increased settlement and with general economic development, the Maritime colonies evolved types of productive activity best suited to their respective local conditions. In Nova Scotia there was concentration on the cod fisheries and the codfish trade, on shipbuilding, and on the provisions trade with the West Indies. In New

Brunswick circumstances co-operated to establish pre-eminently the production and trade in square pine timber, and the closely allied activity of ship-buiding. These pursuits could be profitable in competitive world markets only if costs were low, and in each case the cost of provisions constituted a leading element in the total picture. Mercantile methods of thought led readily to the assumption that reliance for provisions should be placed only upon local sources of supply. Local agriculture, it was taken for granted, should expand to keep pace with commercial requirements.

In line with such reasoning, Maritime governments extended varied aids to domestic agriculture throughout the pre-Confederation period. They subsidized cereal, or bread-corn production; they imported livestock and subsidized its distribution; they established agricultural societies and agricultural boards, providing them with annual revenues for agricultural purposes; they made tentative beginnings in agricultural education.

Though persistent, the efforts to encourage Maritime agriculture took but a trifling portion of annual provincial budgets. Such efforts were unsuccessful in producing a domestic agriculture adequate to commercial needs. Prince Edward Island alone among the Maritime colonies became an agricultural colony, and that without substantial agricultural subsidies. Alternative opportunities on the Island, of greater attractiveness than those of agricultural pursuits, were early exhausted. In Nova Scotia and New Brunswick, however, alternative opportunities continued to be much more attractive, and at Confederation these colonies were more dependent on outside agricultural supplies than ever before.

CHAPTER IV

THE ST. LAWRENCE REGION, 1760-1850

THE completeness of the collapse of the French empire in America by 1763 was a measure of France's failure to integrate that empire on a sound agricultural base.[1] In 1763 there were 65,000 French on the St. Lawrence, while the English in the Thirteen Colonies totalled "perhaps a million and a half."[2] Fishing and sugar-raising areas were not conducive to agriculture; the fur trade barely tolerated it; yet along the fur-trade route appeared the only possible location for an expanding agricultural settlement. The size of the population on the St. Lawrence in 1763 made a cruel mockery of over a century and a half of mercantilistic effort by the French to lay an agricultural foundation for a diversified commercial empire. Far from providing a regular and substantial export of provisions, the French agricultural area frequently had to import foodstuffs for its own needs. French Canadians made more use of the rod and gun than of agricultural implements.[3] Winters and wolves practically prohibited sheep-raising. Farmers were in debt and money was scarce; yet the inhabitants had too many horses and too few cattle.[4] All this Governor Murray reported along with his opinion that with very slight cultivation "all sorts of grain are here easily produced, and in great abundance," and that the lands were suitable for flax and hemp, of which little was grown.[5]

1. British Designs

Britain would not waste these golden opportunities. Newly-acquired territories had to conform to the colonial pattern and yield their full potentialities. The Board of Trade wrote that Canada was a place "where Planting, perpetual Settlement and Cultivation ought

[1]See Chapter II.

[2]Creighton, *Commercial Empire of the St. Lawrence*, p. 12.

[3]Report of the State of the Government of Quebec in Canada, by General Murray, June 5, 1762, Public Archives of Canada, Ottawa. See Canadian Archives, *Constitutional Documents*, in Canada, *Sessional Papers*, 1907, no. 18.

[4]*Ibid.* Murray thought, however, that horses were fed to the troops in order to disguise the high prices charged by those selling food to the government.

[5]*Ibid.* See also Macdonald, *Canada, 1763-1841*, pp. 476 ff.

to be encouraged."⁶ Governor Murray was required to survey the prospects of the colony from the standpoint of agricultural settlement.

Murray magnified the barest traces of agriculture in the Quebec settlement and interpreted each one as a potential constituent of British Empire economy.⁷ The chronic ratio between horses and horned cattle which existed in the settlement he thought could be dealt with by a modification of the horse tax which would yield revenue, and "would serve also to restrain a piece of luxury the people of this Country are too apt to run into, in that respect, and prove a means to encourage the breed of horned Cattle." Fodder requirements were heavy during the long winters, but less for cattle than horses, and cattle "afford a double utility." The tendency toward laziness among the inhabitants, and their addiction to rod and gun, Murray thought would correct itself under the British, since the inhabitants would be deprived of guns and would be free from former monopolies and forced-labour calls.

Murray's attitude towards the cultivation of hemp and flax indicates the typical mercantile viewpoint regarding the function of colonial agriculture. He found the French Canadians already growing these products on lands "well cultivated for this Production." Next steps were obvious to him. "It will be right to turn the thoughts of the people towards the cultivation of this article [hemp], so essential to Great Britain and for which she annually pays great sums to Foreigners. A few premiums properly disposed of, some Germans and Russians skilled in raising and preparing the same and encouraged for that purpose to become settlers here may in a short time greatly improve this most useful branch of Agriculture." More obvious mercantile implications suggested themselves to Murray: "This will be one means of employing the Women and Children during the long winters in breaking and preparing the flax and hemp for exportation, will divert them from manufacturing coarse things for their own use, as it will enable them to purchase those of a better sort manufactured and imported from Great Britain." And again: "Raising hemp and flax for which the lands are in many places extremely proper must be an object of the most serious consideration. And I must repeat here, how useful this must prove to the end

⁶Creighton, *Commercial Empire of the St. Lawrence*, pp. 36-7.
⁷Succeeding citations are from Murray's Report on Quebec.

of promoting agriculture, of employing the Women and Children during the tedious winter months, and of procuring in a short time a vast exportation of that useful commodity for which the returns will be made in British Manufactures."

With navigation on the St. Lawrence closed six months in the year, the colony, Murray argued, could "never vie with our Southern Provinces in the West India Trade." But the prospects were excellent for creating a new cash staple out of potash, "so much demanded by our manufacturers." The preparation of this product would offer "a means to employ the men all Winter in the business of felling and drawing of Wood which time they chiefly dedicate to idleness and smoking."

Modification of St. Lawrence agriculture came with the conquest.[8] Numbers of French seigniors sold their properties in the colony and returned to France. British subjects bought these seigniories and encouraged their settlement by Scottish, Irish, and American families. After 1800 Edward Ellice bought the seigniory of Beauharnois on the south bank of the St. Lawrence, and by 1832 there were 326 Scottish families on his properties.[9] Murray Bay was settled by disbanded troops before 1783. The Eastern Townships contained refugee New England families by 1780, and they began producing livestock for the Quebec and Montreal markets.[10] The Hull settlement begun in 1800 by Philemon Wright was another patch of Anglo-American settlement beyond the edges of French-Canadian habitant agriculture. There was considerable interest in agricultural improvement among the newer British agricultural interests. The many articles on agricultural matters to be found in the *Quebec Gazette* at this time indicate marked attention to new methods of cultivation, wheat and potato culture,[11] and the use of fertilizers. Agricultural societies were formed at Quebec and at Newark (Niagara) by 1792.

Despite Murray's enthusiastic analysis of agricultural prospects in the new British colony, despite the British Proclamation of 1763 prohibiting settlement west of the Alleghanies, and despite a proclamation published by Murray in American newspapers in 1765 calling

[8]Innis (ed.), *Select Documents, 1497–1783*, pp. 434-48.
[9]Macdonald, *Canada, 1763-1841*, pp. 478 ff.
[10]*Ibid.*
[11]Innis (ed.), *Select Documents, 1497-1783*, pp. 572-3.

attention to the generous settlement offers on the St. Lawrence, the agriculture of Quebec did not develop according to expectations.[12] The St. Lawrence had been a fur-trade route, and the most obvious accompaniment of the conquest was the influx of British and New England merchants who came first to feed and clothe the troops and secondly to salvage the fur trade with all its profitable prospects.[13] Neither the habitants nor the French seigniors who remained in the colony were interested in developing commercial agriculture. For twenty years Britain retained the "Southern Provinces" and the entire Maritime region, and British commercial interests were simply not reduced to the point where the uncertain agricultural prospects of the St. Lawrence had to be taken seriously.

Agriculture on the St. Lawrence became significant for the British Empire only after 1783, when Britain had lost sufficient of her colonial agricultural base to appreciate the areas with lesser promise. Even then, interest was not in the geographic regions of French agricultural effort, but farther up the St. Lawrence beyond the seigniories. The Loyalist settlement on the St. Lawrence had neither the magnitude nor the distinctiveness of that in the Maritimes. Six or seven thousand Loyalists may have gone to the former as compared with thirty thousand to the latter region.[14] Even the arrival of the six or seven thousand was spread over several years, some straggling across the line, up the Lake Champlain route, from the first of the war, others coming in a definite group of a few hundred, shipped from New York in 1783, these to be followed by "late Loyalists," and in turn by a stream of land-seekers ending only with the War of 1812. The Loyalists entering the Old Province of Quebec, therefore, were swallowed up in a continuing wave of immigration, and their establishment was not so clearly a project of empire, whether commercial or territorial, as was that of the Maritime group. Governor Haldimand even tried to divert the New York group from the St. Lawrence to the Maritimes, for, he argued, "Fisheries in Nova Scotia and the Island of Cape Breton considered

    [12]Hansen and Brebner, *Mingling of the Canadian and American Peoples*, pp. 41-2.

    [13]*Ibid.;* Creighton, *Commercial Empire of the St. Lawrence*, chap. ii.

    [14]Burt, *Old Province of Quebec*, chap. xv; Cruickshank, *Settlement of the United Empire Loyalists*.

as national and commercial objects are certainly preferable to settlements where agriculture is the sole prospect."[15]

Nevertheless, assistance to Loyalist settlement was the earliest governmental assistance to agriculture in Upper Canada, in territory now Ontario, and contemporary interpretation places it strikingly within the mercantilistic conception of the normal agriculture-commerce relationship. The first Loyalists came unsought, but Haldimand cared for them, first on the seigniory of Sorel, and in 1780 he dispatched families to the upper posts where they might engage in agriculture and thus contribute to the provisioning of the garrisons.[16] Cataraqui had been selected as an asylum for loyalist Indians fleeing from the United States, but Haldimand, hearing that loyalist whites were being sent there too, and that the Indians were agreeable, "in three weeks" became an enthusiastic supporter of the project, defending it in normal mercantilistic sentiments on the grounds that he could "foresee great advantages from this settlement . . . the Royalists settled together in numbers will form a respectable body attached to the interests of Great Britain and capable of being useful upon many occasions. Their industry will in a very few years raise in that fertile tract of country great quantities of wheat and other grains and become a granary for the lower parts of Canada where the crops are precarious . . . and even advantages with regard to the fur trade may result from the settlement at Cataraqui."[17] The purposes of empire were, for the time being, defence and provisions, and with these objects in view Loyalist settlers were given settlement assistance.[18]

[15]Innis and Lower (eds.), *Select Documents, 1783-1885*, p. 11.

[16]Burt states, "His primary motive was to relieve the strain upon the commissariat by creating a local food supply for the garrison. This war-time settlement, it is interesting to note, foreshadows one of his leading ideas in the permanent settlement after the peace" (*Old Province of Quebec*, pp. 364-5). See also Hansen and Brebner, *Mingling of the Canadian and American Peoples*, pp. 48-9.

[17]Innis and Lower (eds.), *Select Documents, 1783-1885*, pp. 10-11.

[18]This assistance included provisions for a year, seed, and the following implements: a plough, a plough share and coulter, a set of drag teeth, a log-chain, an axe, a saw, a hammer, a bill-hook and a grubbing hoe, a pair of hand irons and a cross-cut saw amongst several families. See James, "History of Farming" in *Canada and Its Provinces*, eds. Shortt and Doughty, vol. XVIII, p. 564. Haldimand refused a request for cattle, but several herds were salvaged and driven into Upper Canada in 1784 (Burt, *Old Province of Quebec*, p. 376).

Governor Simcoe's interpretation of settlement and agriculture was the same as expressed by Haldimand.[19] By 1790 population was sweeping westward from the seaboard to envelop the lower lakes, north as well as south.[20] On the matter of defence, Simcoe proposed to settle soldiers on the lake fronts and fill in behind with colonists of doubtful loyalty. As for provisioning prospects, he was more optimistic than Haldimand, reasoning that "Upper Canada is not only capable of satisfying the wants of all its inhabitants, but also of becoming a granary for England, and of creating a considerable trade."[21] This would be, he felt, a "powerful example," arousing great activity in Lower Canada. The corn trade he considered far preferable to the fur trade, the latter monopolized by a few companies, and the corn trade would break the fur-trade monopoly to the advantage of Britain and Canada. Immediately following the first session of the Upper Canada Legislature in the fall of 1791 in Newark (Niagara), Simcoe formed an agricultural society.[22]

In spite of the normal mercantile attitude towards agriculture and settlement expressed successively by Governors Murray, Haldimand, and Simcoe, there were long gaps in the pattern of agricultural aid on the St. Lawrence after 1763. The intention survived well into Simcoe's day, but after the coming of the Loyalists it was a long time before substantial assistance was given towards settlement. This, of course, is to be expected in view of British opinion after 1783 that Canada would sooner or later follow the lead of the Thirteen Colonies, and that, consequently, further defence measures were futile. Since financial aid to immigration and settlement, and to agricultural development, was basically a defence expenditure, it stood condemned by the reasoning which condemned further defence expenditures of any sort. Locally, too, there was no urgent demand for an expanding agriculture, for groups with initiative and with a voice in affairs had no special uses for such activities within the economy. Till the beginnings of the nineteenth century the fur trade

19Innis and Lower (eds.), *Select Documents, 1783-1885*, pp. 18-20; Creighton, *Commercial Empire of the St. Lawrence*, pp. 116 ff.; Hansen and Brebner, *Mingling of the Canadian and American Peoples*, pp. 80-1.

20Creighton, *Commercial Empire of the St. Lawrence*, pp. 89 ff.

21Innis and Lower (eds.), *Select Documents, 1783-1885*, p. 19.

22James, "History of Farming"; see also Talman, "Agricultural Societies of Upper Canada" (Ontario Historical Society, *Papers and Records*, vol. XXVII, 1931), pp. 545-52.

remained unchallenged as the main economic "purpose" of the St. Lawrence. Its provisioning needs were never such as to press heavily on agriculture. Defence had always been the fur trade's requirement in agriculture and the slight interest in agriculture after 1783 was in its defensive aspects. But the Quebec Act had pushed the boundaries of Quebec back to the Ohio, and the St. Lawrence no longer seemed so vulnerable. Besides, the Montreal group was not anxious to have the boundary too sharply drawn, and this frame of mind survived at least until the time of Galt's policy of "incidental protection" in 1859, and fundamentally until the inauguration of the National Policy in 1879.

Earliest agricultural aid legislation in the Canadas concerned hemp-growing, and clearly indicates the defensive role of agriculture within the mercantile framework. On hemp-growing and assistance thereto, local authorities picked up where the home authorities left off. British demands for huge quantities of hemp for sailing vessels, whether merchant or man-o'-war, were largely satisfied from Russia, but such an extra-empire source was held, *ipso facto,* to be a precarious source. If hemp could be grown in the colonies it would serve a variety of mercantile uses: it would provide a staple for export from the colonies which would stimulate British manufacturing and at the same time contribute directly to Empire defence.[23] Governor Murray's comments, mentioned above, bear on these points. A great variety of devices were employed to encourage hemp-growing in practically all British colonies, devices including distribution of seed and information on growing and preparing methods; the establishment of fixed prices for hemp locally grown; bounties on land planted to hemp; premiums for largest fields, best fibre, and seed; the requirement in some cases that land grants be partly laid down to hemp; and the appointment of hemp commissioners to administer the governmental hemp policy.

Hemp-growing possibilities in Canada were investigated about 1787. On the advice of Whitehall, the Executive Council established a committee to investigate the agricultural possibilities of Canada

---

[23]Mackintosh has stressed the staple-crop aspect of hemp culture in British North American colonies. See "Economic Factors in Canadian History" (*Canadian Historical Review,* March, 1923), pp. 12-25. The defence aspect should not be overlooked.

with particular reference to hemp.[24]   In 1789 the newly-formed
Quebec Agricultural Society received a quantity of hemp seed from
the British government for free distribution in the colony, and with
the seed came 1,200 copies of a pamphlet on hemp culture. This
seed was planted in 1790, and the same year Dorchester proclaimed
a fixed price for governmental purchases of hemp seed. For the
next few years, articles in the *Quebec Gazette* kept alive an interest
in hemp culture.

With the turn of the century, European wars so far jeopardized
British hemp supplies from Russia that colonial prospects became
more attractive than ever. Under the prodding of the imperial
government the Lower Canada Legislature in 1801 launched an experimental investigation of hemp-growing possibilities. In 1805 and
1806 the same Legislature supervised and financed the experimental
extravagance of two demonstration farms given over to hemp-
growing.[25] Lower Canada acts of 1802 (42 Geo. III, c. 5) and 1804
(44 Geo. III, c. 8) provided for a board of hemp commissioners
with local committees in Quebec, Three Rivers, and Montreal, and
each act provided £1,200 currency for the encouragement of hemp-
growing. These funds went for seed, for bounties, and for purchasing the fibre at fixed prices. In 1806 Lower Canada appointed an
agent to buy all hemp fibre which might be offered during the next
five years on government account at £43 sterling per ton. Upper
Canada offered similar encouragement to hemp-growing. An early
act "for the further encouragement of the growth and cultivation of
hemp within this province, and the exportation thereof" (1804),
provided £1,000 for purchasing hemp grown in the province, at £40
per ton.[26] An act of 1805 (Upper Canada: 45 Geo. III, c. 10) provided that since £40 a ton was inadequate encouragement, the price
was to be raised to £50. In 1808 the price was raised to £62.10*s.* for
merchantable hemp (Upper Canada: 48 Geo. III, c. 9). Acts of
1816 and 1818 provided £1,000 for the encouragement of hemp cultivation. At the latter end of the 1819-21 depression an act (Upper
Canada: 2 Geo. IV, c. 17, 1822) provided £300 for purchasing and

24Gorham, "Development of Agricultural Administration in Upper and
Lower Canada in the Period before Confederation."
25*Ibid.*
26*Quebec Gazette*, March 24, 1804; *Statutes of Upper Canada*, 44 Geo. III,
c. 11.

erecting hemp machinery "to prepare Hemp for Exportation," and £50 yearly for three years for keeping such machinery in repair. Ten years later John Covert drew £200 which remained unexpended under this act, and for a three-year period drew £50 yearly for repairs.[27]

Despite all the assistance specifically applying to hemp cultivation, and much general encouragement, there is nothing to indicate that the Canadas, or, indeed, any of the North American colonies, ever contributed noticeably to British hemp requirements. However easy the actual growing of hemp may have been, its preparation for market was a different story, with exacting requirement in the way of climatic conditions, and in the skill and care of the labour force. Typical frontier conditions in the colonies, with labour and capital of all sorts scarce in relation to opportunities for land uses, forced all types of production with especially heavy labour requirements far down the scale of desirable occupations.

With the War of 1812-14 the defence aspects of agricultural settlement on the St. Lawrence experienced a temporary revival in the field of practical policy.[28] As in the case of New France it was the mother country that showed concern. Britain had not yet revised her official attitude that emigrants were lost resources wherever they went, and entertaining, as she did, small hope that the Canadas could in the long run be retained, there was little reason for her administrators to show exception in favour of these colonies. The War of 1812-14 demonstrated that the Canadas might be defended and retained but that existing defence forces were inadequate. Settlement seemed the one hope of correcting this inadequacy, provided it was settlement of the right kind—loyal to Britain, preferably comprising men with military training, and, of course, provisioning itself by agricultural activities. The concept of the barrier of loyal British subjects, set forth by Haldimand in 1783 and by Simcoe in the seventeen-nineties,[29] again came to the fore.

[27]Upper Canada Assembly, *Journal*, 1831-2, Public Accounts, p. 3; 1833-4, Public Accounts, p. 8.

[28]See Lower, "Immigration and Settlement in Canada" (*Canadian Historical Review*, March, 1922), pp. 37 ff.

[29]Innis and Lower (eds.), *Select Documents, 1783-1885,* pp. 18-20. The following information on settlement after 1812 is from Lower's article, cited above. See also Hansen and Brebner, *Mingling of the Canadian and American Peoples*, pp. 97-8.

Britain seemed to the British to be the obvious source of settlers of undisputed loyalty, and ex-soldiers to be the class with greatest military capabilities. As early as 1813 Lord Bathurst, the new Colonial Secretary, despatched a body of Scottish emigrants, offering free passage, free land, and aid in settlement, and proposing that bond be exacted against their going to the United States within two years. This group settled in the eastern district of Upper Canada with fair success. Rideau and Drummondville military settlements were located primarily on strategic rather than agricultural considerations. The Rideau settlement was planned as a means of establishing communications from Montreal to Upper Canada *via* the Rideau and Trent rivers, and *via* Lake Simcoe to Lake Huron, for with settlers along the route there would always be provisions, roads, and transport equipment around necessary portages. With the close of the War of 1812-14 the government arranged that disbanded soldiers should receive land on condition of settlement; and that for those who chose to join the Rideau and Drummondville settlements, there should be issued implements and food, and log cabins should be built. Bathurst thought that soldier emigrants, granted free land and other assistance, should be self-supporting within a year of settlement. Within a year, however, this group's complete ignorance of agriculture and especially of frontier agriculture, and their lack of adaptability, had rendered their position hopeless.

For the time being, therefore, the awakened consciousness of the defence requirements of the St. Lawrence led British authorities to assist British emigration to Canada. It also led them to make efforts to keep Americans out of Canada. The war over, every imaginable subterfuge was resorted to in order to keep Americans out, though they persisted in coming. The defence policy, however, was temporary. By 1816 the British government abandoned the policy of assisted passages and general assistance except for discharged soldiers. In 1816 and 1817 civilian emigrants received only free land. The belief reasserted itself that Canada was a lost cause and that further efforts towards its maintenance were useless.

From 1783 to 1815 settlement in the Canadas gradually filled in along the lake shores and river front to form a narrow ribbon from Quebec to Detroit. Though persistent, immigration was not large, from 1783 to 1821 totalling "about equal to the numbers who came in two years of the stirring twenties."[30] Apart from the inhabitants of Quebec and Montreal, agriculture was the concern of everyone, yet excepting aids to hemp culture, encouragement to rural activity was slight. Bush-lot farming was primarily a problem of self-sustenance: wheat, rye, Indian corn, buckwheat, and peas throve, providing bread corns for the household; oats fared badly; hogs, cows, and a few sheep provided further items of diet; oxen were kept for draught, and, if possible, horses for winter sleighs. Prospects for surplus provisions were so slight that stimulation from outside seemed scarcely worth considering. Various agricultural products developed surpluses of limited quantities for individual farmers, or even for areas, and garrisons provided local markets. The government bought flour, salt pork, and peas, thus provisioning troops and at the same time extending limited encouragement to local agriculture.[31] Progress was painfully slow. The War of 1812-14, as far as the Canadas were concerned, cut sharply across the lines of force of a slowly gathering momentum. Agriculture was severely checked in Upper Canada since men were mustered to arms and cattle were driven off for food. In 1813 the Legislature of Upper Canada passed an act "to prohibit the export of grain and other provisions, and also to restrain the distillation of spirituous liquors from grain" (53 Geo. III, c. 3), and in 1814 this act was amended and continued (54 Geo. III, c. 8).[32]

2. The New Staples: Wheat and Timber

During this period fundamental changes in the St. Lawrence economy were in process, changes which were to have far-reaching significance for agriculture and for its relationship to Empire forces. It was during this period that the fur trade finally failed the St. Lawrence, a failure formally recorded in 1821 with the absorption of the North West Company by the Hudson's Bay Company, with the final triumph of the Hudson Bay route over the St. Lawrence River route. This failure was only recorded in 1821; for years previously, the fur trade controlled from the St. Lawrence had reached simultaneously its territorial limits and its end, when expansion had brought its frontiers up sharply at the Pacific and the Arctic. An

30Innis, *Economic History of Canada*, p. 97.
31*Ibid.*, p. 99.
32*Statutes of Upper Canada*, vol. I, Public Acts, 1792-1840.

enterprise which might much longer have survived expansion found a static existence impossible.

But even before fur had departed from the St. Lawrence, the commerce and finance of the route were haltingly visioning the prospects latent in other trades which were for the time being diminutive and uncertain, trades which grew unproclaimed out of the unpromising soil of pioneer drudgery on the upper St. Lawrence, the lower Great Lakes, and the Ottawa River. Timber and wheat were these trades, with potash a distant third. Pioneer farming provided the basis for all three, though potash production was confined to limited areas, and timber and wheat achieved substantial development only when produced under separate specialized conditions. Hardwood forests provided the raw material for potash, and lands supporting hardwood forests were commonly suited for cultivation and cropping. Furthermore, hardwood could be rafted only with difficulty, hence was unsuited for marketing as timber. First steps in the conversion of hardwood bush lots into wheat farms involved cutting, piling, and burning the trees. By leaching, the resultant ashes were converted into an exportable product, potash. The demand for timber, in contrast, was a demand for softwoods, for white pine. This species was found widely, but its finest stands existed on lands ill-adapted to cultivation. Timber was rafted to tidewater, and propelled, till the days of the steam tug, by the force of river current. Accordingly its production in exportable quantities was confined to areas lying close to substantial streams or rivers down which timber rafts could be driven to Montreal or Quebec.[33]

Small export surpluses from Loyalist and post-Loyalist settlements in the upper parts of Canada developed soon after such settlements were established. The Bay of Quinte area soon produced a surplus of wheat which was sold to the government and ground into flour, part going to provision local garrisons and part to England. The first timber raft from the same region went down the St. Lawrence in 1790,[34] and early timber rafts carried potash, wheat, and flour. Philemon Wright first broke the forest on the site of Hull in 1800, and a few years later took the first raft of timber

33To pass over rapids, rafts might be dispersed and reassembled farther down. The real impediment lay in lakes, in large bodies of water without appreciable current and subject to storms.
34Innis, *Economic History of Canada*, p. 111.

down the Ottawa, which later was to develop into the Canadian counterpart of the St. John timber area of New Brunswick. The British preference established after 1800 provided a major impetus to timber exports, but beginnings had already been made. Wheat exports from Quebec reached a peak of over one million bushels in 1802,[35] a figure not matched till 1840. After November, 1820, Canadian wheat was ruled out of the British market by price conditions which called into play the protective features of the Corn Laws.[36]

From these small beginnings, elements significant for later developments appear. Timber and wheat came to displace fur as the staple trades of the St. Lawrence, timber much earlier than wheat. Timber and wheat come to replace fur as providing the dynamic of the St. Lawrence economy. Timber, but more particularly wheat—the newer staples—required improvements of the St. Lawrence never required by fur. These improvements were prodigiously costly in relation to local public finance, involving as they did a thorough-going scheme of canalization which was completed by 1850, only to be followed by a far more costly scheme of railway improvement. These elements were significant for the union of the provinces in 1841, and for Confederation.

Because of the later significance of wheat in the Canadian economy, a few words must be said regarding terminology. Wheat was exported from the St. Lawrence far back in the French régime, and such exports constituted part of the general provisions trade for garrisons, for fisheries, and for sugar plantations. So too did the exports made regularly from New England states, and occasionally from the Maritimes, and also those from Upper Canada till well on into the first half of the nineteenth century. Wheat exports as developed generations later from the Prairie Provinces, however, were not thought of as constituting part of the provisions trade; they had come to constitute an export staple. At some point in the interval wheat exported from Canada had passed from the status of a provision to that of a staple. Definition is difficult and unnecessary here, but the distinction seems to rest on the relative importance of

[35]Innis and Lower (eds.), *Select Documents, 1783-1885,* pp. 265-6.

[36]Gourlay, *Statistical Account of Upper Canada,* General Introduction, p. cccxxv; Lower Canada Assembly, *Journal,* 1821-2, Report of the Grand Committee on Agriculture and Commerce, p. 45.

wheat in the export cargo. If wheat, or wheat and flour, comprised simply one element in the assorted provisions cargo, the cargo also containing perhaps other cereals and meal and salted meats, wheat then would be thought of as a provision. But when wheat came to be exported customarily in such quantities as to move in one-commodity cargoes, then wheat came to be thought of as a staple. Recognition of the staple characteristic in wheat obviously implied a marked advance in its status as an element in the economy, and a corresponding stimulus to the attention of interested groups.

Whether at a particular time wheat was a provision or a staple altered only the degree of interest in its production. In either case profits were to be made in its trade, in its handling, financing, and merchandising. From the early eighteen-hundreds till the eighteen-fifties on the St. Lawrence, there was first of all the trade in timber; there was also a gradually increasing trade in wheat; but with these trades there was always the general provisions trade which required a diversified agriculture as a source of diversified products, and which included wheat among its parts.

On the St. Lawrence between 1800 and 1850, therefore, there were some of the same agricultural-commercial relationships which existed in the Maritimes, particularly in Nova Scotia and in New Brunswick. There was a provisions trade and a timber trade. Were there not, therefore, commercial groups ardently concerned that agriculture should flourish on the St. Lawrence, as there were in the Maritimes? Is there not here the basis for vigorous and persistent efforts on the part of non-agriculturists to stimulate agricultural activities, whatever the strength of agrarian claims upon legislative bodies? Fuller answers to these questions must await an analysis of the period under review. It can be said here that agricultural assistance on the St. Lawrence in the first half of the nineteenth century was trifling in terms of money and was confined almost exclusively to grants in aid of agricultural societies. Such assistance as there was, however, was urged primarily by commercial groups, with some agrarian support in Upper Canada.

3. *Agricultural Policy in Lower Canada*

Difficulties which involved farmer and merchant alike arose out of the War of 1812-14 and contributed to a moderate interest in agricultural encouragement. In both Upper and Lower Canada there was considerable distress, though of different sorts. In Upper Canada agriculture had been devastated by the war, areas were over-run, man-power had been diverted to defence, and livestock had been depleted. It was said that after 1814 if merchants collected their debts, two-thirds of Upper Canadian farmers would be ruined.[37] Lower Canadian difficulties were associated with an agricultural product, wheat, but were commercial rather than agricultural. The wheat trade, so substantial at the turn of the century, all but dis-appeared between 1813 and 1816, was partially restored in 1817 and 1818, only to collapse again in 1819.[38] By 1820 wheat prices were such as to close the British market entirely. Protest was abundant in both Upper and Lower Canada, particularly in the latter.

Significantly, the protests were commercial, though paying lip service to agriculture. In 1816 the Lower Canadian Legislature appointed the first special committee on Canadian agricultural matters; to be followed in 1817 by a "Grand Committee" on agri-culture and commerce, and a separate special committee on the state of agriculture; and in 1818 by a special committee which examined petitions of the newly-formed Montreal and Quebec agri-cultural societies, asking aid.[39] The years 1819-21 were years of commercial depression on the St. Lawrence. In the 1821-2 session the Grand Committee on Agriculture and Commerce—the name giv-ing clues to the interests involved—presented a report which gave still clearer indications of the commercial nature of the problem. Their report stressed the fact that wages, prices, and land values, exports and imports, had all fallen off, partly as a result of un-certainty over British timber preferences, but partly "and principally, by the unexpected operation of the Laws regulating the importation of Corn, Flour and Meal into the United Kingdom, whereby the Grain of this Colony, has since the month of November 1820, been excluded from home consumption in Britain as effectively as foreign grain."[40] There followed the drafting of a petition, revealing still

[37]Innis and Lower (eds.), *Select Documents, 1783-1885*, p. 239.

[38]*Ibid.*, pp. 265-6.

[39]See Quebec (Lower Canada), *Journal of Assembly*, 1816, p. 34 and App. E; 1817, pp. 36, 92, 106, 628; 1818, pp. 9, 42, 46, 82.

[40]Lower Canada Assembly, *Journal,* 1821-2, Report of the Grand Com-mittee on Agriculture and Commerce, p. 45. See also Innis and Lower (eds.), *Select Documents, 1783-1885*, p. 264.

more clearly the interests at stake. The petition to the Lords, Commons, and King begged "That all sorts of Corn or Grain, Flour or Meal of the Agricultural Produce of this Province, be at all times freely admitted for consumption within the United Kingdom."[41] The attempt to see a harmony of interest between commerce and agriculture is evident from the following statement made regarding conditions in Upper Canada in 1821: "The granaries of our farmers, and the stores of our merchants, are now loaded with wheat, and no price whatever can be obtained, while the farmers are in debt and well on the way to losing all they possess."[42] Robert Gourlay and W. L. Mackenzie led the agrarian protest against these conditions,[43] but not even nominal assistance was extended to agriculture in Upper Canada until ten years later despite the continuance of difficult times.

In Lower Canada protests arose in the Assembly, which was the stronghold of rural French-Canadian representation; but the type of reports introduced by the agricultural and agricultural-commercial committees of this body clearly indicate their British mercantile inspiration.[44] The fact that the Assembly was able to agree to implement the financial features of these reports only after two years, suggests that the proposals were those of the British-commercial-executive and French-professional minority, and that while the proposals were nominally designed in aid of agriculture they were opposed by the habitant majority.

Consider the analysis and recommendations embodied in the

[41]Lower Canada Assembly, *Journal,* 1821-2, pp. 49-52.

[42]Innis and Lower (eds.), *Select Documents, 1783-1885,* p. 236. Gourlay reported a protest meeting at Halton in Gore District, November 15, 1821, and listed the resolutions passed there in criticism of the British Corn Laws. See Gourlay, *General Introduction to a Statistical Account of Upper Canada,* p. cccxxv.

[43]See Macdonald, *Canada, 1763-1841,* pp. 355 ff.

[44]French membership on these committees commonly predominated. The members of the 1817 Special Committee on the State of Agriculture were: Taschereau (Chairman), Déligny, Dessaulles, Sherwood, Bondy, Fournier, and Roy. See Lower Canada Assembly, *Journal,* 1817, p. 106. This committee recommended premiums for agriculture, and a board of agriculture "upon a footing closely resembling that which is established in Great Britain" (*ibid.,* p. 628). The French membership was presumably of the professional class, closely allied with the British merchant and executive group, rather than with the habitant.

report of the 1816 agricultural committee of Lower Canada,[45] and
the reaction to this and subsequent reports. The five-man special
committee appointed early in the 1816 session "for the purpose of
enquiring into the present state of Agriculture in this Province, to
mark its decline or progress, whether there exists impediment to
its improvement, and what may be the means proper for its encouragement . . ." investigated by means of questionnaire and reported
with recommendations. They reported that a considerable agricultural progress since the conquest was marred by defects in cultivation, carelessness regarding seed,—particularly in wheat—and deficiency of manures; by the fact that "the instruments of agriculture
now used, are the same as were in use before the conquest"; by the
failure to rear good livestock, since nothing restrained male animals
of all sorts from running at large at all times; and by the fact that
short agricultural seasons were further crowded since "The inhabitant . . . is too much diverted from his work, by attending Courts
of Justice in the Towns, in litigation, or in giving evidence."

The analysis of farming thus presented was the typical British
commentary on frontier agriculture; the recommendations embodied
in the report were as surely British. The eight corrective recommendations urged a board of agriculture for purposes of experimentation and demonstration as in other countries, changes in the
administration of justice to leave farmers on their farms during
the agricultural season,[46] laws to curtail the freedom of livestock
and to encourage its improvement, and laws concerning weed control. A bill for the encouragement of agriculture, submitted by the
committee, made no progress. Two committees in 1817 failed to
secure finances for aid to agriculture, but they made clear the bias
for British institutions. The 1817 Grand Committee on Agriculture
and Commerce resolved "that it is necessary to encourage Agriculture by premiums or rewards and by facilitating the making of
experiments."[47] The same year a special committee inquiring into
the state of agriculture referred to the 1816 report and urged that

[45]Lower Canada Assembly, *Journal,* 1816, App. E.

[46]A bill to facilitate the administration of justice, introduced following the
presentation of this report, became law and was maintained for years,
(*Statutes of Lower Canada:* 57 Geo. III, c. 14). See below, pp. 100-1.

[47]Lower Canada Assembly, *Journal,* 1817, p. 92.

"for the encouragement of Agriculture, premiums ought to be granted, in the same manner as in other countries and that a Board of Agriculture ought to be established, upon a footing closely resembling that which is established in Great Britain."[48] The bill introduced by this committee to effect its recommendations passed only a first reading.[49] Not till the next year did a bill for the encouragement of Lower Canadian agriculture finally become law (Lower Canada: 58 Geo. III, c. 6).

This act was the first of an irregular series extending public aid to agricultural societies in Lower Canada before the union of the provinces. The total aid thus extended was not large, but it is significant because its administration illustrates so clearly the forces at work concerning Lower Canadian agriculture. In 1818 two agricultural societies existed in the chief urban centres of Lower Canada, one in Quebec, organized in 1816, and one in Montreal, formed in 1817. At the same time there was one in formation in Three Rivers. The grant under the agricultural-assistance act of 1818 totalled £2,000, of which £800 was to go to each of the societies of Quebec and Montreal, and £400 to that of Three Rivers. This act, which formed the model for later acts, clearly held that the granting of premiums was to be the basic function of the agricultural societies. Other activities were not prohibited, but two long clauses out of a total of six in the act enumerated in detail the purposes for which "rewards or premiums" might be offered. Grants made to agricultural societies before Union were made irregularly, and after 1818 a dozen acts and ordinances which managed over a score of years to squeeze through the interminable legislative-executive and other bickerings in Lower Canada, aided agricultural societies in the province by a total of from £15,000 to £20,000. At the peak of activity before Union there were, in 1831, district societies in Quebec, Three Rivers, Montreal, and in the Inferior District of St. Francis, and a score of auxiliary societies fostered by the Quebec and Montreal district societies. No central board evolved.

Encouragement to Lower Canadian agriculture in the form of grants in aid of agricultural societies constituted British urban paternalism, a paternalism, therefore, with the doubly alien charac-

48*Ibid.,* p. 628.   49*Ibid.*

teristics of cultural grouping and occupation. Lower Canada did not
develop a central board of the British kind, as developed in Nova
Scotia, but the district societies served the same functions. The
so-called district societies of Quebec, Montreal, and to a lesser extent
of Three Rivers, were urban societies, composed of business men,
merchants, and members of the bureaucracy and clergy, some no
doubt owning farms in the tradition of the landed aristocracy, but
all with a reasonably clear-cut mercantile point of view.[50] The British
character of these societies is evident from reports which give the
names of their members, or of their slates of officers. In 1834, of
sixteen officers of the Quebec agricultural society, at least twelve had
names indicating British extraction.[51]

Such societies understandably failed to secure the co-operation
of actual farmers, particularly the habitant. After 1821 the district
societies were permitted by act to devote part of the government
grant towards fostering auxiliary societies, and efforts were made
to establish such societies. In 1830 William Evans, secretary of the
Montreal society, reported that "Some members of the Committee
[of the society] accompanied the judges when on the inspection of
the growing crops, etc., in July last and explained to the Canadian
Farmers the objects of the Society."[52] The Quebec society busied
itself with the same sort of missionary effort; in 1831 members of
this society "attended these local exhibitions and organized the associations, attending in person to the awarding of the prizes offered

[50]Something of the type of membership in the district societies is indicated
by their self-determined annual dues. On its formation the Quebec society
established annual dues at one guinea, equal to 23s. 4d., per member, and the
Montreal society set its dues at 25s. per member. An act of 1834 which provided for grants to county societies stated that all subscribers of 5s. annually
should be members of such societies, while members of the Catholic and Pro-
testant clergy, of the Legislative and Executive Councils, and of the Assembly,
should be ex officio voting members.

[51]President, John Neilson; Vice-President, Anthony Anderson; Secretary,
Wm. Sheppard; Treasurer, Thos. Wilson; Members of the Committee: John
Anderson, John Murray, Robert Synes, James Clearihue, Barthelemi Lachance,
Thos. Hammond; Honorary Members: Donald McDonald, Andrew Gibson,
Joseph Plain, John Leon, George Eglinton, Wm. Meek. See Report of the
Quebec Agricultural Society, Lower Canada Assembly, Journal, 1834, App.
L. As late as 1848, when legislative reports listed twenty Lower Canadian
and eighteen Upper Canadian agricultural societies, even in Lower Canada the
majority of officers in such societies were British. See ibid., 1848, App. H.

[52]Ibid., 1830, App. I.

. . . steps were taken to put the Parishes in possession of the Law."[53] In 1828-9 the Quebec society reported a want of co-operation on the part of gentlemen residing in the country in the project for local societies.[54] Some success was achieved, however, for in 1831 there were a score of such societies in the districts of Montreal and Quebec.[55]

The conflict between British urban leadership and French-Canadian rural apathy persisted in the agricultural-aid institutions, dividing urban leadership from rural contact, and separating district from local societies. Local societies when formed were either entirely British or were officered by Britishers. District and county societies, therefore, were missionary societies, wherein the British dominant and interloping class sought to convert local agriculturists, partly for mercantile reasons, partly through paternalistic condescension. Lack of co-operation, and diversity of viewpoint, were such that district and local societies held separate exhibitions and ploughing matches for British and for "Canadian practical" farmers; or if they held single shows, there were separate contests and separate prize lists. In a prize list of 1834 reported by the Quebec society, in contests open to all, French Canadians obtained one out of every four prizes.[56]

Most active of the local societies, and most revealing of the results of British uplift efforts, was the County of Beauharnois society, formed in 1828. One of the earliest spots in Lower Canada to attract British settlers, the seigniory of Beauharnois, near Montreal, was partially settled by Glenelg Highlanders in 1802, was later bought by Edward Ellice, son of Alexander Ellice, a London merchant, and under his generous settlement offers was occupied by a considerable number of Scottish families.[57] In 1832 there were 326 Scottish families in the seigniory, though in 1845 French Canadians cultivated two-thirds of it.[58] Ellice supported the agricultural society with cash and breeding stock, and distributed additional stock among the farmers. L. G. Brown and R. H. Norval

53*Ibid.*, 1831, App. L.
54*Ibid.*, 1828-9, App. G.
55*Ibid.*, 1831-2, App. D.
56*Ibid.*, 1834, App. L.
57Macdonald, *Canada, 1763-1841*, pp. 481-2.
58Canada Assembly, *Journal*, 1846, App. J.

signed the society's reports for years as president and secretary, respectively. They often mentioned the progress to be noted among the Canadians, but always as a considerable event and with the greatest condescension. Two years after the society was organized, its British officers could report "a decided improvement within the last two years in the Agriculture of the country, not only among the British, but also, and this the Committee consider a circumstance of greater importance, among the Canadian population; and although the latter has not taken the strong interest in the carrying on and prosperity of the Society that the former have, it has nevertheless, manifested a considerable desire to take advantage of all the benefits the Society is so well calculated to confer."[59] The chief progress was, they thought, in the introduction of potatoes and Indian corn which modified the customary exclusive reliance on wheat, and in the introduction of "the ordinary bastard plough, drawn by two horses," though drivers were still used.[60] In 1834 the Beauharnois officers commented patronizingly that they were "proud to say that the Wheat Crops raised by Canadian Farmers were superior in general to those of the Old Country Farmers, but for other crops the latter rather excel."[61] The hopes expressed for a transformation of habitant cultural practices under the leadership of Britishers were not realized. In 1846 Messrs. Brown and Norval of the Beauharnois society reported that they were still holding separate ploughing matches, one for the British and one for the Canadians, and that the work done at the latter was clumsily done; that Canadian culture in Beauharnois seigniory was most defective, with wheat still persistently grown.[62] In a long list of open awards scarcely a French name appeared. Similarly in 1847, separate ploughing matches were advertised; at the Canadian match only three contestants appeared, and they poorly equipped, so no match was held.[63] At a special cattle show for French-Canadian stock, the officers reported that really no prizes should have been awarded, so poor were the animals.[64] In their report for 1851,[65] Brown and Norval, with some bitterness

[59]Lower Canada Assembly, *Journal*, 1830, App. I.
[60]*Ibid*.
[61]*Ibid*., 1834, App. L.
[62]Canada Assembly, *Journal*, 1846, App. J.
[63]*Ibid*., 1847, Reports of Agricultural Societies, App. E.
[64]*Ibid*.
[65]*Ibid*., 1851. App. J.

and in detail, analysed the difference between British and Canadian agriculture in Lower Canada. They stated that the fundamental principle of the British system of agriculture was the *improvement* of the soil; that of the French-Canadian, its *deterioration*. The great difficulties in the French system, they said, were lack of education and the great number of religious holidays.[66]

The basic clash over agricultural improvement was between the Britisher with recently-acquired traditions of "high" cultivation, and the Canadian habitant with traditions of extensive cultivation much more suitable to frontier conditions. There was also a minor clash *among* Britishers, between British urban interests, some perhaps "gentlemen" farmers, and British rural interests, i.e., British dirt farmers. The Beauharnois County agricultural society illustrates both clashes, the British-Canadian difficulty as already discussed and the urban-rural clash as follows. Brown and Norval in their 1832-3 report[67] criticized the existing system, providing for grants in aid to district societies, which in turn might share with county societies. The district societies, they claimed, absorbed far too great a proportion of the grant, they gave premiums which went chiefly "to wealthy farmers, comprised within a circle not exceeding ten miles around Montreal; a class of persons, who, from the superior advantages they already possess, do not require any such encouragement."[68] Since this quarrel was among Britishers only, it was settled reasonably easily, and legislation of 1834 (Lower Canada: 4 Wm. IV, c. 7) provided that grants go directly to county societies, in proportion to double the local subscriptions, and that accountability be direct to the Legislature. By this time political affairs were at such a stage that agricultural legislation was practically a dead letter.

Lower Canadian agricultural societies regarded the premium system as the normal method of using funds for agricultural improvement. In 1831 the Montreal district society reported offering over 220 premiums. The greater share of the premiums, and funds otherwise used, went towards livestock improvement. The St. Lawrence region did not always produce sufficient cereals for its needs, but it produced cereals with less difficulty than it experienced in the production of

[66]*Ibid.*

[67]Lower Canada Assembly, *Journal,* 1832-3, App. H.

[68]*Ibid.* In 1832, for example, the Beauharnois society received a grant of £33, while the Montreal district society retained £324 for itself.

livestock. The Canadas did not pass through a bread-corn phase in agricultural improvement as did the Maritimes. In 1818 the Montreal district society held a ploughing match and a grain show, but they supervised eight county livestock shows, a "General Cattle Show" at Montreal for horses and cattle, a fat hog show, and a fat ox show.[69] The agricultural societies also imported livestock for auction or service in rural districts, and bonused certain individuals for the importation and maintenance of good breeding stock. None of these activities, however, was on a scale comparable with those of the Maritimes boards and societies. In 1823 the Montreal society purchased two rams and six ewes, Southdowns, from John Young at Halifax.[70] The next year they ordered from England "some short horned cattle of the *Teeswater* or *Holderness* breed."[71] In 1832 the Quebec society spoke of the many applications received "for a share of the small flock of New Leicesters annually procured in this intention."[72] In 1834 the Montreal society spoke of the bulls and other cattle which they had imported and which had been stationed throughout the district "for the improvement of the stock."[73] Sheep and cattle were apparently the only animals imported by the Lower Canadian societies, no record indicating any venture in horses. In fact, beyond the holding of shows and the granting of premiums, and the additional livestock activities just outlined, these agricultural societies have little to their credit.[74]

The truth is that efforts to improve Lower Canadian agriculture throughout the whole period to 1850 and beyond, were trifling and wholly ineffective. Britishers knew of the British Board of Agriculture, the Highland Society of Scotland, and of British "high" methods of cultivation, and they thought it necessary to transplant

[69]*Ibid.*, 1819, App. D.
[70]*Ibid.*, 1823, App. G.
[71]*Ibid.*, 1823-4, App. F.
[72]*Ibid.*, 1832-3, App. H.
[73]*Ibid.*, 1834, App. L.
[74]They imported a few books and a very few implements. In 1822 the Quebec society imported thirteen sets "of the most improved implements" from Britain. These comprised "Twelve Iron double mould Board Drill Ploughs, twelve Iron Drill Harrows, twelve Turnip Barrows, for sowing Turnips, and twelve Turnip Rollers," and an odd set for the district of Gaspé. See *ibid.*, 1823, App. G. In 1845 the Montreal society ordered "two useful implements called Hussey's Reaping Machines." See Canada Assembly, *Journal*, 1846, App. J.

both institutional framework and cultural practice to their new environment. Gentlemen farmers and practical British farmers had similar interests in the matter. Commercial and financial interests with the mercantile point of view regarding agriculture could see sufficient benefits to be derived from a flourishing agriculture to favour the expenditure of a few hundred pounds a year in agricultural bounty.

4. *Tariffs and Transportation*

If, however, as is suggested, the Montreal commercial group were barely luke-warm in their support of aids to Canadian agriculture, what happens to the hypothesis that aids to agriculture have commonly rested on commercial support, even initiative? The hypothesis stood up for the Maritimes. Is it denied on the St. Lawrence? No. With the passing of the fur trade, St. Lawrence commercial interests gradually took an interest in the timber and wheat trades. Timber production required provisioning, the wheat trade required an abundant wheat production, and both trades offered opportunities for profitable investment. But neither provisions nor wheat had to be of Canadian origin, provided they were cheap and abundant. True, from time to time the mercantile conscience found extreme expression in deploring the importation of provisions,[75] just as was the case in Nova Scotia and New Brunswick. But in all these colonies the prime commercial consideration was cheapness and abundance of agricultural produce, and except for periods of severe depression, when conditions might be traced to shortage of money and specie drain, it mattered little whether the products came from a domestic or a foreign hinterland. This indifference was more pronounced on the St. Lawrence than in the Maritimes, for from the earliest days of the fur trade, while a part of the commerce of the St. Lawrence had arisen locally, a far greater part had been derived from the great interior regions. The facts that by the early years of the nineteenth century the trades were in timber and wheat instead of in fur, and that political boundaries now divided the interior plains, did not seem of sufficient importance to the traders to alter their aims.

St. Lawrence merchants had no quarrel with St. Lawrence agriculture. They would gladly see it prosper, and did not begrudge

[75]As, for example, when the Montreal Agricultural Society complained that nineteen-twentieths of the beef consumed in Montreal was produced in the United States. See Lower Canada Assembly, *Journal*, 1821-2, App. F.

a few hundred pounds per year as a gesture towards that end. They were concerned, however, that agricultural welfare should not encroach upon their own prosperity. The issue was clearly drawn in relation to the tariff. As in the Maritime Provinces so on the St. Lawrence, farmers favoured tariffs on agricultural produce while merchants favoured free importation of farm products in order that they might have cheap and abundant produce for trade cargoes, for shipping itself, for timber production, and for local urban consumption. Imperial legislation of 1822 and 1825, particularly the latter, the Huskisson trade acts, opened British colonies to direct trade with foreign countries in all but a very few commodities. Salted fish, fresh and salted provisions, sugar, rum, and fire-arms[76] were still to be imported into British American colonies only from Britain or from other British colonies. Commodities which could enter directly from foreign countries had to enter at specified "free ports" such as Saint John, Halifax, and Quebec, and some in the West Indies. Apart from a negligible free list, all commodities had to pay duty, as for example, 5s. per barrel on flour, 1s. per bushel on wheat, and 15 per cent *ad valorem* on other goods. Besides the "free" ports there were specified warehousing ports, of which Quebec was one, through which goods in transit between the Americas and Europe might pass duty-free.

The trade legislation of the early eighteen-twenties was most ·favourably received by Nova Scotian merchants, since even after paying duties on foreign produce they were better able than before to round out their trade cargoes.[77] Nova Scotian farmers deplored any relaxation of barriers on foreign produce.[78] On the St. Lawrence, by a curious twist of circumstances, just the reverse was true; the farmers were pleased by the legislation, the merchants were greatly annoyed.[79] For the St. Lawrence area the significant factor in the Huskisson legislation was its exclusion of fresh and salted provisions and its imposition of tariff duties on other produce. Until this time the St. Lawrence had been in effect a free-trade area and

[76]Creighton, *Commercial Empire of the St. Lawrence,* p. 233.

[77]Innis, *Cod Fisheries,* p. 255.

[78]Martell, "Achievements of Agricola" (Public Archives of Nova Scotia, *Bulletin:* Halifax, 1940), p. 29.

[79]Creighton, *Commercial Empire of the St. Lawrence,* p. 237.

the striking contrast now was that tariff, and even embargo, barriers were raised against the accepted sources of products for the provisions and wheat trades. Goods for Europe could be warehoused free at Quebec, but when entered at an upper port had already to pay duty before reaching that city.

The vigour with which the St. Lawrence merchants attacked the new structure and overturned it, despite the way in which it was favoured by the farming class, illustrates the point that mercantile interests would tolerate nothing favouring farm prosperity if it threatened to encroach upon mercantile prosperity. Meetings were held,[80] and the merchants' case was put before the imperial authorities so effectively that the legislation was altered within a year, and the restrictions completely modified in the merchants' favour by 1831. In 1826 provision was made that salt beef and pork might enter free if destined for the Newfoundland trade.[81] Legislation of 1827 confirmed the provision of 1826, and extended the trade relaxation so that flour might be bonded free through the Canadas to Quebec; that American timber, lumber, tallow, ashes, fresh meat, and fish might enter free by land or inland navigation; Kingston and Montreal were made warehousing ports, and American products could be bonded through without duty. Finally, in 1831 reciprocity legislation provided that American produce could enter Canada free and could enter the British West Indies as British produce, while duties against "foreign" produce were substantially raised.[82] Lower Canadian merchants sponsored agricultural societies and governmental aid thereto, since only a few thousand pounds at most were involved; tariffs, which would encourage domestic agriculture to an appreciable extent, were not to be tolerated, for many thousands of pounds, and perhaps a principle, were at stake.

Tariffs against American farm produce were enacted by the Canadian government in the eighteen-forties, and some students of the problem have argued that these duties represented a genuine triumph for the Upper Canada farmers in their struggle against commercial privilege.[83] An act of the Canadian Legislature, declared effective August 9, 1843 (6 Vic., c. 31), established a duty of 3s.

---

[80]*Ibid.*, p. 238.   [81]*Ibid.*, p. 239.   [82]*Ibid.*, p. 248.

[83]This argument is embodied in an article by Jones, "Canadian Agricultural Tariff of 1843" (*Canadian Journal of Economics and Political Science*, November, 1941), pp. 528-37.

sterling a quarter on American wheat entering Canada. In November
and December, 1843, duties were imposed (by 7 Vic., c. 1 and 2) on
other American agricultural produce including livestock, meats,
cheese, butter, and coarse grains. In 1846 the duties on wheat
imported for consumption, and on livestock, butter, cheese, meats,
and coarse grains were made permanent.[84] The duties on livestock
were £1.10s. per head for horses, 10s. to £1 on cattle, 5s. on swine,
and 2s. on sheep.[85]

Before this tariff legislation can be interpreted as an agrarian
victory over commercial interests, certain points must be borne in
mind. First, the duty on wheat was small and was imposed by the
provincial government on the understanding that such action would
ensure the removal or a reduction of the duty on Canadian wheat
and flour entering Britain.[86] It was not intended that this duty should
exclude American wheat from Canada. The Canada Corn Act of
1843, passed by the imperial government pursuant to the Canadian
legislation, stabilized the duties on wheat and wheat flour, "the
Produce of the said Province of Canada," at the nominal rate of 1s.
per quarter, and contributed to some expansion in milling capacity
on the St. Lawrence on the basis of the expectation that American
wheat might continue to be imported, milled, and exported to Britain
as "the produce of Canada."[87] The wheat duties, therefore, were
clearly commercial. Second, every session of the Upper Canada
Legislature after 1833 had seen tariff resolutions introduced for the
purpose of securing agricultural protection, but to no avail.[88] Some
of these resolutions had passed the Assembly only to be rejected by
the Legislative Council. The Colonial Office disallowed an Upper
Canada tariff act of 1840 under pressure from the London agents of

[84]By 9 Vic., c. 1. See *ibid.*, p. 535.

[85]*Ibid.*, p. 536.

[86]". . . a degree of protection was facilitated by a dispatch of March 2,
1842, from the Colonial Secretary to Sir Charles Bagot, which could be interpreted to mean that; if Canada placed duties on American wheat, the British
Parliament would remove or reduce the duties on Canadian breadstuffs entering the United Kingdom" (*ibid.*, p. 535). See also Tucker, *Canadian Commercial Revolution*, pp. 89, 103-4. Tucker says, "The provincial law of 1842 . . .
was, so far as the province was concerned, founded on no principle of protection
or revenue, being merely a prerequisite to the Canada Corn Act."

[87]Tucker, *Canadian Commercial Revolution*, pp. 89 ff.

[88]Jones, "Canadian Agricultural Tariff," p. 534.

Quebec and Montreal merchants.[89] Third, late in the eighteen-forties Upper Canada agricultural produce was beginning to overflow generally into the United States, and a tariff ostensibly to prevent farm produce entering Canada was no longer significant to the Upper Canadian farmer.[90] Finally, Upper Canadian farmers during the eighteen-forties were importing increasing quantities of farm implements, notably mowers and reapers, from the United States, and desired the free entry of these articles. The Canadian tariff act of 1847 which provided for duties of $7\frac{1}{2}$ per cent on the bulk of Canadian imports, singled out agricultural machinery for rates of 10 and $12\frac{1}{2}$ per cent.[91] Thus an incipient industrial interest was adding its weight to that of the long-standing commercial interest to assure that agrarian policies should not become embodied in provincial legislation to the detriment of urban groups.

Further illustration of the commercial attitude towards agricultural welfare appears in the question of transportation improvement. Timber and wheat required that the St. Lawrence be canalized; the fur trade had not. As in the case of the fur trade, however, competition with the Hudson River route was the chief pressure. Thus the issue was headed up by the completion of the Erie Canal in 1825, with the resultant probability that New York rather than Montreal or Quebec would draw the profitable trade in wheat from the westward-moving agricultural frontier. Chief barriers on the St. Lawrence route were the Niagara falls and those of the upper St. Lawrence. The former obstacle lay within Upper Canada, and the Welland Canal project was entered upon without immediate opposition from farmers or farm leaders, for the argument of cheaper transportation could easily be made to appeal to agriculturists interested in exports. Clearance of the upper St. Lawrence, on the other hand, required joint action on the part of the Upper and Lower provinces. A nine-foot set of canals was estimated to cost £350,000 for Upper Canada and £236,000 for Lower Canada. On such a

[89]*Ibid.*, p. 535; Innis and Lower (eds.), *Select Documents, 1783-1885*, pp. 361-2.

[90]Montreal still relied on the United States for much of the required provisions, despite the tariff against American produce.

[91]Innis and Lower (eds.), *Select Documents, 1783-1885*, p. 364. The Toronto Board of Trade spoke of "the injury thus inflicted on the Farmer by imposing a higher rate of duty on all Machines for agricultural purposes than on the general imports of the country" (*ibid.*).

project the Lower Canadian Assembly balked completely, for cheaper water transportation, to be obtained at great cost, meant nothing to an agricultural community approaching self-sufficiency. Before long, the Welland Canal scheme and the general St. Lawrence improvement project were interpreted by Upper Canadian agricultural leaders as adverse to agriculture's best interests. Expenditures would certainly be great for any measurable improvement, as witness the Welland Canal development from its earliest years. And from such public expenditures, and ensuing taxation, what had Upper Canadian farmers to expect by way of gain? If the Huskisson duties of 1825 on American produce had led Canadian farmers to entertain any illusions regarding this matter, the immediate attack upon these duties by the provisions traders of the St. Lawrence, and their immediate modification and abolition within a few years, left no doubts in the minds of the well-informed. The design was to have American produce come down the St. Lawrence for entry into local and Empire markets. Every dollar spent by Canadians on the improvement of the St. Lawrence was a dollar's further assurance that American produce would compete with the produce of Upper Canadian farms in local urban markets, such as Montreal, and of more importance, in the distant provisions markets of Britain and the West Indies. By 1828 W. L. Mackenzie was critical of the canal schemes, and other agrarian reformers followed his lead.[92] To make a start on the St. Lawrence rapids improvement, the Upper Canadian Legislature, overriding agricultural interests, provided for governmental borrowing of £350,000 at 6 per cent per annum.[93]

5. *Upper Canada*

Upper Canadian agriculturists before 1850 were unable to secure governmental action constituting any real measure of assistance to agriculture, because commerce and finance were not in a position where *local* agriculture was recognized as essential to their welfare. Agriculturists were not able to block the costly developmental scheme relating to waterways, inimical to their welfare. They were not able to obtain, or to keep more than momentarily, a tariff on American farm produce, when such a tariff would have contributed at least to their immediate welfare. The agricultural tariff of the eighteen-

[92]Creighton, *Commercial Empire of the St. Lawrence*, p. 270.
[93]*Ibid.*, p. 272.

forties came at a time when Upper Canadian farmers were beginning to be more interested in exporting to the United States than in preventing imports from that country.

Aid to Upper Canadian agriculture before 1850 was limited to the same form as in Lower Canada, that is aid to agricultural societies. Upper Canadian grants started later and for the most part were considerably smaller than those in Lower Canada. The bulk of Upper Canadian societies were formed after 1825.[94] Agricultural matters were introduced in the session of 1829 in a Reform House. In his speech, the Governor referred to a communication from the Deputy Postmaster General at Quebec "respecting the impossibility of forwarding the mails with either safety or expedition," and added, "I am persuaded that some better expedient than statute labour must be resorted to, for keeping the Roads in a proper state."[95] A three-member standing committee on agriculture was one of seven established. Buell and Longley moved "that the committee on agriculture be instructed to take into their consideration the establishing of agricultural societies, in this Province, and to submit a plan for carrying the same into effect."[96] Legislation came in 1830 with a four-year act (Upper Canada: 11 Geo. IV, c. 10) providing £100 for any district agricultural society with local subscriptions of £50 "for the purpose of importing valuable live stock, grain, grass seeds, useful implements, or whatever else might conduce to the improvement of agriculture in this province." County societies might share the grant. Payments under this act varied from £500 to £600 per year till 1835, when another Reform House amended and continued the 1830 act for one year (by 5 Wm. IV, c. 11) after the committee of the whole on expiring laws had advised that £1,200 be granted for agricultural societies.[97] In 1836 a select committee "on Agriculture and the improvement of the breeds of animals and seeds of grain, and upon trade and manufactures" eulogized agriculture and attacked the premium system of agricultural assistance as conducted by agricultural societies.[98] The Assembly passed a bill offering £12.10s. in aid of individual township societies; the Council killed

94Talman, "Agricultural Societies of Upper Canada," p. 546.
95Upper Canada Assembly, *Journal*, 1829, p. 5.
96*Ibid.*, p. 25.
97*Ibid.*, 1835, p. 342.
98*Ibid.*, 1836, pp. 51, 331.

the bill by amendment.[99] Under an act of 1837 (7 Wm. IV, c. 23), however, providing £200 per district for agricultural societies, £900 to £1,000 per year issued until 1839, and £1,683 in 1840.

6. *After Union*

After the Union of the Canadas in 1841 encouragement to agriculture continued to involve little but grants in aid of agricultural societies, for both sections of the United Provinces. Diversity of agricultural-aid legislation survived till 1852. Pre-Union legislation was kept in force till the 1844-5 session, the 1834 act of Lower Canada by ordinance (3 Vic., c. 17) and the 1837 Upper Canada act by an 1841 act (4 and 5 Vic., c. 23). Acts of 1844-5 (8 Vic., c. 53 for Lower Canada and c. 54 for Upper Canada) continued the grants to agricultural societies, raising the scale to treble instead of double the local subscriptions, with maxima of £150 per Lower Canadian county and £250 per Upper Canadian district. Grants made under Canadian agricultural-aid legislation varied from £2,400 to £3,350 yearly from 1841 to 1844, the latter sum equalling less than one-third of one per cent of total provincial expenditures which reached £1,100,000 for one year.[100] With the rate of grant raised to treble local subscriptions in 1845, actual grants increased sharply to an average of £9,000 per year, varying from one to one and a half per cent of total provincial expenditures. Continued separation of Upper and Lower Canadian agricultural accounts shows the extreme disorganization of agricultural-aid institutions in "Lower Canada" by and after 1840. In 1835 there had been ten county societies there; in 1841 grants issued to only five, and in 1842 to four. After 1845 there was a marked improvement until three dozen societies received aid in 1850. "Upper Canada" grants issued yearly to fifteen or twenty societies, with twenty-five in 1850. By this time the former sections of the United Provinces were sharing with rough equality in annual grants of approximately £12,000.[101]

Co-ordination of agricultural assistance was a problem so long as contact with the Executive was lacking. Central boards and central agricultural societies long were the only instruments working towards

99*Ibid.*, pp. 51, 331-2.
100Canada Assembly, *Journal*, 1850, App. YY, Expenditures for 1844.
101*Ibid.*

this end. The British Board of Agriculture and the Highland Agricultural Society served as models in all British American colonies. In 1841 Nova Scotia was organizing its third central agricultural board; Prince Edward Island had the Royal Agricultural Society; New York had had a state agricultural board since 1832, responsible for the state fair; and various states had boards administering aid to agricultural societies. Agitation for a similar co-ordinating agency was voiced in Upper Canada by 1843, and under the editorial direction of the *British American Cultivator* of Toronto, the Provincial Agricultural Association and Board of Agriculture was formed in 1846 by delegates from district societies. This was a show-holding body, and in 1846 it conducted the first provincial exhibition at Toronto, giving $880 in premiums, with the help of a $200 grant from the Canada Company. In 1847 the association was incorporated as the Agricultural Association of Upper Canada, an exhibition-holding body, with a directorate appointed by the district agricultural societies. In the same year the Lower Canada Agricultural Society was incorporated, designed to hold exhibitions and to supervise agricultural aid. In 1849 each of these organizations was granted $600 in aid. In 1850 a Board of Agriculture for Upper Canada was created,[102] with the Inspector General as an *ex-officio* member.

Detailed reports submitted to the Legislature by the agricultural societies after 1841 indicate that Lower Canadian societies persisted in distributing funds in premiums, accomplishing little,[103] while Upper Canadian societies became more and more actively engaged in the importation and maintenance of livestock, thus contributing towards the current trend in livestock improvement. The foundation of the pure-bred stock industry in Ontario has been traced to the period 1831-45,[104] and agricultural societies contributed markedly towards these beginnings. Year after year individual societies reported expenditures on livestock activities. In the 1845 reports,[105] for instance, Bathurst District society spent £426 including £70 for premiums, but also bought two Ayrshire bulls for £43, two Woburn boars for £8, had some stock from previous years, and was paying

[102]By *Statutes of Canada*: 13 and 14 Vic., c. 73.

[103]Exceptionally active societies were found in the Eastern Townships and in one or two communities near Montreal.

[104]See James, "History of Farming," p. 561.

[105]Canada Assembly, *Journal,* 1846, App. J.

a stock-keeper £87 per year. The County of Drummond society spent much less (£151) but owned a bull and bought four rams and five ewes. The St. Thomas branch of the London society reported expenses for keeping four bulls. In 1847 the Bathurst society was again in the lead with the importation of an entire horse, a Durham bull, and some boars. For a groom for the horse and for keepers of horse, bulls, and boars, they paid £140. Their receipts included £1 "for use of animals," and £5 for sale of animals. Similar reports appear over the years from a number of Upper Canadian societies. Apart from notable exceptions, Lower Canadian societies were inactive by comparison. In 1849 reports came from forty-eight agricultural societies,[106] thirty-two from Upper and sixteen from Lower Canada. Of the thirty-two Upper Canadian societies, at least a dozen reported livestock activities; of the Lower Canadian, only two or three.

7. "Divers Abuses"

An analysis of agricultural policy on the St. Lawrence would be incomplete without consideration of legislative and administrative efforts to deal with a miscellany of petty agricultural problems. In both Lower and Upper Canada the period ending in 1850 was characterized largely by a frontier agriculture, with, of course, a steadily growing area of "old" settlements, never far from the frontier. Newer settlements always butted headlong into, or against, the forest, and their special problems were those of a pioneer agriculture forcing its way into heavily timbered areas, never with adequate capital to render the work anything less than painful, never with adequate buildings and fences to keep animals from straying and trespass, and from destruction by wild animals. Roads and relief were perennial problems. In Lower Canada the whole was complicated by the cultural clash between habitants on the one hand, and British commercial and agricultural invaders on the other, by the failure of the British to understand French law and custom concerning the farmer's status in the administration of justice and his obligation to prevent trespass among his neighbours. British interests found what to them was an intolerable casualness in these matters, and their persistent agitation[107] was partly responsible for

106Ibid., 1849, App. Q.
107For instance, the Montreal Agricultural Society hammered away in its annual reports, and in other ways, on the subject of male animals running at large, till finally the "divers abuses" act was passed.

legislation to facilitate the administration of justice, and to provide "for the remedy of divers abuses prejudicial to agriculture."

In Lower Canada the question of the administration of rural justice, of the "administration of justice in small causes,"[108] formed an important part of the broad question of the extent to which English law and procedure, and the English system of courts, should displace corresponding French institutions after the conquest. After 1764 various attempts to establish the system of Justices of the Peace and Circuit Courts were unsuccessful; Justices of the Peace were a British institution and therefore unwelcome. Under the Quebec Act the "Circle" was tried.[109] Meanwhile the administration of justice interfered greatly with agriculture, because the administration was poorly done and took so much of the habitant's time. Long and arduous winters left but a short growing season for the work involved in cereal husbandry, and at the same time made cereal husbandry necessary instead of animal husbandry. Furthermore, with forests cleared away and with snow covering thus made less reliable, fall-sown cereals winter killed, and spring sowings became necessary. All field work, therefore, had to be crowded into a short growing season, and farmers could not afford time to attend court sessions held in town. Yet attendance at court was essential to the bare minimum of justice in small causes.[110]

The same problems survived beyond the Constitutional Act. The special committee of the Lower Canadian Legislature, 1816, found existing agriculture "not in a flourishing state" and, as previously noted, attributed the prevailing inadequacy in cultivation to short seasons and to the fact that "The inhabitant has too little time, and is too much diverted from his work, by attending Courts of Justice in the Towns, in litigation, and in giving evidence."[111] One of several of their recommendations was for "a law for preventing

108For a discussion of this problem see Neatby, *Administration of Justice under the Quebec Act*, pp. 275 ff.

109See *ibid.*

110A petition from la Prairie for a "Circle" outlined a situation where a farmer could withhold wages, knowing that the man could not take time to go to Montreal to sue. The trespass of farm animals caused considerable damage —large farmers let their cattle go *abandon* as soon as their fields were cleared, and smaller farmers, having helped the larger ones with their harvest, could not take time to go to court to secure damages. See *ibid.*, p. 279.

111Lower Canada Assembly, *Journal*, 1816, App. E.

the husbandman from being diverted from his work, by going to towns to sue or give evidence in trivial and common matters, which may be decided in the Parish."[112] An act conforming to this recommendation was passed in 1817 (Lower Canada: 57 Geo. III, c. 14) and was continued until 1827 when its subject matter was incorporated into "divers abuses" legislation. The series of acts beginning in 1817 "to facilitate the Administration of Justice in certain small matters therein mentioned, in the Country Parishes," empowered "the nearest Justice of the Peace within the County" to hear cases involving line fences, ditches, and damages done by livestock. For such cases "experts" might be selected, two by the plaintiff, two by the defendant, and a fifth by the Justice of the Peace if he thought necessary. On the advice of the experts, the Justice of the Peace might require work to be done, or assess damages up to £3 including costs.

Pioneer agricultural communities suffer much from weeds and stray livestock. Extensive methods of cultivation fall short of effective control for either. Straying animals retard field husbandry through the destruction of crops, fences, and buildings, and discourage improvement in animal husbandry through the irresponsible biological effectiveness of ubiquitous scrub males. The French-Canadian custom regulating the freedom of stock, *l'abandon des animaux* (or simply *l'abandon*) permitted animals to go at large from fall to spring, supposedly after the old crop was garnered and before the new one could be damaged by grazing animals. Abuses were obvious, and the custom was "abolished" by legislation in 1790 (30 Geo. III, c. 4), "An Act or Ordinance for preventing Cattle from going at large, or *l'Abandon des Animaux.*" Besides abolishing *l'abandon* this act required that fences should be kept up at all seasons, prohibited the removal of fences and the straying of any farm stock on others' property or on highways, provided fines for specified offences, and permitted the impounding of animals till fines and damages should be paid.

By 1816 *l'abandon* was no longer evident, but the special committee on agriculture noted divers abuses concerning weeds and straying animals.[113] They recommended laws to prohibit the straying of stallions at all times, and that of rams before November 20 of

112*Ibid.*   113*Ibid.*

each year, and to prevent negligent persons from causing damage to their neighbours "by their Thistles and their Weeds." From 1819 on, the Montreal agricultural society dinned away at livestock abuses, deploring the increasing numbers of dogs so destructive to sheep, and the straying of scrub male animals of all kinds. A bill for the "more efficacious remedy for divers abuses prejudicial to agricultural improvement" was given first reading in 1818, but not till 1824 was there passed the first of a long series of acts "for the more speedy remedy of divers abuses" (Lower Canada: 4 Geo. IV, c. 33), which lasted with amendments throughout the pre-Confederation period. The acts comprised from thirty-nine to sixty-four sections each and dealt rather literally with "divers abuses." Under the administration of Justices of the Peace, penalties were provided for a multitude of specified trespasses of man, of beast, and of weed seeds; freeholders were required to appoint "fence viewers" and inspectors of drains; road overseers were to destroy weeds along roads. The solidly British, Montreal district agricultural society felt that the passage of the 1824 Divers Abuses Act was a part of its own specific accomplishments, and when urging its renewal in 1826 gave the opinion of its officers that the act "though but partially put into effect in this District, has produced more beneficial effects and tended more to promote the grand objects intended by its wise enactments, than all that had been previously done for our Agriculture."[114]

Miscellaneous agricultural problems in Lower Canada included such diverse elements as bad roads, oppressive mill charges, and the continuous marauding of wild animals. Roads have constituted an endless problem. A century after the first rough road joined Montreal and Quebec in 1735,[115] Lower Canadian roads were of four classes: (1) post roads or "front" roads, (2) back roads, parallel to the front roads, (3) cross roads, and (4) branch roads to the seigniory mill.[116] Summer traffic was difficult enough, but the habitant custom of hitching a single horse to the *traineau, berline,* or *cariole* (a low sledge) made winter travel extremely hard. The type of hitch left the road unsuited for teams, and with the alternate tightening and slackening of the chain, the shafts gouged craters in

114*Ibid.,* 1826, App. E.
115Innis (ed.), *Select Documents, 1497-1783,* p. 397.
116Innis and Lower (eds.), *Select Documents, 1783-1885,* pp. 57-8.

the road which were called *cahots* by the French and "cowholes" by the English. Habitants were required by law to carry shovel, pick, and hoe with which to level the road after them.[117] Persistent dissatisfaction led in 1829 to an appropriation of £200 to enable the district agricultural societies to conduct experiments "for ascertaining the best mode of fixing the Shafts of Winter Carriages in order to prevent the formation of *Cahots*."[118] Experiments were not conducted since snowfall was inadequate, but English officers of agricultural societies were sure they already knew the causes well enough. In 1839 a determined attack was made upon the problem by an ordinance which prescribed in detail the type and specifications of sleighs permissible on five specified post roads.[119]

Inadequacy of capital showed itself in general shortage of processing equipment, notably oatmills, and in recurring complaints of extortionate charges. Regulation had been sporadic during the French régime. By 1830 the tolls for grinding wheat had been set by law in Lower Canada, and the custom existed of exacting a fourteenth "for the multure of all kinds of Grain," though this amount was not specified by law.[120] Recurring failures of wheat crops forced inhabitants into raising oats and other coarse grains. "Speculative monopolists" who had established oatmeal mills charged exorbitantly for grinding oats, their tolls ranging up to 5*d*. or 6*d*. per bushel, or as much as one-fourth of the grain if paid in kind, besides which they retained the "dust and seeds which are most essentially useful for feeding of cattle."[121] Legislative committees considering petitions for assistance to oatmills recommended that the customary toll of one-fourteenth be legalized, but no such action was taken.

Wild animals, wolves and bears, were a constant threat to livestock on clearance farms. A Lower Canadian act of 1831 (1

117*Ibid.*

118*Statutes of Lower Canada*, 9 Geo. IV, c. 71 (1829). See also Lower Canada Assembly, *Journal*, 1834, p. 259.

1192 Vic., c. 34 (1839), An Ordinance to provide for the improvement, during the Winter season, of the principal Post Roads from various parts of the Province to Montreal.

120Lower Canada Assembly, *Journal*, 1831, pp. 187-8, Report of the Standing Committee on Agriculture on Petitions regarding Oatmill Charges.

121*Ibid.*, 1830, pp. 208-9.

Wm. IV, c. 6) "to encourage the Destruction of Wolves. . . . Whereas it is expedient to endeavor to arrest the ravages committed among sheep and cattle by wolves," provided a bounty of £2.10s. per wolf killed by an inhabitant within six miles of an inhabited place. The general terms of this statute were continued throughout the pre-Confederation period.[122]

Since Upper Canada was planned as an agricultural province, the early enactment of legislation dealing with matters of rural concern is not surprising. In 1792 the Legislature passed an act (32 Geo. III, c. 7) "to regulate the toll to be taken in Mills." This act forbade any mill owner from taking more than one-twelfth of any grain for grinding and bolting. The act was still in force in the Confederation period.[123] In 1794 the Legislature sought by act (34 Geo. III, c. 8) to prevent damage to property by the straying of domestic animals. This act introduced the principle of impounding with penalties, and in modified form it was extended by later acts (such as 43 Geo. III, c. 10, 1803) until municipal organization developed sufficiently so that townships were enabled to establish their own regulations relating to stock movements. Acts of 1835 and 1837 (5 Wm. IV, c. 8 and 1 Vic., c. 21) consolidated previous legislation which had outlined the duties of township officers, and provided that freeholders and householders in the various townships should lay down their own livestock rules, within the limits of the specific details set forth in the acts for guidance to pound-keepers. This system persisted throughout the pre-Confederation period.[124] In 1793 legislation had provided for "fence viewing" by overseers of highways and roads. In 1834 townships were permitted (by 4 Wm. IV, c. 12) to appoint three to eighteen fence viewers; and in 1839 (by 2 Vic., c. 18), this act was made permanent. Legislation to encourage the destruction of wolves in Upper Canada was passed in 1809 (49 Geo. III, c. 3), embodying the bounty principle. Later legislation continued the bounty at £1.10s., or $6.00, payable by county treasurers.[125]

[122]See *Consolidated Statutes for Lower Canada*, 1860.

[123]See *Consolidated Statutes of Upper Canada*, 1859, c. 48. This act embodied a $40.00 penalty.

[124]*Ibid.*, c. 54.

[125]*Ibid.*, c. 60.

8. *Changes in the Purposes of Canadian Agriculture*: *The Frontier Role*

Considered as a whole the assistance extended by government to Upper and Lower Canadian agriculture before 1850 was trifling in amount, formal (even ritualistic) in conception, and indicates that encouragement to agriculture was no essential part of the real interests of government. The comparative neglect of agriculture was not an outcome of growing laissez-faire sentiment. Current philosophies of government did not prevent vigorous governmental efforts to stimulate agriculture in Nova Scotia and New Brunswick, for agriculture seemed important to the leading economic interests of those colonies. More significantly, laissez-faire sentiment did not prevent government on the St. Lawrence from contributing heavily before 1850 to the promotion and financing of river improvement, for such improvement seemed essential to the economic purposes of the St. Lawrence region. Agriculture in Canada during the same period called forth gestures of encouragement, and little more, for the basic reason that Canadian agriculture seemed of little consequence in the economic purposes of the region.

The hypothesis as set forth in Chapter I is that Canadian agriculture has been related functionally to empire (territorial and economic) in providing defence, in provisioning staple trades, and in providing investment opportunities on the agricultural frontier. By 1820 agriculture on the St. Lawrence had given up its defensive role. Provisioning was still important, and some arguments for encouraging domestic agriculture were based on the desirability of more adequate local sources; but with abundant American supplies immediately to hand, such arguments were unconvincing. Finally before 1850, perhaps much earlier, Upper Canadian farms were supplying surplus wheat in sufficient quantities to warrant the suggestion that Canadian agriculture was now the basis for a new staple trade. This development was based in turn on a rapid expansion of the Canadian agricultural frontier. Commerce and finance were interested in the new staple trade. Fur-trading interests had shifted their attentions to timber and to wheat even while the North West Company nominally held the fur trade to the St. Lawrence. But, as in provisions so in wheat, Canadian supplies were trifling compared to quantities which *might* be secured in the American hinterland. Geography was the stumbling block, for American provisions and wheat had three potential channels to seaboard: the Mississippi, the Mohawk and Hudson Rivers, and the St. Lawrence. When the Americans opened the Erie barge canal in 1825 the issue was clear; the Canadas would have to improve the St. Lawrence in marked degree, or the Canadian groups interested in provisions and wheat would have to reconcile themselves to reliance on local sources. That Canadian governments were willing to put millions into river improvement where they doled out thousands towards agricultural improvement may be taken as a measure of the possibilities which they saw in American, as compared with domestic, agriculture. In the period before 1850 agriculture remained important for empire in its economic sense, but American agriculture rather than Canadian was significant.

Looking forward, however, the time was to come (and that before Confederation) when Canadian agricultural expansion appeared to be the only possible solution, if a doubtful one, for the problems of the Canadian economy. The analysis of that situation must be left for the following chapter, but such analysis develops understandably only in the light of the working of certain obscure forces within the decades prior to 1850. Actually, Canadian commercial and financial interests before 1850 relied more on local, or non-American, agricultural phenomena than they thought.[126] Their reliance was associated with the great influx of British and continental immigration to the St. Lawrence, an influx which stands by any test as one of the major factors of the quarter-century from 1825 to 1850. This immigration was an agricultural phenomenon in the sense that the pioneer communities of Upper Canada, where the great bulk of the newcomers went, held few opportunities for them except to clear and till the soil. Immigration was of immediate interest to commerce and finance in two ways: first, it provided cargoes for Canada-bound timber ships,[127] and second, its settlement processes required quantities of manufactured goods, tools, and comparatively primitive implements, building supplies, and general hardware, as well as clothing and home furnishings.

126What they thought regarding this reliance is inferred from their general apathy towards local agricultural improvement.

127See Innis, "Unused Capacity as a Factor in Canadian Economic History" (*Canadian Journal of Economics and Political Science*, February, 1936), pp. 1-15.

More will be said in later chapters regarding the economic significance of immigration and settlement, but the general case must now be outlined. Investment, or "capital fixation," is an essential feature of the establishment of new economic activity whether in new or in old regions. Physical facilities, capital equipment, must be provided, and while the complexity and volume of such equipment may vary widely depending upon the type of activity involved and upon the stage of the industrial arts, nevertheless some quantity of such equipment is indispensable. The point is readily illustrated in terms of the recent establishment and expansion of Canadian base-metal production, or of the pulp and paper industry. The fundamental necessity for capital equipment was as surely present in the establishment and expansion of the cod fisheries and the fur trade in early colonial days. The establishment of such equipment, a process which economists currently call "investment," is important not only for the region and industry directly concerned. If the process occurs on a substantial scale it is bound to be reflected throughout the whole national and even international economy in high indices of employment, wage payments, incomes, and in a greater or lesser degree of general prosperity. To individual business men, to financiers, merchants, transportation interests, and industrialists the capital-creation processes offer opportunities for profitable investment.

Agriculture conforms fully to the above analysis. To establish agricultural production in new regions, or to expand the area or variety of agricultural activity, there is necessary the establishment of suitable capital equipment. The economic significance of agricultural expansion can be interpreted in the light of this fact. The economic significance of immigration and settlement requires no different interpretation. Immigration, settlement, and agricultural expansion are complementary parts of a single, coherent picture.

The "frontier role" of agriculture now becomes obvious. Whatever may be the essential features of the agricultural frontier for the historian, the sociologist, or the political scientist, for the economist the frontier's essential features are its investment opportunities. In fact, for the economist such questions as whether or not the frontier is exclusively an agricultural concept, or whether or not it must be looked for "on the hither edge of free land," are quite beside the point. The frontier at any point of time is whatever place and whatever economic activity gives rise to investment opportunities on a substantial scale.

These considerations contribute towards an understanding of the changes taking place in the functions of St. Lawrence agriculture in the period 1825-50. The magnitude of the investment required for the establishment of agricultural production in a new region varies directly with the extent of the new settlement, and with the degree to which current local agriculture can rely on mechanized, or capitalistic, methods of production; and inversely with the degree to which the new region is self-sufficient. Settlement on the St. Lawrence between 1825 and 1850 could well be contrasted in these respects with the settlement of the Prairie Provinces after 1900, being clearly of lesser extent, compelled to use tools and implements of a much more primitive nature, and much more self-sufficient than the latter. In the years after 1900 the capital fixation involved in the opening of the Canadian West was sufficient to vitalize and integrate the Dominion,[128] and was the central economic factor of the time, vastly greater in absolute and relative volume than similar processes between 1825 and 1850. Nevertheless, as increasing numbers of immigrants poured through Quebec and Montreal and onward towards the lower Great Lakes region, an increasing structure of capital fixtures was necessary in transportation and transit-housing facilities; in the rough merchandising and service equipment of the pioneer village; in milling equipment for grains, wool, lumber, and tan-bark; and in the instruments and implements of the farm and of the farm home, however primitive they might be. As for the problem of unbalanced cargo, after two hundred years during which the staple trade of the St. Lawrence, the fur trade, could find bare tolerance for a movement of settlers and settlers' effects from Europe to Canada, the situation at last was changed so that the new staples—timber and wheat—favoured the movement of settlers and their effects, since these would bear a part of the overhead which would otherwise result from returning westward in ballast.

These factors were at work between 1825 and 1850, but their significance was not fully realized. Immigration was heavy and it was profitable for various groups, but it was taken for granted and few efforts were made to encourage either immigration or settle-

[128]See Mackintosh, *Economic Background of Dominion-Provincial Relations*, chaps. v, vi.

ment. Dr. Thomas Rolph acted as Canadian emigration agent in the United Kingdom from 1839 to 1842,[129] was awarded £500 for his services[130] by the provincial government, and was apparently the only emigrant agent which Canada had abroad earlier than the eighteen-fifties. Immigration agencies in Canada had been established by Britain in 1828 and were partially financed by annual imperial grants as late as 1854.[131] Land-grant regulations were somewhat relaxed during the eighteen-forties, but the provincial government made no great efforts to settle the free grants. Immigrants, it is clear, did not need to settle on the St. Lawrence in order to serve as return cargo, or, for that matter, in order to admit St. Lawrence commercial and financial interests to the field of profitable investment. So long as immigrants came by way of the St. Lawrence they could go as far into American territory as they liked for all it immediately concerned St. Lawrence shipping and transportation interests.[132] As for capital fixation, the belief was that once the St. Lawrence River improvements were completed, the Canadian route would handle much of the inward traffic of the United States, as well as much of the outward. Agriculture, immigration, and agricultural settlement were significant for St. Lawrence carriers, merchants, and investors, but in the light of the hopes pinned on the completion of St. Lawrence River improvements, American agriculture and agricultural settlement were of much greater importance than were those on the St. Lawrence.

9. Summary

British plans for Quebec, formulated officially immediately upon the conquest of that colony, envisaged a colonial area where agricultural prospects would be developed to conform with mercantile requirements. Habitant indifference, however, combined with the basic agricultural difficulties of the region to nullify these plans. Following the Revolutionary War the imperial government assisted the settlement on the St. Lawrence of Loyalists from the United

---

[129]Canada Assembly, *Journal,* 1842, pp. 63-6.

[130]*Ibid.,* 1843, App. A (Public Accounts).

[131]See Report of the Select Committee on Emigration, Canada Assembly, *Journal,* 1860, App. no. 4; *ibid.,* 1863 (first session), App. no. 3.

[132]In fact, years later the Grand Trunk Railway Company was accused of selling, in Britain, "through" tickets to the United States in preference to tickets to Canada.

States, and later of military and other small groups from the Old Country, the avowed purposes being those of defence and provisioning. By 1820 the defence problem was no longer urgent, and other reasons for extending financial aid to local agriculture were not yet apparent. From that time until 1850, while there was always the formality of agricultural organization and agricultural grants, instituted and supported by commercial interests, there was little heart in the encouragement process. From 1825 to 1850 agricultural settlement on the upper St. Lawrence increased tremendously on the basis of Old Country immigration. Wheat production increased to the point where it constituted a staple export. The processes of immigration and settlement during this period, however, were spontaneous, unsought, and for the most part unassisted.

Out of this unprecedented influx of immigration, with its accompanying agricultural settlement, there evolved the realization of a new commercial purpose in agricultural expansion. Immigrants had to be transported, housed, fed, and clothed; and their settlement on the land required the accumulation of capital equipment. This equipment was slight and partly home-made in the early eighteen-hundreds, but always included a nucleus of items necessarily manufactured and purchased rather than home-made. As the decades passed and improvements were evolved in household hardware, tools, and implements, the manufactured portion of a settler's requirements increased, and the commercial interest in the establishment of new agricultural settlement increased correspondingly. The process here discussed is currently known as "investment," or "capital fixation." By 1850 the volume of settlement which had characterized the preceding decades, along with the steady improvement in agricultural techniques which made agricultural capital more complex and less likely to be home-made, had established and demonstrated a substantial new reason for commercial interest in agricultural expansion. It only remained for the rate of agricultural expansion on the St. Lawrence to be checked in order that its importance for commercial prosperity be made evident. This occurred during the eighteen-fifties.

CHAPTER V

THE AGRICULTURAL FRONTIER AND CONFEDERATION

ECONOMIC, constitutional, and political phenomena[1] associated with the British abandonment of the system of colonial preferences and Navigation Acts at the middle of the nineteenth century had revolutionary effect in the colonies. World-wide depression, European and British crop failures, and the "Famine Migration" of 1847, combined with local crop shortages and commercial difficulties to create distress and unrest in British North America. The loss of British preference and the repeal of the Navigation Laws were among the factors contributing to a desire in Canada for closer economic relationships with the United States.[2] The immediate question was, however, would the St. Lawrence canals, finally completed by 1848, achieve their purpose in drawing trade from the western states? The Canadian canals and the Canadian route as a whole had some advantages over the Erie Canal and the Mohawk-Hudson River route,[3] but comparative ocean freight rates from New York and Montreal were such as to set the balance firmly against the latter port and against the route which it represented.[4] Besides, by 1850, the United States were well into the railway era, and their railways by fitful stages, first supplementing waterways and later striking out on their own, had come to tap the Mississippi valley. With the Great Western link from Niagara to Windsor-Detroit, railways linked New York and Chicago by 1855. North-south feeders tapped the Canadian area as a hinterland: the Ogdensburg railway tapped the border above the St. Lawrence rapids, linking Ogdensburg in 1850 with Rouse's Point, where lines joined up with Boston and New York; railways connected Montreal and Boston in 1851, and Montreal and New York in 1852; by the early eighteen-fifties American railways had termini at Niagara and Detroit, the Niagara terminus tapping the western Canadian peninsula.

The struggle was not only to bring American produce down the St. Lawrence; it was also to keep Canadian produce from going

[1] See Tucker, *Canadian Commercial Revolution, passim.*
[2] Wilgus, *Railway Interrelations of the United States and Canada,* p. 38.
[3] Tucker, *Canadian Commercial Revolution,* pp. 55 ff.
[4] *Ibid.,* p. 62.

down the Hudson. American drawback legislation[5] in 1845 and after enabled Canadian exports from the upper regions to go out *via* New York. Upper Canadian farmers and even merchants thought less of the Canadian canals, as they saw cheap export channels opening up by way of the United States. Lower Canadian farmers—habitants—were indifferent as ever, except in their opposition to financial burdens. Montreal merchants were more concerned than ever. The transformation came by 1850 when the industrial expansion in eastern American centres provided an American market of great and profitable proportions for meats, livestock, poultry, eggs, dairy products, and coarse grains; and American railways touching or approaching the border provided the means for getting these products there.[6]

Upper Canadian farmers had been protectionist from early days, in the face of the American provisioning of St. Lawrence trade and commerce, and in constant opposition to the merchants' insistence on free entry of American produce. Short-lived agrarian triumph accompanying the Huskisson trade legislation of the middle eighteen-twenties, which imposed duties on American produce, collapsed with the modification and removal of these duties by 1831.[7] The duties imposed on American agricultural products by the Canadian Legislature in the middle eighteen-forties were countered in 1847 by discriminatory duties on the importation of agricultural machinery, and, in any case, were rendered ineffectual because by 1850 agricultural produce was flowing from Canada to the United States instead of in the other direction.[8] Upper Canadian farmers were no sooner granted a measure of nominal protection than they were led by changing circumstances to favour free trade, and by the early eighteen-fifties were readily persuaded of the advantages which might arise from reciprocity with the United States.[9]

1. The Bureau of Agriculture

Meanwhile considerable changes were made in the machinery for administering assistance to Canadian agriculture. Organization

[5]*Ibid.*, pp. 63, 118-19, 210-12; Innis and Lower (eds.), *Select Documents, 1783-1885*, p. 347.
[6]Jones, "History of Agriculture in the Province of Canada," pp. 126 ff.
[7]See above, pp. 91-2.
[8]See above, pp. 92-4.
[9]Masters, *Reciprocity Treaty of 1854*, p. 6.

was broadened and specialized functionally, and co-ordinated in responsibility. The movement towards co-ordination of agricultural administrative machinery, long advocated as in conformity with practice in Britain, various states of the Union, and other colonies such as Nova Scotia and Prince Edward Island, began in 1847 with the incorporation of the Lower Canada Agricultural Society (by 10 & 11 Vic., c. 60), and of the Agricultural Association of Upper Canada (by 10 & 11 Vic., c. 61) ; was carried forward by an act of 1850 (13 & 14 Vic., c. 73) which established the Board of Agriculture of Upper Canada, with the Inspector General as an *ex officio* member; and was brought to its culmination by legislation in 1852 (16 Vic., c. 11 and c. 18) which finally centralized the agricultural organization of the province under a member of the Executive Council. The 1852 acts overhauled existing legislation for agricultural organization, brought the structure for the two parts of the province closely into line for the first time, and provided potential centralization through the creation of a bureau of agriculture to be headed by a member of the Executive Council. Chapter 11 repealed all existing legislation concerning agricultural organization, but reconstituted the Upper Canada Board of Agriculture and the Upper Canada Agricultural Association, provided for parallel institutions in Lower Canada, and provided the constitution for Upper Canada township and county agricultural societies. A separate act of the same year (16 Vic., c. 18) outlined the constitution for Lower Canada county societies. The reasoning of the main act was that existing agricultural administrative institutions were helpful, "but in the absence of a suitable provision for the collection and dissemination in an authentic form of facts and statistics relating to Agriculture, the full benefit of these Associations is not attained."[10]

The legislation of 1852 created an hierarchy of agricultural institutions which was co-ordinated, balanced, and parallel in the two parts of the United Province. Heading up the structure was the Bureau of Agriculture "attached to one of the Public Departments, and the Head of such Department . . . shall in respect thereof be known as the minister of Agriculture."[11] Subsidiary organizations in each part of the province comprised (a) an agricultural board designed to supervise local societies, (b) an agricultural association

[10]*Statutes of Canada*, 1852, c. 11, s. 1.
[11]*Ibid.*, s. 2.

charged with conducting annual exhibitions, and (c) county and township agricultural societies with farmer membership subscribing 5s. per member annually. The agricultural boards in Canada East and Canada West were the active co-ordinating agencies for the societies and associations. The Minister of Agriculture, the presidents of the respective agricultural associations, and professors of agriculture in colleges, universities, and other educational institutions, were *ex officio* members of the boards of agriculture, and eight other members were selected from nominations made by local agricultural societies. Agricultural societies were now to report to the Board of Agriculture in each section of the province instead of directly to the Legislature, as formerly, and instead of to the Bureau of Agriculture, as might be supposed. The boards were to certify to the Bureau of Agriculture the annual amounts of grant due to each society, based on a ratio trebling local subscriptions up to a maximum grant of £250 per county;[12] then to issue and supervise the expenditure of the grants. In addition, the boards were enjoined by law to move, with the approval of the Minister of Agriculture, to establish a "model, illustrative or experimental farm"; to establish an agricultural museum; to import improved animals, grain, seeds, vegetables, and new and improved implements; to improve agriculture by every available means, and to publish records and transactions and all useful information.

Agricultural societies continued under the new supervision with little alteration. Upper Canada societies continued to stress efforts to improve local livestock, particularly by importing animals and hiring them to members by the season, or in other ways making them available to the farming community.[13] With forty-two counties in Upper Canada in 1853, total grants might equal £9,450, or approximately $40,000.[14] In 1853 every county had a society, except for Leeds and Grenville counties which had a united society.[15] Data for local societies follow.

12Less 10 per cent deducted and diverted to the Agricultural Association in each part of the province. Each association drew £1,000 yearly besides, to aid in exhibition-holding activities.

13*Journal and Transactions of the Board of Agriculture of Upper Canada,* vol. I, pp. 14-15.

14Forty-two counties at a maximum grant of £250 per county, less 10 per cent for the Agricultural Association.

15*Journal and Transactions of the Board of Agriculture of Upper Canada.*

LOCAL AGRICULTURAL SOCIETIES IN UPPER AND LOWER CANADA*

| | Upper Canada | | Lower Canada | |
| | Number of | Provincial | Number of | Provincial |
Year	county societies	grant	county societies	grant
1849	14	£3,411	29†	£3,974
1850	25	6,166	39†	5,720
1851	19	5,147	43†	5,771
1852	24	5,889	45	5,905
1853	39	6,857	52	6,827
1854	41	8,597	56	7,571
1855	41	8,143	56	7,517
1856	40	8,253	39	7,702
1857	42	8,669	60	11,849
1858	53	$47,275	56	$41,436

*Compiled from annual Public Accounts, Canada Assembly, *Journal*.
†Including three district societies.

Nominal head of the entire structure was the Minister of Agriculture, the head of one of the public departments and enjoined by law to administer the Bureau of Agriculture. A real opportunity for supervision was granted him, for he was to be *ex officio* member of the provincial boards of agriculture of Upper and Lower Canada, which position would automatically place him on the council of the provincial agricultural associations as well. Specific duties of the Minister, however, were few, really only three: (1) to receive, pass upon, and record applications for patents of inventions; (2) to act as chairman of the Board of Registration and Statistics,[16] and thus to have charge of the census and of statistical returns; (3) and to "institute inquiries and collect useful facts and statistics relating to the Agricultural interests of the Province, and to adopt measures for disseminating or publishing the same in such manner and form

[16]The Board of Registration and Statistics was constituted in 1847 by 10 and 11 Vic., c. 14, "An Act for Taking the Census of this Province, and Obtaining Statistical Information Therein." The Board comprised the Receiver General, the Secretary of the Province, and the Inspector General, with a governmentally-appointed secretary. The Board was to prepare and circulate census forms; the first "General Census" was to be taken in February and March, 1848, another in February and March, 1850, and every five years thereafter. More generally, the Board was to "have general supervision of the Statistics of the Province," reporting annually to the Legislature, "which said report shall contain all such information relative to the Trade, Manufactures, Agriculture and Population of the Province as they may be able to obtain."

as he may find best adapted to promote improvement within the Province, and to encourage immigration from other countries."[17]

The formal structure for the administration of agricultural aid in Canada was left untouched by an act of 1857 (20 Vic., c. 32) which embodied the 1852 legislation practically intact, providing in addition for the promotion of mechanical science, setting up boards of arts and manufactures to parallel the boards of agriculture, thus symbolizing the growing industrialization of the Lake Ontario region. An act of 1862 (25 Vic., c. 7) provided that "The Bureau of Agriculture shall be . . . a separate Public Department, under the direction and management of the Minister of Agriculture." This act assigned to the Minister of Agriculture "the official superintendence and management of all matters relative to Immigration into this Province from Europe, or from America or any other country," as well as the superintendence of colonization, whether of newcomers or of residents of older parts of the province.

2. *Commerce and the Canadian and American Agricultural Frontiers*

Throughout the period from 1850 to 1867, as before and since, agricultural policy continued to be related to commerce and to the commercial functions of agriculture. Agricultural societies and agricultural boards could carry on in orthodox fashion, spending eighty to one hundred thousand dollars of governmental bounty per year, one to two per cent of the provincial budget, and contributing, in Upper Canada at least, to the development of animal husbandry. This development was nicely adapted to changes in American markets caused by American industrialization and increased specialization on wheat-growing, and at the same time countered the difficulties of Canadian agriculture associated with progressive exhaustion of Upper Canadian soils under persistent frontier wheat-growing, and with the westward march of insect pests (the wheat midge and the Hessian fly), and the fungus, rust.[18] Improvement of agricultural production in the St. Lawrence valley was thought to warrant some effort. Exports of agricultural produce from Canada to the United States had considerable beginnings just at mid-

[17]*Statutes of Canada*, 16 Vic., c. 11 (1852), s. 6.

[18]Hind, *Eighty Years' Progress in British North America*, p. 36; *Essay on Insects and Diseases Injurious to the Wheat Crops*, *passim*.

century and were stimulated by the Reciprocity Treaty and more particularly by the Civil War.[19] Cattle exports from Canada, almost exclusively to the United States, increased from 8,300 in 1850 to 147,000 in 1866; barley and rye from 67,000 bushels in 1850 to 6,350,000 bushels in 1866; oats from 668,000 bushels in 1850 to 3,600,000 bushels in 1860, and 5,916,000 bushels in 1864.[20]

This trade was profitable for merchants and transportation companies as well as for primary producers, and it fully justified certain efforts towards encouragement to primary production. But the main objects and purposes of the St. Lawrence were different. The St. Lawrence had never tolerated the suggestion of self-sufficiency. Since its earliest settlement, and as late as within a generation of Confederation, the St. Lawrence had been in fact a trade route, the basis of vast empire in the commercial sense. The fur trade was gone, and the spread and intensification of settlement and agriculture in Upper Canada might suggest (to the superficial analyst) a considerable change in emphasis. So far as population groupings were concerned, by far the greatest proportion were "dirt" farmers, but they were not self-sufficient producers. They did supply a high proportion of their own requirements, and conversely they consumed a high proportion of what they produced. But they also bought and sold, and it was what they bought and sold that made agricultural encouragement worth while for non-agriculturists. In the second quarter of the nineteenth century something of the commercial significance of an expanding agricultural area had become evident. It had become evident that however self-sufficient and self-contained a farm family might become once it was established on a pioneer farm, the processes of migration and settlement in their very nature entailed dependence upon transportation and stopping-house facilities, and upon the producers of whatever simple capital equipment could neither be dispensed with nor produced on the farm, and which the settler could afford. These processes were, of course, associated with migration and settlement, rather than with subsequent agricultural production, and whatever the degree to which the evolving community became self-contained, or, in fact, whatever its

[19]Jones, "History of Agriculture in the Province of Canada," pp. 126 ff.; Saunders, "Reciprocity Treaty of 1854" (*Canadian Journal of Economics and Political Science*, February, 1936), pp. 41-53.

[20]Creighton, *British North America at Confederation*, p. 18.

success or failure, there were profitable investment opportunities associated with the original transfer and installation of prospective farm populations. Furthermore, even if migrants went beyond the Canadas into the United States, so long as they came *via* the Canadian route, much of the essential commercial interest in their migration was preserved for Canadians, and was worth consideration.

After 1850, and as late perhaps as 1930, the chief non-agrarian interest in Canadian agriculture has related to the investment processes accompanying the transfer of great streams of population from Europe and Britain, and later from the United States, to frontier agricultural regions, first on the St. Lawrence and later on the prairies. If we consider the significance of the frontier to lie chiefly in its capital fixation processes, and in the way in which the whole economy is thus vitalized, it becomes worth while to search for the frontier activities of the Canadian economy at the various phases in its history. Clearly the fur trade, constantly expanding, offered the frontier function for, and transmitted frontier vitality to, the St. Lawrence economy for two hundred years after Champlain's earliest settlements. With the North West Company eventually crowded against the Arctic and the Pacific, however, the further expansion essential to a frontier condition was prevented, and fur thus ended its commercial service to the St. Lawrence. Timber took over the frontier role and filled it till mid-century. By 1850 it was evident that in the settlement of the Upper Canadian lowlands, agriculture was in effect shouldering the frontier function, and in fact had been doing so increasingly since immigration began to pour in, in the middle twenties.

Before 1850 the vitalizing effects of the steadily expanding Canadian agricultural frontier were not fully appreciated. The whole process was taken for granted, and the really big commercial and financial stakes were always thought to lie in the American hinterland and its traffic, and to await merely the completion of the Canadian canal system. The same attitude carried on into the early eighteen-fifties. As immigration regained a healthy and moderate abundance after the 1847 tragedy, settlement filled in the vacancies in the better lands in the western parts of Upper Canada, and was associated with a considerable degree of farm and urban prosperity. This, however, was accepted as a matter of course, while urban interests, forwarding merchants and financiers, continued to measure the prospects attaching to the American hinterland. The Canadian canal system was patently a failure in its major objectives from the very days of its completion, partly because of comparative ocean rates from New York and Montreal, but partly also because of American progress in railway-building. Canadian canals were obsolescent while still under construction. If there remained anything of interest to Canadian merchants in the American hinterland, nothing short of a Canadian railway structure, a "grand trunk" railroad linking the Canadian-American western boundary (at Sarnia or Windsor) with an all-winter seaport, would suffice to give the Canadian route a competitive chance. In fact, many forces were at work to make an entrée to the American West increasingly attractive. European food shortages helped to drive great floods of migrants to the new continent, particularly to the United States, and they, as well as older settlers, poured westward towards and beyond the Mississippi, to create and maintain a steadily moving American agricultural frontier. In comparison to the commercial spoils awaiting the diversion of American traffic to Canadian channels, provided the comparative transportation handicap could be overcome, the profits to be made in servicing the Canadian agricultural frontier were trifling. The American prospect was sufficient to induce the Canadas to turn their backs on their gigantic canal project, practically before it was completed, and to embark upon a scheme of railway construction more ambitious than anything before thought possible.

In 1850 there were sixty miles of railway in Canada; in 1860 there were over two thousand.[21] By 1867 sixteen companies had spent $146,000,000 for 2,188 miles of railway in Canada.[22] As the structure towards the west was planned to tap the carrying trade of the American grain states, so in the east it was directed towards winter outlets for the St. Lawrence valley by way of north Atlantic ports. In the attempt to salvage the St. Lawrence route between 1850 and 1867, 2,000 miles of railway were superimposed on an obsolete canal system.[23] If developmental costs were heavy before

[21]Glazebrook, *History of Transportation in Canada*, p. 172.

[22]*Ibid.*, p. 173.

[23]Canadian canals did not long accommodate the larger vessels appearing on the lakes. By 1860 even the Welland Canal was too small for one-quarter of the lake grain vessels, and by 1871, for three-quarters. See Creighton, *British North America at Confederation*, p. 14.

1850 they were prodigious thereafter. The railways failed as the canals before them. The Great Western, an important unit in Canadian railway mileage, actually served to divert American traffic through Canada West at what we might call its narrowest point, and thus to aid American railways in their already one-sided competition with the Canadian railway system. The Grand Trunk was bankrupt by 1860; it did not gain access to Chicago until 1880. Governmental expenditures over these years included comparatively trifling sums spent on colonization roads. Figures for these expenditures were $2,016,000 from Union till 1852, and $2,566,000 from Union till 1860, inclusive.[24] The size of such expenditures directed exclusively towards local improvement, compared with the expenditures on railways, indicates something of the relative significance in the Canadian scheme of things of local development as compared with the possibility of establishing effective contact with American territory.

By 1850, however, merchants, forwarders, and financiers were not indifferent to the Canadian agricultural frontier and its lucrative employments. They had taken these for granted, and might have continued so to do had not the vitality of the frontier completely vanished from the Canadian situation. Some warning of impermanence in the onward movement was given by the immigration panic of 1847 and by some decline in immigrant numbers in succeeding years. By 1854 immigrant numbers were again high, at 60,000 equalling two-thirds of the 1847 figure. But in 1855, with local depression in Canada and with war prosperity in Britain and Ireland, numbers were halved, not to recover any considerable proportions before Confederation. After the widespread crisis of 1857 immigration to Canada fell to a trickle for three years, and during the eighteen-sixties was slight. Migrants were pouring into the United States. They did not come to Canada; they did not come via the St. Lawrence; after 1855 they added insult to injury by crossing hurriedly through the western peninsula by way of the Great Western Railway, touching lightly on Canadian soil and escaping as quickly as possible into the American West. The Crimean War forced the price of Canadian wheat up to a phenomenal peak of

[24]Report of the Select Committee on Emigration, Canada Assembly, *Journal*, 1861, App. no. 1.

$2.40 a bushel in Toronto in 1856,[25] and railway-building contributed to a concurrent though short-lived boom in all branches of agricultural and urban activity. But in 1857 the collapse was sudden and of offsetting proportions. With or without local prosperity, however, by the middle eighteen-fifties the forward sweep of the St. Lawrence agricultural frontier was ended; the crown lands available for disposal in the western parts of Upper Canada were progressively poorer in quality.

3. The Bureau of Agriculture as Immigration Agency

The functional relationship of Canadian agriculture to the other elements in the Canadian economy between 1850 and 1867 is made clear by the activities and attitudes of the Bureau of Agriculture[26] following its establishment in 1852. Apart from cursory supervision of the agricultural hierarchy, the Bureau and the eleven successive Ministers of Agriculture consistently considered their function to be the stimulation of traffic for the Canadian transportation system. The Bureau was in effect a traffic agency, the leading traffic agency in Canada before Confederation. The act which constituted the Bureau set the stage for such activity without stressing it in providing that agricultural statistics should be collected and disseminated "to promote improvement in the Province, and to encourage immigration from other countries."[27] Bureau heads, the Ministers of Agriculture, from Malcolm Cameron onward consistently interpreted "improvement within the Province" to mean the solution of the developmental-overhead problem of the province, and this to be dependent upon the securing of ever-increased traffic. Immigration would provide this increased traffic, so that the encouragement of immigration and the fostering of internal improvement constituted a single task. Settlement within Canada offered the additional transportation and merchandising prospect of an outbound staple,

[25]Jones, "History of Agriculture in the Province of Canada," pp. 126 ff.

[26]The act of 1862 (25 Vic., c. 7) changed the Bureau to a department, the Department of Agriculture of Canada, and this formed the basis of the federal Department of Agriculture constituted by act in 1868 (31 Vic., c. 53).

[27]Statutes of Canada, 16 Vic., c. 11 (1852), s. 6. Suggesting the increasing industrialization of the St. Lawrence during the eighteen-fifties, this section was broadened in the 1857 act to relate statistical enquiries to "Agricultural, Mechanical and Manufacturing Interests." See Statutes of Canada, 20 Vic., c. 32.

and it was accordingly desirable that immigrants should stay in Canada. But even if migrants went on to the United States, so long as they came *via* Canada, *via* Quebec and the St. Lawrence, they were contributing cash for their fare, cartage and keep to Canadian interests, and this was all there was in immediate prospect from any migrant, whether he stopped in Canada or went beyond. The immediate concern was not that immigrants went to the United States instead of to Canada, but that they went to the States through New York instead of through Quebec.

The Bureau of Agriculture was essentially an immigration agency, and the first one in the Canadas.[28] The first Minister of Agriculture, the Honourable Malcolm Cameron, considered the encouragement of immigration his first, and almost his exclusive, "agricultural" function. Mr. Kirkwood was appointed agent to Britain, to gather information on flax culture and also "to disseminate information on the resources of the country Canada as relating to immigration."[29] In order to obtain information for Kirkwood, Cameron circularized Montreal forwarding houses to obtain comparative information concerning the Quebec and New York routes, information as to comparative distances, conveyances, expenses, luggage allowed, charges for excess luggage, types of vessel, and other general factors.[30] For further material, Cameron sought success stories from former immigrants. In January, 1853, he forwarded questionnaires to twenty-eight persons, officials and acquaintances of his own, with covering letters asking the recipients to get the questionnaires filled out by successful immigrants and explaining that the completed forms were to be sent to the native parish of the immigrant, "that his friends and acquaintances there

28Dr. Thomas Rolph had acted as Canadian Emigration Agent in the United Kingdom during the years 1839-42, and claimed to have combatted by correspondence, lectures, and letters to the press, much of the publicity favouring the United States and Australia. See above, p. 109.

29First Annual Report of the Minister of Agriculture, August 20, 1854, Canada Assembly, *Journal*, 1854-5, App. II. The Minister of Agriculture instructed Kirkwood to proceed to England, Ireland, and Belgium if necessary; also that he should give "all the information which can be had on the subject of Emigration to this Province by lectures or letters to the people among whom you may travel." See Letter Books of the Bureau of Agriculture, Public Archives of Canada, Cameron to Kirkwood, February, 1853, no. 94, p. 59.

30*Ibid.*, circular signed Malcolm Cameron, Dec. 28, 1852, no. 15.

may judge of the inducements that Canada offers to Emigrants from the mother country."[31] Not all former immigrants, however, could represent Canada's inducements in a way suitable for the purpose involved. Cameron added, "This, of course, is a delicate matter, and can only be rendered serviceable to the country by a very judicious selection of the persons to be questioned."[32] Sending a copy of the questionnaire to E. W. Thompson, Chairman of the Board of Agriculture at Toronto, Cameron mentioned that Kirkwood was going to England, and suggested "and if you know a successful man in the Gore or in Esquesing who came out poor and penniless and has succeeded, get his history on that sheet and return it."[33]

Ministers of Agriculture relied heavily on pamphlets and other published materials to stimulate immigration. Cameron authorized publication in German of "a small work comprising a series of articles on the capabilities of the Province," as well as a comprehensive dispatch by Lord Elgin.[34] These with several thousand copies of the railway map of the province were specially prepared and forwarded for distribution in Europe.[35] In 1857 the Honourable P. M. Vankoughnet, then Minister of Agriculture, reported that Mr. Hutton of the Bureau of Agriculture had prepared a twenty-four-page pamphlet embodying full information on "the condition, geographic position, climate, soil, productions, capabilities, Educational and Municipal institutions of the country; and the wages of labourers of all classes, etc., etc."[36] Of this pamphlet the Bureau of Agriculture had printed 12,000 English, 6,000 German, 5,000 Norwegian, and 4,000 French copies, and sent them to Europe for distribution. Help was secured there from Sir Cusack Roney, Secretary in London for the Grand Trunk Railway Company, from

[31]Ibid., Jan. 18, 1853, no. 25.

[32]Ibid.

[33]Ibid., Cameron to Thompson, Jan. 4, 1853, no. 16.

[34]Cameron authorized Peter Eby of Berlin, C.W., to print five thousand copies of Lord Elgin's dispatch in German, for £25, four thousand to be delivered to the Bureau of Agriculture and the rest distributed in the local German settlements (ibid., Cameron to Eby, June 1, 1853, no 92). Cameron also authorized Mr. Sinn of Quebec to have prepared "the cheap edition" of Mr. Teuscher's pamphlet for distribution in Germany (ibid., Cameron to Sinn, June 11, 1853, no. 107).

[35]Report of the Minister of Agriculture, Canada Assembly, Journal, 1854-5, App. II.

[36]Ibid., 1857, App. no. 54.

emigration commissioners, foreign consuls, large ship-owners, and newspaper proprietors. The same year the Bureau circulated a pamphlet written by T. P. French, resident agent on the Ottawa and Opeongo road, "giving particular information as to what Settlers on the Free Grants . . . have to provide themselves with."[37] Also the Bureau bought and distributed six hundred copies of a "well-known little work," Mrs. Traill's *The Female Emigrant's Guide.* The purchase of these copies for £100 was partly designed as assistance to Mrs. Traill.

Complying with the statutory requirement that the Bureau of Agriculture should secure statistical information as a basis for encouraging immigration, Vankoughnet started, and his successors followed, the practice of circularizing annually the reeves and mayors of municipalities to learn the numbers and kinds of immigrants needed in various localities.[38] From 160 replies in 1857 he gathered that there was local need for 24,000 immigrants, including 9,300 farm servants and labourers, 3,600 female servants, 5,765 boys and girls, 900 "mechanics," and 4,500 undefined.

The commercial crisis of 1857 forced retrenchment of immigration activities, but with most of the depression over by 1859, the Bureau of Agriculture intensified its efforts in this direction, using both pamphlets and European agencies.[39] In 1859 Mr. A. B. Hawke, formerly Emigration Agent at Toronto, was sent to establish an agency at Liverpool. Pamphlets advertising Canada were printed in German, Norwegian, and English, and a map of Canada, put out by the Crown Lands Department and indicating the free-grant roads, was distributed widely. In 1860 the Bureau of Agriculture's pamphlet *Canada* was revised in second and third editions totalling 25,000 copies, translated into French, German, and Norwegian, and distributed in Britain and Ireland, Prussia, Germany, Norway, and France.[40] In February, 1860, Mr. Wagner, a Prussian, lately a provincial surveyor in the Ottawa country, was sent to Germany loaded with maps, pamphlets, and the Honourable A. T. Galt's brochure, *Canada, 1849 to 1859,* translated into German. Mr. C.

37*Ibid.*

38*Ibid.*, and succeeding reports.

39Report of the Minister of Agriculture, Canada, *Sessional Papers,* 1860, no. 22, pp. 22-3.

40*Ibid.,* 1861, no. 23.

Closter was sent to Norway, and Helge Hangan, a settler in Lower Canada, on leaving for Norway was given maps and pamphlets. After travelling and lecturing on the prospects of Canada, Hangan chartered two vessels to sail with Norwegian migrants from Drontheim and Lossoten, respectively. Meanwhile A. B. Hawke maintained the Liverpool office. In 1861 more agents were sent abroad, for Ireland and western Europe.[41] There was, however, no certainty regarding policy. In 1862 the agents were recalled on the advice of the legislative Committee on Emigration and Colonization.[42] Immigration was unsatisfactory; the Civil-War demand for labour in the United States was advanced hopefully as an excuse; but whatever the reason, encouragement efforts were not meeting with success.

In encouraging immigration as a means towards commercial prosperity, the Bureau of Agriculture relied on more than literature and special agents. Pamphlets and travelling speakers stressed the advantages of the Quebec immigration route as compared with that by New York, and of Canada as a place for permanent settlement as compared with the United States. The 1860 legislative committee on emigration voiced the most common and most carefully cultivated faith regarding Canadian prospects for newcomers when it said: "The strongest attraction which Canada can offer to the European emigrant, is, *cheap or free, cultivable* land."[43] A few careful thinkers such as T. D. McGee, Minister of Agriculture from 1864 till his death in 1868, realized[44] that "cultivable land" was a relative term, the comparison always being between Canadian lands and lands on the American frontier already marching well beyond the Mississippi. But the common reasoning was that Canadian free grants should be at least a fair competitive match for American lands available only at a price.

4. Land Policy: The Ottawa-Huron Tract

In the eighteen-fifties the Canadian government acting through its Crown Lands Department and its Bureau of Agriculture set out

[41]*Ibid.*, 1862, no. 32.
[42]*Ibid.*, 1863, no. 4.
[43]Canada Assembly, *Journal*, 1860, App. no. 4, p. 9.
[44]See, for example, his report on immigration presented to the Executive Council, *Minutes of the Executive Council*, Public Archives of Canada, Series E, State Book Y, May 9, 1863.

to revive the spotty Canadian tradition of free-land grants.[45] By 1830 a planless free-grant policy had impoverished the Canadian domain, had enriched friends of the Executive, had isolated settlers, and had contributed substantially to the Upper Canadian Rebellion of 1837. Simcoe had offered free grants along Yonge Street north of Toronto. The Public Lands Act of 1841 (4 and 5 Vic., c. 100) permitted the Governor to grant fifty acres to settlers "along the line of Public Roads," and this section remained in the 1849 revision of the Public Lands Act (12 Vic., c. 31).[46] The free-grant section of the Public Lands Act of 1853 (16 Vic., c. 159, s. 9)[47] was more generous; it raised the individual grant to one hundred acres, and directed it towards developmental purposes. The Governor might "appropriate as free grants any Public Lands in this Province to actual settlers, upon or in the vicinity of any Public Roads in any new settlements which shall or may be opened through the Lands of the Crown."

This legislation is the basis of the colonization efforts pursued so vigorously by the Ministers of Agriculture and the Agricultural Bureau after 1854 in a desperate attempt to attract immigration to Canada. By the middle eighteen-fifties the better crown lands in the Upper Canada peninsula were nearly if not quite exhausted, and there remained only the "Ottawa-Huron tract," the territory between the Ottawa River and Georgian Bay, to the north of existing settle-

[45]Jones, "History of Agriculture in the Province of Canada," pp. 182-93; Morrison, "Principle of Free Grants in the Land Act of 1841" (*Canadian Historical Review*, December, 1933), pp. 392-407; Sage, "Some Aspects of the Frontier in Canadian History" (Canadian Historical Association, *Report*, 1928), pp. 62-72; Macdonald, *Canada, 1763-1841, passim.*

[46]Free-grant legislation opened several important Upper Canadian roads, and whole areas with them. The Garafraxa or Owen Sound road, from Fergus to Owen Sound, completed in 1842, was soon completely settled. There were also the "Toronto Line," or Toronto and Sydenham road, completed in 1849 from Chatsworth to Shelburne; the Durham road, Garafraxa to Kincardine, completed by 1853; and the Elora and Saugeen road, nearly completed by 1855. All attracted settlers. See Jones, "History of Agriculture in the Province of Canada"; Morrison, "Principle of Free Grants in the Land Act of 1841."

[47]Section 14 of this act permitted the reservation of one-quarter of the proceeds of School Land sales and one-fifth of those of Crown Land sales "as a fund for public improvement within the county," to be expended by the provincial government. Sums thus secured went for local roads and bridges.

ments. In 1853 Dr. John Rolph changed from the post of Commissioner of Crown Lands to that of President of the Executive Council and thus became *ex officio* Minister of Agriculture. He took with him the administration of colonization roads in Upper Canada and laid before the Council his plans for a new era in colonization and settlement.[48] The two areas which to him presented "the most favorable character for agricultural settlement" were "the School Tract on Lake Huron and such other vacant public lands as are connected with it," and the eastern region, which, he said, "may be comprehended between the Georgian Bay and the Ottawa in the rear of the frontier settlements." For the latter region Rolph proposed a system of main free-grant roads, east-west, and north-south; one, the Ottawa and Opeongo, from Renfrew to Lake Opeongo; one from Pembroke to Mattawan to the River Nipissing; north and south, the Hastings and the Addington. These roads, particularly the east-west ones he considered as traversing good agricultural regions. The Ottawa and Opeongo, for instance, he considered to be "bordered by excellent land covered with hardwood."[49]

Opinion on such a project wavered for a year or two. The committee on public lands in 1855 was non-committal despite urging by important witnesses. In 1856 the Commissioner of Crown Lands described the Ottawa-Huron tract as the best area available for colonization, since lumber camps provided a ready market for farm produce. It must have been common knowledge that regions where lumber camps abounded at that time were red- and white-pine areas and that such areas held little agricultural prospect. Yet the urging of Ministers of Agriculture and of Crown Lands Commissioners were indicative of the pressure of the situation. Immigration had to be fostered; movement and expansion must be restored to the Canadian agricultural frontier. That the region contemplated for new settlement in the middle eighteen-fifties lies in the neighbourhood of the present-day Algonquin Park is sufficient to indicate something of the stakes involved in the hopeless gamble. In 1855 the government set out on a policy of colonization road construction, combined with the pushing of free grants upon these roads, designed

[48]Letter Books of the Bureau of Agriculture, Public Archives of Canada, Report to the Honourable Executive Council, by John Rolph, Sept. 12, 1853, no. 158.
[49]*Ibid.*

to settle the Ottawa-Huron tract,[50] and to re-establish a Canadian agricultural frontier on the margins of the Precambrian Shield. Annually $100,000 were voted "for colonization purposes" and devoted to the extension of colonization, or free-grant, roads equally in Upper and Lower Canada.

It has been argued in other studies that the east-west road projects in the Ottawa-Huron tract were developed to aid the lumbermen, and that it was the lumbermen, notably John Egan, who persuaded the government to apply the free-grant principle to such roads, since lumbermen wanted sources of cheap supplies close at hand.[51] Pressure from lumber interests was undoubtedly present and formative. In 1853 Dr. Rolph advised that the Hastings and Addington roads be developed only as winter roads[52]—generally of little use to settlers but all that lumbermen required. The willingness of the lumber interests to have farmers establish themselves in situations with no long-run prospects for survival may not be surprising, but the willingness of government to conspire towards that end under the guise of "aid to agriculture," is.

Ministers of Agriculture and governmental departments of Canada had greater stakes in view in attempting to establish settlement within the Ottawa-Huron tract than merely the smoothing of the pathway for local timber kings. Inmmigration had come to be regarded as necessary to prosperity in Canada, and immigrants would come to Canada and stay in Canada only if there was room and opportunity for them. In first advancing the rounded scheme of colonization roads for the Ottawa-Huron tract Dr. Rolph stressed their agricultural possibilities and their potential contribution towards the solution of the immigration problem, in the following words:

> The Minister of Agriculture has the honor to report that the extension of Agriculture in Canada West, the encouragement of immigration and the inducement of immigrants upon arriving among us to settle in the Country, will be most effectively promoted by opening those fertile regions, the value of which is very imperfectly known and cannot especially by newcomers be now satisfactorily examined by them. It is not consistent with the policy of rapid settlement of the public lands that they should be so entirely in a

---

[50]Canada Legislative Council, *Sessional Papers,* 1857, no. 54. Report of the Minister of Agriculture.

[51]Jones, "History of Agriculture in the Province of Canada."

[52]Report to the Honourable Executive Council (John Rolph).

wilderness as to be almost inaccessible and thus discourage exploration by the rising generation among us and render such exploration almost impossible to settlers from abroad.   This contrasts strongly with the facility with which all can examine and determine the value and advantages of any portion of the western parts of the United States, whither go too many of the Immigrants (as well as too many Canadians).[53]

The prairies, Dr. Rolph added, offered natural roads, not available in the forest; hence colonization road building was essential to establish communications tributary to rivers and railways.

In 1856 Vankoughnet, then Minister of Agriculture, advertised the free grants "To Emigrants and Others Seeking Lands for Settlement."[54] He claimed that in the Ottawa-Huron tract there was "an abundance of the very best of land for farming purposes." This land, he argued, could be cleared for about £4 currency per acre, which amount the first average wheat crop would nearly repay, while land values doubled every ten years regardless of any improvement by the settler. The Ottawa country, he said, "lying south of Lake Nipissing and of the great River Ottawa . . . is capable of sustaining a population of *Eight Millions of People.*"[55]

Correspondence and annual reports of Ministers of Agriculture, and various statements by the permanent officers of the Bureau of Agriculture, emphasize the immigrant-bait function of the free grants along the colonization roads in the Ottawa-Huron tract. They also make it clear that the free-grant system was not the parallel of the later Canadian homestead system. Throughout the eighteen-fifties crown lands were considered a source of revenue, and free grants were designed to attract immigration which, in turn, among its various purposes, would valorize crown lands through which roads were run. A letter written in 1857 by Hutton, Secretary of the Bureau of Agriculture, makes these relationships clear:

> Mr. V[ankoughnet, Minister of Agriculture], gave me the excellent articles from the Bulletin, &c. . . I much fear there is too much importance attached to the extent of the *free grants*—they form a *comparatively very narrow strip* and are only intended as *channels to lead the stream of population* to the lands which are for sale at the rear of them.   Thus the Hastings Road is 74 miles long with narrow lots of 100 acres each laid out the whole length for Free Gifts—the land outside these will, I hear, be *sold* at 4/ currency per acre and

---

[53]*Ibid.*
[54]Canada Assembly, *Journal,* 1857, App. no. 54.
[55]*Ibid.*

ten years to pay—*almost* equivalent to a grant certainly, but Mr. V. seems anxious that there should be no misunderstanding about the extent of the Free Grants.[56]

The logical evolution of the idea that the whole economy could be vitalized by a steadily expanding agricultural frontier required the abandonment of a land-sale policy and the adoption of the free-homestead system. Land sales might facilitate public financing, in the narrow budgetary sense, but this was a negligible consideration in relation to potential fruits in terms of general prosperity which were coming to be recognized as the concomitant of an abundant and continuous immigration. During the eighteen-fifties the revenue idea survived, but it was fast giving away before the broader idea of the vitalizing possibilities inherent in the public domain. Free grants were given on conditions of immediate settlement, erection of domicile, minimum cultivation, and actual residence. Even crown lands reserved for sale were sold only for settlement, at least nominally, while prices and terms of sale were adapted to this end. Hutton made these points in answer to the request of an American who asked a grant of 400,000 acres which he proposed to colonize with Germans. Hutton stated: "It is not the present policy of the Canadian government either to grant or sell large blocks of land except on actual and immediate settlement, i.e., *one month* only is allowed from the time of choosing each lot, to the time of *actual* settlement thereon."[57] He added that crown lands in the rear of free grants were for sale at 4*s.* currency (3/3 sterling) per acre, with ten years to pay at 6 per cent interest, the terms established by the Crown Lands Department.

Supervision of colonization roads was not allotted to the Bureau of Agriculture by legislation until 1862 (25 Vic., c. 7) and then only optionally. It is significant that the Bureau supervised the colonization-road fund in Upper Canada from 1853 to 1862, but took over the Lower Canada fund only in 1862, and then only for a year or so. Colonization roads were as closely related to agriculture in Lower as in Upper Canada. Why did the Bureau of Agriculture control one and not the other?

[56]Letter Books of the Bureau of Agriculture, Hutton to Sir Cusack P. Roney, Secretary in London for the Grand Trunk Railway, Feb. 25, 1857, no. 66. The letter refers to a series of publicity documents put out by Roney. Italics are Hutton's.

[57]*Ibid.*, Hutton to Klieber, Camden, N.J., March 9, 1857, no. 82.

The answer to this question is clear. As an immigration agency the Bureau of Agriculture worked strenuously to groom local agriculture and agricultural prospects so that migrants might be attracted. New areas had to be found and opened up if Canada was to offer any effective competition with the United States in the European immigration markets. Upper Canada had the Ottawa-Huron tract which offered a last desperate prospect. Lower Canada also had unopened territories, and Lower Canada was annually awarded half the colonization-road fund. But the Lower Canadian situation held no interest for the Bureau of Agriculture because, whatever might be done in the way of extending colonization roads, Lower Canada would not tolerate immigration. There was the "racial" question, the fear that habitant culture would be endangered, that the Canadian vote would be swallowed up, besides the basic fact that Lower Canada was suffering from over-crowding despite the vast nearby areas lying untouched. Lower Canada had a colonization problem, but it was a question of finding room for, and persuading to settle, its own "surplus" population, which since 1837 had been steadily, if in uncertain numbers, draining into the United States.[58] But even if this colonization problem could be met, it was not on a parallel with the hoped-for Upper Canadian colonization of immigrants. To move farmers' sons from old and over-crowded parishes into new ones near at hand would contribute nothing to the prosperity of transportation and travel-agency systems; and once there, even the process of carving out and establishing a new farmstead meant practically nothing commercially, for habitant methods of pioneering were not to any appreciable extent dependent upon the purchase of shop-made equipment. As habitant farming was to a very high degree self-contained, non-commercial, so too would be the colonization process, as one aspect of habitant practice.

Consequently the Canadian Bureau of Agriculture, and the government generally, had vast interest in Upper Canadian colonization but little in Lower Canadian colonization. Annually, half of the

[58]Report of the Special Committee on Emigration, Canada Legislative Council, *Sessional Papers*, 1857, no. 47; Report of the Select Committee on Colonization, Canada Assembly, *Journal*, 1860, App. no. 5; Report of the Select Committee on the Colonization of Wild Lands in Lower Canada, *ibid.*, 1862, App. no. 1; Report of Select Standing Committee on Immigration and Colonization, *ibid.*, 1864, App. no. 7. See also Hansen, *Mingling of the Canadian and American Peoples*, chap. VI.

Colonization Fund was expended in Lower Canada, under the nominal supervision of the Commissioner of Crown Lands. Actually, the funds were dissipated on a multitude of local projects in the old parishes.[59] In 1862 the Minister of Agriculture took over supervision of the Lower Canadian colonization fund and made elaborate plans[60] to reorganize the system around five trunk roads so that new territories might be opened up. In 1864 the Department of Agriculture gave up the recently-acquired task, for which it had such slight regard.

Individuals and committees expressed satisfaction with the progress of Upper Canada colonization roads. The 1861 Committee on Emigration under McGee thought that the Ottawa-Huron tract with 485 miles of roads completed had nearly enough main roads.[61] Lumbermen found them convenient for bringing in supplies. But years before Confederation the whole venture into the Ottawa-Huron tract was recognized as a failure. Old settlers took up land on the free-grant roads, cleared off the timber, and moved on. Not that there was any concern that old settlers rather than new immigrants went to the free grants. It was held normal and advisable that new immigrants hire out as farm labourers for a period of months or a year or so to gain experience in new conditions, as well as to acquire cash for settlement needs. If only old settlers or their sons would go and develop the free grants! But these went in as timber farmers, stripped the timber, and left. If they had capital they went to buy land on the American agricultural frontier.

Officials of the Bureau of Agriculture showed considerable discretion concerning the qualities and quantities of immigration held desirable. In the first place, while they considered the free grants to be the chief attraction to immigrants, nevertheless they realized that newcomers would be helpless upon the free grants, that they should hire out if they had no capital, or buy cleared farms if they had.[62]

[59]Report of the Select Committee on Emigration, Canada Assembly, *Journal*, 1861, App. no. 1.

[60]Report of the Minister of Agriculture to the Executive Council, *Minutes of the Executive Council*, Public Archives of Canada, Series E, State Book X, June 28, 1862.

[61]Canada Assembly, *Journal*, 1861, App. no. 1.

[62]"The sons of our old Settlers are the best Pioneers of the Forest, and the Emigrants *without capital* are best employed in supplying their places, whilst those *having capital* are wiser to purchase clearances. Immense mis-

Secondly, they thought in terms of immigrants whose native environment would fit them for the bush life of the Canadian frontier. Norwegians and Swedes they thought of as most suitable.[63] There was great disappointment when Norwegians and Swedes passed Canada by for the Michigan timber areas. Not only environment but also occupation was held important. Typical of the Bureau's attitude was Hutton's statement: "We do not wish for a great number of tradesmen nor clerks nor quill drivers of any kind, but chiefly farm and domestic servants, boys and girls over 12 years of age and farmers with some capital."[64] Hutton was steadily opposed to the entry of clerks, "quill drivers," teachers of any kind, literary persons, and gentlemen without money.[65] The season of the year at which migrants arrived was also important.[66] Too often immigrants were gathered slowly throughout the summer months, were embarked well past midsummer, and debarked in Canada late in the fall, with employment already shrinking towards a seasonal winter low. Finally, the Bureau of Agriculture was far from seeking unlimited immigration even of the most suitable kinds. There was the realization that Canadian opportunities were not unlimited. Particularly was this true after the slump of 1857. Early in 1858 Hutton wrote to an English firm that "Canada suffered so much by these hard times that we are very unwilling to encourage *indiscriminate Immigration*."[67]

Significantly enough the Bureau had repeated cause to complain about the propaganda work of C. P. Roney, secretary to the Grand Trunk Railway. Roney was completely unguarded in publicizing Canadian immigration attractions. Officials in Canada wanted traffic

---

chief may be done by forcing Emigration to the Free Grants if Emigrants have mistaken views with regard to the difficulties of a forest life. The 'Free Grants' would be a very small boon to a great majority of raw Emigrants" (Letter Books of the Bureau of Agriculture, Hutton to Roney, Sept. 29, 1856, no. 239; italics Hutton's).

63*Ibid.,* Hutton to French, July 7, 1856; Hutton to Buchanan, Aug. 7, 1856; Hutton to Roney, Feb. 25, 1857.

64*Ibid,* Hutton to Buchanan, Oct. 10, 1857.

65See for example *ibid.,* Hutton to an English enquirer, Feb. 27, 1858; Hutton to Wilson, April 19, 1858.

66*Ibid.,* Hutton to a London firm, Oct. 16, 1856.

67*Ibid.,* Hutton to an English firm, Feb. 27, 1858; italics Hutton's. See also Taché to Dixon, Jan. 25, 1866.

for railways and canals and all the desirable results associated with an abundant immigration; but they were fully aware of their responsibility for indigent immigrants. The Grand Trunk's immediate purposes were served once the immigrant's ticket was bought. In 1858 Hutton complained to Wilson, Professor of Agriculture at Edinburgh: "There was an article lately in the *Morning Herald* calculated to do much mischief—the resources, etc., of Canada were quite *overdrawn. I hear* that it was written by Sir Cusack P. Roney. We are rather anxious in this Department to *chasten* people's ideas of Canada."[68]

5. *Failure of the Canadian Agricultural Frontier: Agricultural Purposes in Confederation*

However, neither in their efforts towards the encouragement of immigration nor in their insistence on selective standards were Ministers of Agriculture able to take comfort in the decade or more before Confederation. Immigration in 1854, numbering 60,000[69] and second in size only to the calamitous total of 1847, seemed to justify eager efforts towards further promotion. Best of all, 53,000 of these immigrants came by way of Quebec, and though immigration officials estimated[70] that less than half of the total remained in Canada, nevertheless in travelling *via* Quebec they were providing return cargo for Canadian timber and grain vessels, and traffic for Canadian canals and other service facilities. But stated concisely, after 1854 scarcely a single year brought immigration sufficient to satisfy the hopes of St. Lawrence transportation and service industries. Estimated entries[71] in 1857 were 72,000, but only 32,000 came *via* Quebec, and only 33,000 were estimated to remain in Canada. Average Quebec entries of 10,000 per year between 1858 and 1860, inclusive, increased to a 20,000 annual average from 1861 to 1865; but both figures were a mere mockery of expectations. An increasing stream entered Canada at the Niagara suspension bridge, not to stay, but passing hastily *en route* to western American territory.

In facing the immigration dilemma the Bureau of Agriculture was at the heart of one of the most crucial problems of the day. In

[68]*Ibid.,* Hutton to Wilson, April 19, 1858; italics Hutton's.
[69]Canada Assembly, *Journal,* 1854-5, App. DDD.
[70]*Ibid.*
[71]For immigration data see annual reports of A. C. Buchanan, Chief Emigrant Agent, Canada Assembly, *Journals.*

nine years, 1857-65 inclusive, thirteen House committees reported on various aspects of immigration and colonization; in 1860 three reported. Each year's reports strengthened the tone of defeat sounded by those preceding. Contributory causes were easy to discover. The Crimean and Italian wars, "by taking many thousands of hands out of the labor market, by exciting the spirit of martial adventure among certain orders of men, and by suggesting restrictions on the free egress of emigrants to some of the German Governments, partially diminished the volume of the exodus."[72] In the decade of the eighteen-fifties, four million persons left Europe for the United States, Australia, and Canada, and "the newer countries of the world lost a productive force of at least 500,000 by the Crimean and Italian wars."[73]

As emigration dwindled, competition for settlers became more acute. The competition between Canada and the United States was as old as that between New England and New France or between New England and Newfoundland. The competition of Australian colonies was comparatively new. In 1837 and 1853, New South Wales and Van Dieman's Land, respectively, had ceased to be penal settlements. In 1853 the Gibbon Wakefield system of colonization by great companies was given up by the Colonial Office and local governments secured the revenues from their lands. Then gold discoveries were made, and the six Australian colonies set out with all their energies to increase the flow of immigration to their shores.[74] More irksome to Canadians, because more obvious, was the comparison between the dribble of Canadian immigration and the stream pouring into the United States. By 1860 New York was drawing seven immigrants for every one going to Quebec.[75] Ocean rates were partly responsible. In 1863 fares from Liverpool to Quebec were £4.5s. sterling; to New York, £3.10s. sterling; while prepaid passages, secured in New York, were as low as $18.00 or £2.10s.[76] Agents for American land and railway companies were tireless promoters. The Civil War raised factory wages in the United States to most attractive levels.

[72]Report of the Select Committee on Emigration (T. D. McGee, Chairman), Canada Assembly, *Journal*, 1860, App. no. 4, p. 6.

[73]*Ibid.*   [74]*Ibid.*, pp. 7-8.   [75]*Ibid.*

[76]Third Report of the Select Committee on Immigration and Colonization, Canada Assembly, *Journal*, 1863 (first session), App. no. 3.

The real dilemma, the really disturbing factor, however, was that, small as was Canada's immigration, her opportunities were smaller. It was common then as since to consider Canada a land of boundless resources, of unlimited fertile land. Yet thoughtful persons realized this was wrong. From the middle eighteen-fifties onward, Buchanan, reporting annually as Chief Emigrant Agent for Canada, was seldom hopeful regarding opportunities for newcomers.[77] Some years he admitted that the small immigration had been salutary, for employment was limited. The clearest statement of the relationship between immigration and opportunities was given by Thomas D'Arcy McGee. Under the pressure of industrial distress in Britain in the early eighteen-sixties, the Secretary of State for the Colonies approached the Canadian government with a proposal for assisted settlement. McGee, President of the Executive Council, prepared a report on the matter. He reviewed briefly Canada's immigration policy, and admitted that Canadian population was trifling in comparison to territory. He went on, however:

> Formerly, the great Immigration epochs of this country, were coincident with the execution of the great public works of the country, the Rideau Canal in 1827, the Saint Lawrence Canals in 1832, the Welland and Beauharnois in 1841-2. The construction of railways also, between the years 1850 and 1857 attracted a large amount of immigrant labor, and by the wages thus provided enabled a large proportion of those so employed to remain as permanent settlers in the province. Unfortunately for the benevolent plans of many advocates of an extensive operative immigration from England to this country there are at present no extensive public works, in course of construction, upon which employment and wages might be found, for persons accustomed to artificial rather than agricultural occupations. Should such an immigration therefore take place on a large scale there is reason to apprehend that great suffering would result....[78]

The various committees appointed to consider the immigration problem put forward dozens of trivial proposals[79] concerning agents and agencies, boards of emigration commissioners, quarantine, landing sheds, and lavatories. But their proposals concerned superficialities. Colonization roads represented the one real hope advanced in

[77]See Canada Assembly, *Journal*, Appendices, annually.

[78]See *Minutes of the Executive Council*, Public Archives of Canada, Series E, State Book Y, May 9, 1863.

[79]See, for example, Report of the Select Committee on Emigration, Canada Assembly, *Journal*, 1860, App. no. 4; Second Report of the Committee on Immigration and Colonization, *ibid.*, 1863 (first session), App. no. 3.

Canada after 1850; and this was exploded by 1860. American railways had reached the Mississippi; Iowa and Minnesota could clearly grow wheat; Minnesota was admitted as a State of the Union in 1858. American homestead legislation of 1862 was merely the last straw, for by 1860, free grants in Ontario's Ottawa-Huron tract could not compete with lands which had to be paid for in the midwestern states. While Upper Canada could offer only forest land, much of it pine and far from markets, American land companies were offering, first, land with "wood, water and hay," and, well before Confederation, land "ready for the plough." Canadian attempts to bait developmental schemes with offers of settlement on timber lands, on pine lands, were rewarded by the ultimate problem that settlers came to be timber-settlers, bogus settlers, interested only in stripping the timber and then moving on.

By the early eighteen-sixties there came the knowledge, overdue by a decade, that the Canadian agricultural frontier had disappeared and that it could not be recreated within the St. Lawrence drainage basin. These facts were discouraging, not because the frontier reappeared across the international boundary, in the midwestern states,[80] but because Canada was lagging behind the United States in railway construction just as she had lagged in canal development. The Grand Trunk Railway linked Sarnia and Portland by 1860, but did not reach Chicago till 1880. St. Lawrence interests were trebly thwarted: in failing to obtain immigrants; in failing to keep the migrants who did come *via* Quebec; and in failing to tap the agricultural trade developing in the midwestern states. By 1860 Upper Canada was facing the problem which had already baffled Lower Canada for a quarter of a century, the problem of keeping her native sons.

By Confederation, then, there had come the realization of two facts of significance for Canadian agriculture and agricultural policy: first, that neither canals nor railways would enable the St. Lawrence valley to attract the commerce of the advancing American frontier, either inward or outward, and second, that it was hopeless to think of recreating a Canadian agricultural frontier any place on the St. Lawrence. The conclusive establishment of these facts eventually forced the major gamble of attempting to establish

[80]Sage, "Some Aspects of the Frontier in Canadian History" (Canadian Historical Association, *Report*, 1928), pp. 62-72.

agriculture in the North West Territories. The outcome of this plunge was wholly uncertain for decades after the decision was made, but after 1900 the results amply justified the risks. The North-West finally provided the Canadian agricultural frontier which it had been found impossible to re-establish on the St. Lawrence.

While the Canadian government was still putting forward efforts to tap the trade of the American West, and to expand the circumference of Canadian agriculture, straws in the wind showed increasingly serious consideration of the one remaining possibility, the agricultural entry of the Canadian North-West. In 1857 the British House of Commons gave special attention to the Hudson's Bay Company's stewardship of Rupert's Land, held by charter nearly two hundred years old. A select committee[81] inquired at length into the administration of the Company, but directed particular attention to the agricultural and settlement possibilities in the North West Territories. The best-informed witnesses, undoubtedly also the most biased, held agricultural prospects in the North-West to be negligible, and no one could cite experience to prove them wrong. Nevertheless the committee recommended that the western regions be ceded to Canada.[82] The same year Captain Palliser was sent out with an expedition under instructions by the Colonial Office to explore the North-West and determine its prospects in terms of timber, minerals, and agricultural capabilities; also to discover whether and what improvement in routes of entry would make for immigration and settlement results commensurate with the cost. Palliser's name is lastingly associated with the description of the southern areas of the Prairie Provinces as a "triangle" of infertile land.[83] Furthermore, Palliser reasoned that an all-Canadian route

81British Parliamentary Papers, 1857, Minutes of Evidence and Report of the Select Committee on the Hudson's Bay Company. See also Trotter, Canadian Federation, chaps. xvi, xvii. In subsequent chapters Professor Trotter outlines the growth of Canadian interest in the North-West in the eighteen-fifties and sixties. His interpretation is suggested by his statement that "The notion, often expressed, that the acquisition of the North-West by the new Dominion was a fortunate afterthought, has little basis in fact" (ibid., p. 222).

82Mackintosh, Prairie Settlement, p. 30.

83Ibid., pp. 30-5; Papers Relative to Exploration by Captain Palliser (British Parliamentary Papers, 1863). Palliser continued explorations in the West till 1860.

to the West would be useless in competition with available American routes. Nevertheless, outside the triangle of infertile land, Palliser reported vast fertile areas suitable for settlement largely in what we now know as the Park Belt. The same year Canada sent an exploration party to the West, best known of its members being S. J. Dawson as surveyor, and Professor H. Y. Hind as geologist and naturalist.[84] Their assignment was expressly to explore a route from Lake Superior to the Red River Settlement. In 1858 the expedition went in two parts, that under Dawson charged with continuing the survey of the transportation route, and that under Hind charged with exploring the valleys of the Assiniboine and the Saskatchewan. The reports of the Canadian expeditions[85] did not suggest perfection in western settlement prospects, but they drew the parallel with American experience. They suggested that the chief western agricultural problems concerned lack of markets rather than climatic and soil conditions.

Explorations before Confederation were far from removing prevailing doubts over the agricultural possibilities of the North-West. They revealed, however, a growing interest in whatever might develop there. Other signs of this interest occurred. As early as 1856 the President of the Executive Council, *ex officio* Minister of Agriculture, declared that Canada's western boundary should be on the Pacific. The Grand Trunk Railway people, notably E. W. Watkin, president of the railway in the eighteen-sixties, saw the solution to their own difficulties in a Pacific railway.[86] George Brown, persistently ridiculing in the *Globe*[87] all the efforts of "P. Weevil" Vankoughnet as Minister of Agriculture, particularly the latter's efforts to encourage local settlements on the free grants, just as persistently argued the merits of the great North-West as a prospective agricultural region. Brown used everything available in the way of favourable evidence: the reports of explorers, travellers, and correspondents, the isothermal theory, and the analogy of American experience. Whatever the arguments, and whatever their

[84]Mackintosh, *Prairie Settlement*, pp. 35 ff.

[85]Hind, *Narrative of the Canadian Red River Exploring Expedition; North-West Territory Reports of Progress;* Dawson, *Report on Exploration.*

[86]Glazebrook, *History of Transportation in Canada*, pp. 193-4.

[87]See, for example, *Toronto Globe*, Dec. 4, Dec. 20, 1856; Feb. 27, April 25, May 1, and June 5, 1857.

acceptance, the ultimate logic of the situation was that the agricultural prospects of the North-West, however slim, were the only remaining hope for the commerce, finance, transportation, and other service industries of the St. Lawrence. By 1860 a new interest existed to pin its hopes on the agricultural frontier, wherever it might again be set in motion: manufacturing was by this time far enough advanced to recognize the importance of secure and ever-expanding domestic markets.

Commonly expressed in the Confederation debates were the related thoughts that Canada's ills would vanish if immigration could be assured, and that union of the provinces was the best, if not the only, means towards such assurance. George Brown expressed the point as follows: "On this question of immigration turns, in my opinion, the whole future success of this great scheme [of Confederation] which we are now discussing. Why, Sir, there is hardly a political or financial or social problem suggested by this Union that does not find its best solution in a large influx of immigration. . . . I go for a Union of the Provinces because it will give a new start to immigration into our country."[88] Maritime leaders such as Tupper and Chandler voiced the same general opinions.[89] There was, of course, no assurance that the provinces would share equally in the benefits of western development. Canada, the St. Lawrence province, was clearly in a position to skim the best of the results. Said McGiverin: "What then may we not expect our great North-West to become? If we had it opened up, Canada would be the carriers of its produce, as the Middle States are the carriers of the Western States, and the manufacturers of its goods as the Eastern States are now the manufacturers of the goods consumed by the West."[90] Many thought that the West would provide ample benefits to go around.

A variety of factors, political as well as economic, impelled the British North American colonies towards Confederation; but in a very real sense Confederation was the constitutional instrument designed to permit Canada, the province, to re-establish an agricultural frontier to which it would have exclusive entrée. The prizes

[88]*Canadian Confederation Debates*, pp. 102-3, as quoted by Creighton in *British North America at Confederation*, pp. 47-8.
[89]*Ibid.*
[90]Cited by Creighton, *ibid.*, p. 42.

were to be found in remuneration for the provision of transportation services for settlers and their effects inward, and for their produce outward, and for the provision of all the varied capital equipment necessary for the creation of an agricultural frontier. Acre for acre, the servicing of the prairie frontier offered less prospect for profitable enterprise than did timber lands, for clearing was unnecessary, and each acre would absorb less in the way of capital and human resources; but there were so many more prairie acres.

A very substantial proportion of the functions projected for the Dominion government concerned immigration and colonization. The Department of Agriculture was the most important link beween Canada, the province, and Canada, the Dominion. It was long the most important department in the Dominion structure of government, for it carried forward the immigration functions of the provincial Department of Agriculture, and for many years concentrated its attentions upon these functions alone. Since the federal government was so largely created as an agency for the colonization of the West it follows that the Dominion government would grow strong throughout the years during which it was performing this function, and would weaken once this was accomplished—unless in the meantime the central government should discover new and vital purposes.

6. Summary

By 1850 commercial prosperity on the St. Lawrence relied more heavily on agriculture than ever before. Wheat was by this time a staple Canadian export and it was felt to be imperative that the export trade therein should continue to expand and should, at all costs, be secured to the Canadian export route—the St. Lawrence. Developmental energies were expended on canals and railways because of the belief that American agricultural exports might be diverted from the Hudson to the St. Lawrence if only adequate improvements were made to the latter route, and that commercial opportunities in Canadian agriculture were comparatively unimportant. Canadian agricultural expansion before 1850, however, had had decidedly profitable features, and after 1850 the efforts to tap the American West by means of a "grand trunk" railway were accompanied by activities and expenditures designed to bring floods of immigrants to Canada and to maintain the previous rate of

Canadian agricultural expansion. The Bureau of Agriculture, organized in 1852, was in fact an immigration and colonization agency. Land-grant regulations were liberalized and colonization roads were opened through the Ottawa-Huron tract.

Agricultural encouragement in the Province of Canada from 1850 to 1867 comprised chiefly the assistance and promotion of immigration and settlement. However, the attempt to compete with the United States for European emigrants was ineffective. The area which the government sought to colonize, the Ottawa-Huron tract, lay within the margins of the Precambrian Shield in northern Ontario, its heart today being occupied by a national park, with all that that implies in terms of agricultural possibilities. Pine lands within this area had no attraction for settlers by comparison with the lands offered on the American frontier. Settlement in the United States moved westward steadily and without geographic interruption. Against the forward movement of a Canadian agricultural frontier there lay a thousand miles of the Precambrian Shield, a thousand miles of rock and forest. Beyond that were the prairie portions of Rupert's Land, still under the control of the Hudson's Bay Company. It was barely possible that these territories might possess agricultural capabilities. So far this was completely unproven, one way or the other, but Hudson's Bay Company officials were careful to discourage any planning along these lines. In the prairie region, however, beyond the thousand-mile barrier, there lay the last desperate chance, and to secure this chance was one of the important purposes underlying the sponsorship of Confederation by the Province of Canada.

PART TWO

FEDERAL AGRICULTURAL POLICY

CHAPTER VI

THE DIVISION OF POWERS AT CONFEDERATION

DISSATISFACTION with agricultural development in the various British North American colonies, particularly in Canada, was one of the strongest forces working toward Confederation. In an important sense Confederation was a measure of agricultural assistance as clearly as were grants to agricultural boards and agricultural societies. The huge investment in transportation and service industries, and more recently in manufacturing enterprise, in the St. Lawrence River valley called for ready and, if possible, undisputed access to a forward-moving agricultural frontier, domestic or foreign. Such a frontier existed in the United States, of unprecedented scope; but this frontier was less and less accessible to Canadian activity. Efforts to reconstruct a Canadian frontier after 1850 were fruitless. American experience beyond the Mississippi, however, suggested the possibility that similar good fortune might await agricultural establishment north of the forty-ninth parallel of latitude, west of the Precambrian barrier. The encompassing of the vast western territories would require the united efforts of the British North American colonies. It would require developmental expenditure on a scale hitherto unknown in British territory. It would require, and make possible, immigration and settlement in non-American territory in a measure approaching the enviable American record. It would surely compensate for the shortcomings of agriculture in the existing colonies.

1. Concurrent Jurisdiction

It was no mere coincidence that "agriculture" and "immigration" were linked in the discussions at the Quebec Conference (1864) and were singled out for uniform treatment in the division-of-powers clauses of the British North America Act (1867). Agricultural "progress" had come to be regarded as dependent upon continued immigration, for the progress expected of agriculture was that it should constantly expand and constantly require servicing by commercial, financial, industrial, and transportation interests. Since by 1860 continued expansion could occur only in the western territories, still to be acquired, and since the proposed Dominion government was designed to administer those territories, it followed that this newly-planned governmental body should perform at least some of the functions relating to agriculture and immigration. Certain aspects of agriculture and immigration, on the other hand, were purely local in nature; that is to say, they were not essential to the grand strategy of Confederation. Settlement in the old provinces, for example, had so obviously exhausted all prospects of expansion for any reasonable future period that land titles and settlement policies in these provinces might well be left with the provincial administrations. Similarly, what little might be done, comparatively speaking, in the way of encouraging the agriculture in these provinces by continued grants in aid, importations of livestock, and even by agricultural education, was not on a scale sufficient to weigh in Confederation projects.

At the Quebec Conference it was accepted with little opposition that agriculture and immigration should, under Confederation, be objects of concurrent jurisdiction.[1] Mr. Coles of Prince Edward Island suggested that the federal government should have exclusive control over immigration and settlement. Jonathan McCully of Nova Scotia urged that the federal government have nothing to do with these subjects. Mr. Tupper and others, however, elaborated their support of concurrent jurisdiction. Said Mr. Mowat (Canada): "The items of Agriculture and Immigration should be vested in both Federal and Local Governments. Danger often arises where there is exclusive jurisdiction, and not so often in cases of concurrent jurisdiction. In municipal matters the county and township council often have concurrent jurisdiction."[2] Thomas D'Arcy McGee implied concurrent jurisdiction in discussing immigration: "The General Government," he said, "may draw attention to this country for settlement. The only permanent attraction we can offer is cheap land, free institutions, etc. I propose that the Local Legislatures should be bound to let immigrants have lands as hitherto. Immigrants should feel that they came to British America as a whole, and that they are free to choose lands where they like."[3]

[1]Pope (ed.), *Confederation Documents*, pp. 80-1.

[2]*Ibid.*

[3]*Ibid.* Elsewhere McGee was more specific. Reporting as Minister of Agriculture in 1866 he said: "I cannot but express my satisfaction, that under the proposed plan of Colonial Union, the subject of Agriculture should be made one of concurrent jurisdiction. . . . I am not insensible to the difficulties

As McGee's remarks indicate, the question of jurisdiction over agriculture and immigration could not be settled without reference to the position of crown lands, for crown lands provided the standard attraction for immigrants. By the time the Quebec discussions got around to agriculture and immigration it was taken for granted that crown lands should remain with the provincial governments. Answering Mr. Coles's suggestion for exclusive federal control over immigration and settlement, Mr. Tupper said: "I approve of some things being of a concurrent character. We should confine the jurisdiction neither to one nor the other exclusively. The same remark applies to Immigration, which is intimately connected with the Crown Lands, and these are under the Local Governments."[4]

The Quebec Resolutions provided that both the provincial and federal governments should be competent to make laws respecting agriculture and immigration. Section 95 of the British North America Act provided that provincial Legislatures might make laws relating to "Agriculture in the Province, and to Immigration into the Province," while the Parliament of Canada might make laws "in relation to Agriculture in all or any of the Provinces, and to Immigration into all or any of the Provinces." To avert conflict of jurisdiction the same section provided that "any Law of the Legislature of a Province relative to Agriculture or to Immigration, shall have effect in and for the Province as long and as far only as it is not repugnant to any Act of the Parliament of Canada." Further in line with the Quebec discussions the British North America Act specified provincial control of crown lands in the four provinces originally concerned. Among the exclusive powers of provincial Legislatures, Section 92 of the Act listed "(5) The management and sale of public lands belonging to the Province and of the timber and woods thereon," and "(13) Property and civil rights in the Province." Section 109 secured to "the several provinces of Ontario, Quebec, Nova Scotia, and New Brunswick" all lands, mines, and minerals within their borders.

---

which lie in the way of devising a thoroughly good system of general supervision capable of embracing all these Provinces. But the United States, with a wider area, and more varied productions, have, since July 1862, succeeded in establishing and carrying out such a general system of supervision and direction." See Canada, *Sessional Papers,* 1866, no. 5, p. 3.

[4]Pope, *Confederation Documents.*

2. *Reorganization of Agricultural Agencies After 1867*

The division of powers under the British North America Act called for administrative readjustments, because the federal government was to share in the jurisdiction over agriculture and immigration. Agricultural organization had reached a considerable degree of centralization in each of the several provinces. Nova Scotia, New Brunswick, and the Canadas all had central agricultural boards supervising agricultural societies and administering the annual grants in aid extended to these institutions by the provincial Legislatures. The Royal Agricultural Society in Prince Edward Island, forty years old by Confederation and incorporated in 1849, was in decline after 1860. It had formerly given whatever agricultural leadership there was in the Island, but the collapse of its stock-farm venture in 1858 had discouraged its membership and brought it into disrepute. Agricultural organizations in all the provinces were concerned mainly with spending governmental funds towards a measure of livestock improvement. Neither the Maritimes nor the Canadas, nor even the Genessee valley of New York State, could compete with the flood of wheat pouring in from the western American frontier.

In the Canadas, agricultural organization was more complex and more highly centralized than in the Maritimes.[5] Central boards in Upper and Lower Canada supervised the work of county and township agricultural societies, as in the Maritimes, while agricultural associations specialized in the administration of annual provincial fairs. Of more significance was the Department of Agriculture for the Canadas, situated at Ottawa, a separate department since 1862 and a bureau of government since 1852, which from its inception had been presided over by a Minister of the Crown. The ostensible purpose in the creation and maintenance of the Agricultural Department had been to tie the agricultural hierarchy, its activities leavened by grants in aid, more closely into the scheme of parliamentary responsibility. As pointed out in the previous chapter, the provincial Department of Agriculture retained only nominal supervision over the agricultural hierarchy and concentrated its whole energies upon immigration and colonization, activities mentioned only incidentally in the act of 1852 (16 Vic., c. 11) which created the bureau.

5See above, pp. 97-9, 112-6.

What place was there for the Dominion government in the heirarchy of agricultural agencies? It is clear that the new constitutional unit was not designed to concern itself with such petty matters as the supervision of annual grants to local agricultural societies. The provision for concurrent jurisdiction assured, on the one hand, that the provincial governments should retain this minor responsibility, and, on the other hand, that the Dominion government should have the right to intervene in the broader and more significant elements which pertained to agriculture and immigration according to the commercial interpretation which had gradually developed in the pre-Confederation period. The agricultural boards of the Maritime Provinces had little, if any, concern with problems of immigration and settlement, and their main function, that of supervision over agricultural societies, remained untouched by the creation of the Dominion government. New Brunswick and Nova Scotia retained their pre-Confederation structure of central boards and local societies, with inconsequential changes until later when secretaries responsible to the local Legislatures were provided for the care of agricultural matters.[6] Prince Edward Island continued to finance the governmental stock farm under the supervision of a governmental committee.

In the Canadas the situation was different. The offices of the Department of Agriculture of the Province of Canada were located in Ottawa at the time of Confederation, and Ottawa was declared the capital of the new Dominion. McGee had suggested shortly before Confederation that the provincial Department of Agriculture might, because of its considerable experience, take over the agricultural duties contemplated for the Dominion.[7] An act of 1868

[6]In 1871 New Brunswick repealed acts of 1854, 1855, 1859, 1860, and 1862, relating to agricultural societies and the Central Board, and gathered the whole structure within the purview of a single act (34 Vic., c. 35). In 1875 by 38 Vic., c. 12, the Central Board gave way to a Secretary of Agriculture to be appointed by the Governor in Council. Nova Scotia made only minor amendments (by 34 Vic., c. 13, 1871, and 35 Vic., c. 27, 1872) in her agricultural organization until 1873 when a "Government Member," a member of the Executive Council, was appointed to the Central Board, and more particularly till 1885 when the Board gave way to a government-appointed Secretary of Agriculture. See Martell and Harvey, "From Central Board to Secretary of Agriculture" (Public Archives of Nova Scotia, *Bulletin:* Halifax, 1940).

[7]Report of the Minister of Agriculture, Canada, *Sessional Papers*, 1866, no. 5, p. 3.

provided for the organization of a federal Department of Agriculture and defined the scope of its authority under nine headings.[8]   In conformity with McGee's suggestions the provincial Department of Agriculture became the Dominion Department of Agriculture, carrying forward its personnel and offices practically intact.[9]   The new department was given functions nominally almost identical with those of the preceding provincial department, but would, of course, exercise them over a wider geographic area; over New Brunswick and Nova Scotia as well as Ontario and Quebec, to begin with, and over whatever additional territory should be added to the Dominion of Canada.   Within this wide area the function listed as "agriculture" was interpreted as excluding supervision of agricultural boards and societies.   This activity was lèft with the provincial governments of New Brunswick and Nova Scotia and handed over to the governments of the newly created Provinces of Ontario and Quebec.   This limitation, imposed upon the scope of authority of the Department of Agriculture at Ottawa as it was transformed from a provincial to a federal department, was only a minor limitation, for over the years since its inception as a bureau in 1852, the provincial executive office dealing with agriculture in the Canadas had taken but slight and steadily decreasing interest in the affairs of the subordinate boards and societies.

Ontario and Quebec were left to reorganize their agricultural agencies to suit the altered circumstances.   Ontario took over existing institutions unchanged and incorporated pre-Confederation agricultural legislation into the new provincial codes.[10]   Societies, the agricultural association, and the agricultural board were continued,

---

[8]*Statutes of Canada*, 31 Vic., c. 53 (1868).   The headings were: 1. Agriculture; 2. Immigration and Emigration; 3. Public Health and Quarantine; 4. The Marine and Emigrant Hospital at Quebec; 5. Arts and Manufactures; 6. The Census, Statistics and the Registration of Statistics; 7. Patents of Invention; 8. Copyright; 9. Industrial Designs and Trade Marks.

[9]Thomas D'Arcy McGee was Minister of Agriculture of the Province of Canada in 1867, but did not survive to see the transformation from provincial to federal department by act of May 22, 1868.   Three of the provincial employees at Ottawa were transferred to Quebec because they had been working with colonization roads in that province.   The other employees, including the Deputy Minister, J. C. Taché, and a score of clerks and messengers, constituted the personnel of the new federal Department of Agriculture.   See Report of the Minister of Agriculture, Canada, *Sessional Papers*, 1869, no. 76, pp. 2-3.

[10]*Statutes of Ontario*, 31 Vic., c. 29 (1868).

now to be responsible to the Bureau of Agriculture and Arts within the Department of the Commissioner of Agriculture and Public Works. The Ontario Agricultural College was established in 1873. Quebec established a Department of Agriculture and Public Works and took the opportunity of replacing the agricultural board and association with a distinctive Council of Agriculture.[11]

3. *Reorganization of Immigration Services*

With Confederation the Dominion government generally, and the Department of Agriculture in particular, turned to consider the prospects for immigration. The concurrent-powers provision caused no immediate dispute so far as it related to agriculture, for the federal government was long only slightly interested in agriculture in any direct meaning of the word. The situation relating to immigration was different, for the Dominion Department of Agriculture proceeded to consider it one of its primary purposes, while at the same time the provinces hung jealously to their equity in the immigration processes. An individual province might admit the broad federal interest in immigration to British North America, but it could not be indifferent regarding the provincial incidence of settlement. Each province wanted an expanding population. Conflicting as were the provincial claims, the federal government could not ignore them, at least in the early Confederation years, for as yet all immigrants to the Dominion had to settle in one or another of the four provinces which it comprised. After the western territories had been added to the Dominion, in 1870, the federal government had regions of its own to colonize; it became autonomous as a colonizing agency, and in disputes over immigration it could force the eastern provinces into line by the threat that in any case its main interest lay in western settlement.

Until the acquisition of the western territories the Dominion government felt its hands tied in the matter of immigration. The Select Standing Committee on Immigration and Colonization, appointed in 1868 by the Dominion House of Commons, took up the whole problem of Dominion jurisdiction over immigration and colonization under the British North America Act. They pointed

[11]*Statutes of Quebec*, 32 Vic., c. 15 (1869), in *Statutes of Quebec, 1883, Title Fifth*, c. 1.

out[12] that Clause 92, Subsection 5, and Clause 109 of the Act ruled colonization out as a subject for committee consideration, reasoning that: "These clauses seem to place every interest in connection with the public lands and their settlement beyond the purview of this Committee, and to limit their inquiries and supervision of immigration matters simply to the sanitary arrangements for the reception of immigrants, the management of existing agencies, and the transit of immigrants within the Dominion."[13] Leading ministers in the provincial governments were asked their interpretation of the division of powers under Clause 95. They were also asked to state the conditions under which lands were granted in their respective provinces.[14]

The parliamentary committee, therefore, were fully aware of the interdependence between immigration and land policy. In speaking of provincial lands they advised that "The mode of disposing of these lands should be at once inviting and encouraging," and expressed the hope that "the public policy in regard to them will be quite as liberal as that which appears to have succeeded in the United States."[15] The system of immigration encouragement to Canada prior to Confederation had, they stated, been without satisfactory results, nor was it "adapted to be so under the law which has placed the public lands under the control of the Provincial Legislatures." The provincial and Dominion governments would have to come to some understanding on these matters. Finally, however, the committee glimpsed the ultimate solution, the basic economic purpose of Confederation; that is, the colonization of the North West Territories under federal supervision. They said:

> The prospective acquisition by Canada of the fertile lands in the valley of the Saskatchewan and its tributaries is, no doubt, interesting thousands who purpose to migrate from the Parent Country to one of its dependencies. In the present state of the relations between the North-West Territory and Canada no precise plan for its settlement can be recommended or even considered by your Committee, but they submit that, without any unnecessary delay, so much

---

12See Report of the Standing Committee on Immigration and Colonization, Canada House of Commons, *Journal*, 1868, App. no. 8, p. 1.

13*Ibid.*

14*Ibid.* This report outlines the replies received from provincial ministers, and thus embodies a statement of land-grant policies in the four provinces at the time of Confederation.

15*Ibid.*, p. 10.

of these lands as are fitted for agricultural purposes should be made accessible, through British territory, and offered on such terms as will be attractive to a class of settlers who desire to enjoy the fruits of their industry under the security of British laws and institutions.[16]

In the face of provincial reluctance to yield any share in immigration activities[17] the Dominion government sought by means of conferences to arrange for co-operative action in the matter. At the first immigration conference, held in Ottawa in October, 1868, Macdonald and Chapais, the Prime Minister and the Minister of Agriculture, respectively, represented the Dominion, and delegates attended from Ontario, Quebec, and New Brunswick.[18] The delegates agreed,[19] subject to the approval of their respective governments, that the Dominion government should administer and finance the various quarantine establishments in the seaboard provinces, should maintain and finance one or more immigration agencies in Britain and one or more on the continent, as well as the eight or ten such agencies within the Dominion of Canada. They agreed that the provinces should establish "an efficient system of Emigrant Agency within their respective Territories" to be related "as much as possible, with a liberal policy for the settlement and colonization of the uncultivated lands."[20] But the provinces refused to give up their rights of entry to Britain and Europe, so that the agreement contained a minute permitting each province to appoint agents in Europe or elsewhere as it thought proper.

The governments of the Dominion, of Ontario, Quebec, and New Brunswick adopted the conference proposals. To implement the federal responsibility the Dominion government passed its first immigration act,[21] embodying the relevant features of the agreement, and establishing a scale of immigrant duties. The Nova Scotian government "regretted" that it had to refuse to co-operate "in the enlarged scheme of immigration" because of financial difficulties.[22]

[16]*Ibid.*, p. 9.

[17]See evidence of Mr. Lowe of the federal Department of Agriculture before the Select Committee on Immigration and Colonization, Canada House of Commons, *Journal*, 1875, App. no. 4, p. 7.

[18]Report of the Standing Committee on Immigration and Colonization, Canada House of Commons, *Journal*, 1869, App. no. 7.

[19]*Ibid.*, pp. 3-4.

[20]*Ibid.*, p. 4.

[21]*Statutes of Canada*, 32-33 Vic., c. 10 (1869).

[22]Canada, *Sessional Papers*, 1869, no. 67, p. 8.

The provinces joined in the co-operative scheme of immigration promotion with varying degrees of activity. Nova Scotia was completely unco-operative till 1871. New Brunswick was willing to assist, but had limited local scope. Quebec continued, as throughout the pre-Confederation period, to stress colonization of native sons rather than the encouragement of foreign immigration. Ontario took full advantage of the conference permission to enter foreign immigrant markets. In 1869 the Ontario government reported[23] that they had appointed Mr. White of Hamilton to act as the special Emigration Commissioner from Ontario to Great Britain, that they had provided him with thousands of posters and pamphlets, that four hundred mayors and reeves had been circularized to learn the local labour needs, that the provincial government was voting $185,000 for colonization roads, locks, and surveys, and $10,000[24] for immigration, and that they were prepared to provide destitute immigrants with food and passage from Toronto to their railway destination.

The provinces worked together and with the Dominion only with the greatest difficulty. They clamoured so for assistance that in 1872 the Dominion government voted $70,000 as a special grant towards provincial immigration services. Quebec and Nova Scotia took advantage of the grant of funds to appoint European agents. The grant was repeated in 1873. The provinces quarreled over the distribution of the burden of inland transportation aids.[25] Ontario complained of her geographic disadvantage and secured federal agreement to share in the transportation of immigrants from Quebec to Ontario. Quebec and New Brunswick had to be accorded comparable concessions. Nova Scotia refused to pay transportation for immigrants even within her own borders.

By 1874 these wranglings made some new arrangement imperative. At a conference in Ottawa "It was generally admitted in the discussions which took place, that separate and individual action of

23Report of the Standing Committee on Immigration and Colonization, Canada House of Commons, *Journal,* 1869, App. no. 7, p. 6.

24They spent $25,000, making up the excess of $15,000 by vote in 1870, besides voting $25,000 for 1870. See Report of the Standing Committee on Immigration and Colonization, Canada House of Commons, *Journal,* 1870, App. no. 5, p. 2.

25Report of the Proceedings of a Conference on the Subject of Immigration, Canada, *Sessional Papers,* 1875, no. 40, App. no. 1.

the Provinces in promoting immigration, by means of agents in the United Kingdom and the European Continent, led not only to waste of strength and unnecessary expense and divided counsels, but in some cases to actual conflicts, which had an injuriously prejudicial effect on the minds of intending emigrants."[26] Consequently the control of all matters connected with the promotion of immigration from Britain and Europe was, by agreement, turned over to the Minister of Agriculture at Ottawa, and while the provinces might appoint sub-agents, these were to be under the direction of federal authorities.[27]

Significantly related to this provincial retreat was the fact that by 1870 the Dominion government had come into possession of the North West Territories, an area with unprecedented potentialities for the settlement of newcomers. At the immigration conference of October, 1869, attended by representatives of the Dominion government and those of Ontario and Quebec, Sir John Macdonald mentioned a project to appoint "some special agent for immigration into the North-West section of Canada, when the organization of that newly acquired territory is completed."[28] The 1871 immigration conference at Ottawa was attended by representatives of the Dominion, of Ontario, Quebec, New Brunswick, Nova Scotia, British Columbia, and Manitoba.[29] It was the first attendance of Nova Scotia, and, significantly in relation to the expanding scene of enterprise, it was the first attendance of British Columbia and of Manitoba. New elements in the resultant agreement related to the Dominion's pledges that: "It will maintain a liberal policy for the settlement and colonization of Crown lands in Manitoba and the Northwest Territories," and that "It will disseminate such information with reference to the Dominion generally and to Manitoba and the North West Territory in particular as may be deemed necessary for the advancement of immigration."[30] These pledges were renewed at the 1874 conference, to continue for five years, plus an additional

[26]Report of the Minister of Agriculture, Canada, *Sessional Papers*, 1875, no. 40, p. x.

[27]*Ibid.*, p. xi and App. no. 1.

[28]Report of the Standing Committee on Immigration and Colonization, Canada House of Commons, *Journal*, 1870, App. no. 5, p. 12.

[29]Report of the Minister of Agriculture, Canada, *Sessional Papers*, 1872, no. 2A, pp. 12-13.

[30]*Ibid.*

five years failing notice of discontinuance. Becoming engrossed in the colonization of her own territories, Manitoba and the North West, and in the encouragement of immigration to make that colonization possible, the Dominion government no longer needed to heed provincial claims for a share in immigration activities. Constitutionally the Dominion was to share control over immigration with the provinces; geographic factors in the shape of the expanding West made this unnecessary.

4. *Federal Agricultural Policy*

The pre-Confederation pattern of attention to agriculture and immigration in the Canadas served also as the pattern for the post-Confederation period. Provincial governments retained what might be called the traditional instruments of agricultural encouragement, chiefly the financing and supervision of agricultural societies, the assistance of shows and exhibitions, and whatever elementary beginnings there were by way of agricultural education. These were instruments of agricultural encouragement, but the provincial interest in the encouragement of agriculture after Confederation should be clearly distinguished from that of the federal government. The federal interest was in agricultural development and expansion, in the establishment of agriculture in new regions, in immigration and settlement, an interest, incidentally, which tended at times to depress the values of agricultural land and products in the longer established Canadian regions and thus to counteract instead of to complement provincial efforts. The federal government's interest in agriculture was essentially an interest in agricultural commerce and finance, in the opportunities for the profitable servicing of a rapidly expanding agricultural frontier. To a very considerable extent the constitutional provision that the Dominion government should share in the jurisdiction over agriculture and immigration was but an amplification of the clause which gave the Dominion government exclusive jurisdiction over trade and commerce.

The federal-provincial division of interest in agriculture which was taken for granted in 1867 and the immediately succeeding years was maintained on clear-cut lines for decades. As the following chapters will make plain, the Dominion government in general and the Dominion Departments of Agriculture and of the Interior in particular set themselves the task of developing the West as an agricultural region. This aim necessitated immigration and land settlement; it induced encouragement to the live cattle trade and the establishment of experimental farms; it led to the supervision of the grain trade. So great was the early federal engrossment with immigration promotion that in the eighteen-eighties officials of the Dominion Department of Agriculture admitted that since Confederation they had performed scarcely any agricultural functions. They had extended grants to exhibitions, gathered statistics, and supervised cattle quarantine and inspection, and had done nothing more "in relation to agriculture."[31]

The extreme simplicity in the federal-provincial division of agricultural interest has not survived to the present day. Gradually both Dominion and provincial governments have extended their range of agricultural activities. The activities carried on under the supervision of the various departments of agriculture have become so complex that any attempt to list or classify them concisely, let alone to analyse them in detail, would be quite beyond the bounds of a study of agricultural policy. This and the following chapters seek to analyse the agricultural policy of the Dominion government, but even within the limits of the federal field the activities analysed are illustrative rather than exhaustive.

Despite growing complexity of governmental activity the hypothesis is put forward here that the Dominion government's interest in agriculture has remained primarily a commercial interest. Exactness requires use of the word "primarily" instead of "exclusively." Elaboration of the main hypothesis and of its qualifications must wait for later chapters but general points may be noted as in the following paragraphs.

In the first place, as pointed out earlier in this study, commercial as well as financial and industrial interests are by no means always distinguishable from agricultural interests. Even in the short run, agriculture has at times been well satisfied with policy sponsored or at least tolerated by commercial and other urban groups.

In the second place, in the gradual multiplication of agricultural activities by both Dominion and provincial governments sharp delineation of interest is not always possible. Provinces have shown marked interest in the commercial aspects of agriculture, as witness the assistance extended by prairie governments to agricultural

[31]Canada House of Commons, *Journal*, 1884, App. no. 6, p. 102.

co-operatives since the early nineteen-hundreds,[32] the Saskatchewan legislative attempt to establish a compulsory wheat pool in 1931,[33] and the generally more recent attempts by provincial governments to establish effective control over the marketing of natural products.[34] Certain agricultural activities of the Dominion government, on the other hand, cannot be attributed to commercial prompting. Examples of such activities are the federal assistance to agricultural education extended under the Agricultural Aid Act of 1912,[35] and the half-hearted federal venture into the field of long-term agricultural credit under the Canadian Farm Loan Act of 1927.[36]

The Prairie Farm Rehabilitation Act of 1935[37] and the activities conducted thereunder by the federal government may or may not be regarded as emergency measures of agricultural assistance relating only to conditions of crisis. It seems certain, however, that the federal Department of Agriculture must increasingly cast about for new ways in which to demonstrate its interest in Canadian agriculture. The re-establishment and expansion of the Canadian agricultural frontier was the central interest of the federal Department of Agriculture, and was, indeed, the central agricultural interest of the federal government, from Confederation till as late as 1930. This interest found its fulfilment in the establishment of

[32]For elaboration of this point see Patton, *Grain Growers' Cooperation in Western Canada, passim.*

[33]*Statutes of Saskatchewan,* 21 Geo. V, c. 87 and c. 88 (1931).

[34]For an analysis of the development and current status of efforts along these lines in British Columbia see the *Report of His Honour Judge A. M. Harper on the Various Schemes established under the Authority of the "Natural Products Marketing (British Columbia) Act."* Provincial marketing legislation includes the following: *Statutes of Alberta,* 3 Geo. VI, c. 3 (1939); *Revised Statutes of British Columbia,* 1 Ed. VIII, c. 165 (1936); *Statutes of Manitoba,* 3 Geo. VI, c. 46 (1939); *Statutes of New Brunswick,* 1 Geo. VI, c. 52-53 (1937); *Statutes of Nova Scotia,* 3 Geo. VI, c. 4, part XII (1939); *Revised Statutes of Ontario,* 1 Geo. VI, c. 75 (1937); *Statutes of Prince Edward Island,* 4 Geo. VI, c. 40 (1940); *Statutes of Quebec,* 25-26 Geo. V, c. 30 (1935).

[35]*Statutes of Canada,* 2 Geo. V, c. 3 (1912), and 3-4 Geo. V, c. 5 (1913). See also Gettys, *Administration of Canadian Conditional Grants,* chap. II; Maxwell, *Federal Subsidies to the Provincial Governments in Canada,* chap. xv.

[36]*Statutes of Canada,* 17 Geo. V, c. 43 (1927). Dominion legislation providing for the establishment of a central mortgage bank, *Statutes of Canada,* 3 Geo. VI, c. 40 (1939), has not been put into effect.

[37]*Statutes of Canada,* 25-26 Geo. V, c. 23 (1935).

the wheat economy, the major capital structure for which was completed by the end of the nineteen-twenties.

5. *Summary*

Dissatisfaction of commercial, financial, and transportation interests with the rate of agricultural development on the St. Lawrence was one of the strongest forces working towards Confederation. The prospect was that the western territories north of the forty-ninth parallel could be acquired from the Hudson's Bay Company and would offer scope for an agricultural expansion similar to that occurring in the United States. Immigration and agricultural settlement would be the major concomitant activities. The federal government would administer these activities and would assure the central provinces (Ontario and Quebec) of the commercial advantages accompanying the anticipated expansion. Since agricultural expansion in the old provinces was clearly at an end for any discernible future period, there would be no point in depriving them of control over their lands or over their immediate agricultural processes. This control, accordingly, the existing provinces were allowed to retain, and with it went control over and responsibility for local settlement and for whatever nominal encouragement might issue to local agriculture through agricultural boards and societies. Over agriculture and immigration the federal government and the provinces were granted concurrent jurisdiction. The provinces jealously protested the encroachment of the new administrative authority, the Dominion government, into these fields, but after 1870 the dispute ceased to have significance because the federal government by this time had exclusive control over the western territories and had little concern over what the eastern provinces did or did not do regarding immigration and settlement within their own restricted sphere. Immigration and settlement, agricultural expansion and the commercial prospects in Canadian agriculture came to relate almost exclusively to the future of the Canadian West. These prospects continued as the measure of federal interest in Canadian agriculture.

CHAPTER VII

THE ENCOURAGEMENT OF IMMIGRATION AND SETTLEMENT

In 1884 it was stated[1] that the Dominion Department of Agriculture had so far performed practically no agricultural functions, and that it had received no general agricultural grant. This was true if agricultural functions are thought to relate to the supervision of grants in aid of agricultural societies and of livestock importation. The Department of Agriculture of the Province of Canada had shown little interest in these activities and, when it became the corresponding department for the federal government, it did not change its basic purposes. While federal and provincial authorities in the early post-Confederation years had great difficulty in co-ordinating their efforts relating to immigration, they had no trouble over agriculture, for the federal government, and particularly the federal Department of Agriculture, had no desire to busy itself with the "small change" of agricultural paternalism, the distribution of grants to agricultural boards and societies.

1. Purposes of the West

The agricultural significance of Confederation lay in the realization, firmly established by the eighteen-fifties, that immigration, agricultural settlement, and wheat production could work together to provide an expanding frontier which would vitalize an economy, no matter how cumbersome that economy might be. This had been demonstrated by events in Canada from 1825 to 1850; and was continuously evident in the United States. Confederation was necessary to afford Canada the geographic locus for the restoration of such a frontier. With all the best, and much of the fair, agricultural land occupied in the eastern provinces, the federal government became in fact the administrator of the western empire in trust for the original provinces of the Dominion, particularly the central provinces. To fulfil the frontier role in the Canadian economy, Canadian agriculture had to be attractive to immigrant labour and capital. This was as true for the new territories in the West as it had been in the East.

[1] Canada House of Commons, *Journal*, 1884, App. no. 6, p. 102.

These facts imposed definite obligations upon the federal government in the administration of the West. First in order was the necessity that title to the western territories be secured and that provision be made for legislative and executive controls over the newly-acquired regions. Further requirements comprised a satisfactory land-grant system, a means of communication, and means whereby potential immigrants might be attracted to the new Canadian domain. In all these points the competition of the United States was a prime consideration. Since the passage of the American Homestead Act in 1862, nothing short of an equally generous measure would suffice for Canada. As for the communication system, it should be adequate and accessible on payment of reasonable fares if possible, but at any cost it would have to be all-Canadian (or more pointedly, all non-American) to prevent the possible diversion of immigrants on their way inward, and of export produce on its way out. The Grand Trunk proposal[2] to enter the Canadian West *via* Chicago could not be entertained. The attempt to attract immigrants to Canada had long met with intense competition from the United States, and for thirty years after Confederation this competition did not abate. Added to this was the competition offered in the emigration markets by the various Australian colonies. Within twenty years of Confederation it became apparent that free grants of western lands, even after railway communications had been established, were not enough to divert the flow of European emigrants to Canadian territory. Wheat-growing on the Canadian plains was much too hazardous in the existing state of knowledge of soil and climatic conditions. In 1886 the Dominion experimental farm system was instituted primarily in the hope that the capabilities of western agriculture might be improved.[3]

Complex as were the constitutional and political features associated with Canada's acquisition of title to the North West Territories, they need not delay us here.[4] By the time the transfer was completed, in June, 1870, the Manitoba Act had created the first new province in the West, and a year later provision was made for the government of the remaining territories by an appointed Council.

[2]Glazebrook, *History of Transportation in Canada*, p. 193.
[3]See below, Chapter IX.
[4]See Morton and Martin, *History of Prairie Settlement and "Dominion Lands" Policy*, pp. 41 ff.

But legal control of the western territories was a bare beginning. The Dominion government had to demonstrate an ability to hold the areas against the westward and northward sweep of the American frontier. Between 1850 and 1860 the population of Minnesota (exclusive of Indians) increased from 6,000 to 172,000,[5] and communications between Fort Garry and Minneapolis were well established. The chartering of the Northern Pacific in 1864, after that of the Union Pacific in 1862, stressed the northward pressures in American expansion. By 1870 John A. Macdonald admitted it to be obvious that "the United States Government are resolved to do all they can, short of war, to get possession of the western territory, and we must take immediate and vigorous steps to counteract them."[6]

In the Canadian West, therefore, there was a sharp revival of the defence function of agriculture. American railroad expansion in the West would have to be countered by an all-Canadian railroad to and through the Canadian West.[7] Western lands would build such a railroad if they were valorized, but they could be valorized only by agricultural settlement on a prodigious scale. This could be effected only if immigration were greatly increased, and here again western lands provided the basic consideration; they were expected to provide the chief attraction.

Western lands therefore had a dual role: to finance railroads, and to entice settlers. For these purposes the lands in the Canadian West were held and administered by the Dominion government, from the time of the passage of the Manitoba Act[8] in 1870 until 1930.

[5]Mackintosh, *Prairie Settlement*, p. 27.

[6]Pope, *Correspondence of Sir John A. Macdonald* as quoted in Morton and Martin, *History of Prairie Settlement*, pp. 225-6.

[7]Macdonald said, early in 1870: "One of the first things is to show unmistakably our resolve to build the Pacific Railway" (*ibid.*).

[8]*Statutes of Canada*, 33 Vic., c. 3 (1870). Section 30 of this act provided that: "All ungranted or waste lands in the Province shall be . . . vested in the Crown, and administered by the Government of Canada for the purposes of the Dominion." Much has been said concerning this lawmaker's euphemism, "purposes of the Dominion." It has been argued that the purposes of the Dominion were railroads and settlement. See Morton and Martin, *History of Prairie Settlement*, pp. 220-8. The Dominion government retained title to western lands to make possible railroads and settlement, but these in turn were merely means to an end, the end being the recreation of a Canadian agricultural frontier.

Chester Martin has analysed this matter in detail.[9] He has not, however, made it sufficiently clear that there was a conflict between the two functions of western lands, a conflict which survived until the lands were freed from the railroad-building burdens in the eighteen-nineties. The point is that, at best, only free grants of land would suffice to draw immigrants to Canada in competition with the attractions of Australia or of the United States. But if railroads were to be built out of the proceeds of land disposal, these lands would have to be granted to a railway company or companies, which in turn would expect to sell the land to prospective settlers. If it be argued that there was plenty of land in the West for disposal in both ways, it is still true that a *bona fide* free-grant system would interfere with a sales policy, at least temporarily. Besides, the quantity of good land contiguous to a single east-west railroad line was far from unlimited in amount. Even the Dominion government clung to the hope of deriving revenue from land sales.[10]

The conflict between the two immediate purposes of western lands had its effect in land-grant policy. The adoption of the free-homestead system for western Canada was taken for granted practically from 1862, the date of its adoption in the United States.[11] Drafted tentatively in Orders-in-Council of March, April, and May, 1871, the homestead provision was embodied in the Dominion Lands Act which the House passed "almost perfunctorily," and which received assent in April, 1872. But this act nullified the homestead policy by reserving a belt of land twenty miles wide on each side of the proposed railway line for the railway and the government, none of which land might be homesteaded.[12] Homesteading privileges were

[9]Morton and Martin, *History of Prairie Settlement*, pp. 220-8.

[10]The Dominion Lands Act of 1872 (35 Vic., c. 23) anticipated the sale of lands within the forty-mile zone by railway *and* by government.

[11]Thomas D'Arcy McGee, Minister of Agriculture, commenting on the American immigration and land-settlement system in his annual report for 1865, stated: "As part of an improved system of immigration for this country, I had intended to offer for Your Excellency's approval, a Homestead Law, and to discuss generally our present policy in the disposition of the public lands. But the imminency of Confederation has been given and accepted as a sufficient reason, for not urging the adoption of improvements, which could not go into full operation before a new power would be charged with the general subject." See Province of Canada, *Sessional Papers*, 1866, no. 5, p. 15.

[12]Morton and Martin, *History of Prairie Settlement*, p. 396.

gradually liberalized, particularly in 1882 when, in effect, all even-numbered sections of Dominion lands became available for home-stead.[13] The Canadian Pacific Railway urged this liberalization of governmental policy;[14] naturally enough, for the railway would gain from such a policy through greater traffic and through the valoriza-tion of their own lands. Nevertheless, railway lands dominated the picture until the railway land-grant system was discarded in 1894.

Further modifications in land policy are indicated in later pages, but the impression is inescapable that the uncertainty over land policy and the detail of its administration inclined the Dominion govern-ment for a generation to lose sight of its own western purposes. So far as the West was concerned the Dominion government was an agency designed to open a Canadian agricultural frontier west of the Precambrian barrier. The two most important federal depart-ments from this viewpoint were those of Agriculture and the Interior, the latter organized in 1873. In the pre-Confederation tradition the Department of Agriculture conducted the activities towards the promotion of immigration. The Department of the Interior, with its Dominion Lands Branch, was created to conduct the survey and allocation of western agricultural lands for the hordes of immigrants whose arrival was anticipated once the basic commu-nication system was completed. These agencies worked hard to promote immigration and western settlement. The government was right in assuming that all such plans awaited the completion of a through railroad, and that lands might foot the bill. But in their zeal that the lands should finance the railway, they tended to forget that the railway was itself a means to other ends, those of immigration and settlement, and that the railway was in turn worthless unless land policy were generous enough to secure these ends. The free-grant policy employed with various modifications in Upper Canada from 1841 to 1867 had failed partly because advocates of this policy were never clear whether its purpose was to assure a rapid population growth or to give value to unalienated governmental lands as well as

[13]*Ibid.*, pp. 396 ff.

[14]In 1881 the Minister of Railways, speaking of the Canadian Pacific Rail-way, said: "No policy did the syndicate press more strongly upon us than that of settling the land as fast as we could. They said we should be only too glad to plant a free settler upon every acre belonging to the Government" (as quoted in *ibid.*, p. 399). There seems, however, little basis for surprise at this policy; it was not the C.P.R. land which was to be homesteaded free by settlers.

those in private and corporate hands. The homestead policy instituted in the West in 1872 was stranded on the same uncertainty for at least twenty years.

2. The Department of Agriculture as Immigration Agency

The Department of Agriculture supervised the immigration branch until 1892 when this branch was turned over to the Department of the Interior.[15] Considerable energy with slight imagination went into the promotion programme. The main elements in this programme had been developed before Confederation. Starting with the faith that the basic attraction for immigrants lay in free land, the immigration authorities maintained agencies abroad, well stocked with maps and pamphlets and prospectuses extolling the virtues of Canada. Agencies were maintained in Canada at points of debarkation and at interior distributing centres, where immigrants were supplied with information as well as relief and transportation aid. An "emigrant" hospital at Quebec and certain port physicians offered a minimum of medical care for sick arrivals. The immigrant act of 1869 (32-33 Vic., c. 10) embodied the Dominion-provincial agreement on concurrent immigration jurisdiction, and set passenger duties at $1.00 per person over one year of age, if sanctioned by government at point of departure, and $1.50 if not so sanctioned. An immigrant act of 1872 (35 Vic., c. 28) cancelled all immigrant duties except for a levy of $2.00 per person over one year of age, carried by a vessel with no surgeon and with health inadequately cared for.

Before and after Confederation, confidence in the effectiveness of the European immigration agency had its ups and downs. The maintenance of such agencies was costly, and at times they produced too few, or too poverty-stricken, migrants. Nevertheless the Dominion Department of Agriculture employed such agencies extensively. The 1877 Committee on Immigration and Colonization, answering

[15]In evidence before the Select Standing Committee on Agriculture and Colonization, 1892, John Lowe, then Deputy Minister of Agriculture, said in part (p. 139) that the transfer had been made "for the reason, mainly, of associating that subject [immigration] with the settlement of Dominion lands; and also for economy of administration.... It has happened in the past, and particularly at times when there have been unusually large immigrations, that the two departments [Agriculture, and the Interior] have not always been in touch" (Canada House of Commons, *Journal*, 1892, App. no. 2, p. 139).

charges that immigration costs were too high in view of the decline of immigration, pointed out that the staff of paid agents abroad had been reduced to thirteen, not, however, indicating how large it had previously been.[16] The new government in 1879 cleaned house on the foreign services, recalling nine travelling and lecturing agents at the expiration of their terms of office.[17] In 1880 Sir A. T. Galt was appointed Canadian High Commissioner in England and was given the superintendence of Canadian emigration agencies for Europe and Britain. These agencies were· kept supplied with pamphlet material outlining Canadian attractions in glowing terms, and in various languages. In eighteen months ending June, 1873, the Department of Agriculture, through its immigration agencies, had distributed 1,815,000 pamphlets in English, French, German, and Flemish.[18] Among the titles were such names as *Information for Intending Emigrants, Journey to Manitoba, Manitoba and Immigration, Our Great West,* and *Canada vs. Nebraska.* In 1887 the Department of Agriculture issued three million publications.[19]

Immigration agencies in eastern Canada provided immigrants with information, lodging, and where necessary, food, medical care, and inland transport. The latter service was easily subject to abuse. In 1868 Mr. J. C. Taché, Deputy Minister of Agriculture, stated that "It is a notorious fact, that many emigrants are advised before leaving Europe, by agents of forwarding companies or by friends, who have preceded them by the way of the St. Lawrence, to plead poverty, on their reaching Quebec or other places where our agents are located in order to get their passage free. . . . The great bulk of the emigrants so transported, I have every reason to believe, and for many I have evidence of it, have been immigrants destined for the United States."[20] By 1868 the policy was to pay no inland

[16]Report of the Select Standing Committee on Immigration and Colonization, Canada House of Commons, *Journal*, 1877, App. no. 6, p. 6.

[17]Report of the Minister of Agriculture, Canada, *Sessional Papers*, 1879, no. 9, p. xxviii.

[18]Report of the Committee on Immigration and Colonization (Lowe's evidence), Canada House of Commons, *Journal*, 1873, App. no. 7, p. 3.

[19]Report of the Select Standing Committee on Agriculture and Colonization, Canada House of Commons, *Journal*, 1888, App. no. 5, p. 77.

[20]Report of the Standing Committee on Immigration and Colonization, Canada House of Commons, *Journal*, 1868, App. no. 8, p. 8.

passages "unless in exceptional and very peculiar circumstances."[21] The eastern agencies, however, were maintained until the Department of the Interior took over the services in 1892 and closed all except those at ports of entry.[22] With the acquisition of the West it became necessary to establish agencies to care for the migrants into western areas. The first appointments were made in 1871; a Mr. McMicken to be stationed at Winnipeg, and a Mr. Provencher to carry a roving commission.[23] With the creation of the Department of the Interior in 1873, land offices for the West were also established. There was certain resultant over-lapping and friction between the western immigration and land offices, which difficulties were removed only in 1892 when the Department of the Interior relieved the Department of Agriculture of immigration functions.

The Dominion government instituted two financial procedures in immigration promotion in an attempt to cope with the intense competition of the United States and of the Australian States. They began to pay commissions, or per capita rewards, to passenger agents in the employ of steamship companies; and they established a system of passenger warrants, providing reduced fares for selected classes of immigrants. Both policies began in 1872. The system of passenger warrants was discontinued in 1888.

By 1872 the North Atlantic steamship companies (Allan, Dominion, Temperley, and Anchor) had established a conference effectively setting steerage or emigrant rates for "Ocean Adults" from Liverpool to any North Atlantic port at £6.6s. sterling.[24] Governmental policy of the day was averse to intervening in such cases, even if intervention were possible, for, it was reasoned, freedom of contract must be recognized whether contributory to competition or to monopoly. But the Canadian government's long-established tradition of developmental subsidies made the passenger warrant system the obvious cure for the monopoly burdens imposed upon the immigration traffic. Let the members of the steamship

[21]*Ibid.*

[22]Report of the Select Standing Committee on Agriculture and Colonization, Canada House of Commons, *Journal*, 1892, App. no. 2, pp. 139 ff.

[23]Report of the Minister of Agriculture, Canada, *Sessional Papers*, 1872, no. 2A, p. 11.

[24]*Ibid.*, 1875, no. 40, p. vii. An "ocean adult" was anyone over eight years of age.

conference secure their monopoly profits, it was argued, but at the same time let the emigrants have cheap fares; the government would pay the difference. The system instituted in 1872, accordingly, was that the person declaring an intention to migrate to Canada should be issued a "passenger warrant" entitling him to passage at a specified lower rate, the Canadian government paying to the steam-ship company the difference between this rate and some rate never made public. All applications for passenger warrants went before the London immigration office and required the certificate of a clergyman or magistrate attesting the applicant's intention to settle in Canada.[25]

The cost of Canadian passenger warrants varied slightly from year to year and was commonly graduated for age and immigration categories. For 1872, while the conference fares were held at £6.6s., the passenger warrant permitted adult passage for £4.5s., with children in proportion. For 1873 the general passenger warrant fare was raised to £4.15s., but special warrants were instituted at £2.5s. "to be confined exclusively to families of indigent agricultural labourers and female domestic servants."[26] With the temporary collapse of the Atlantic conference in May, 1874, standard fares fell from £6.6s. to £3, but the special warrant at £2.5s. was still greatly in demand.[27] The conference pulled itself together in 1875 and restored the level of rates, first at £5.5s., and finally at £6.6s. in 1876, where they were held for years. Until 1880 the Canadian passenger warrants were constant at £4.5s. to £4.15s. for the general ones, and at £2.5s. for the special class. Various alterations were made during the eighteen-eighties, but none of major importance until the abolition of the system in 1888.

The costs and results of the passenger warrant system cannot be closely measured. The government would not reveal how much it subsidized any single passenger, maintaining that such subsidy was a matter of confidential agreement between the government and the various steamship lines. For any given year the general conference rates and the special rates granted under passenger warrant were

[25]Report of the Select Committee on Immigration and Colonization (Lowe's evidence), Canada House of Commons, *Journal*, 1876, App. no 8, pp. 6 ff.
[26]*Ibid.*, 1875, App. no. 4, pp. 3 ff.
[27]*Ibid.*, pp. 5-6.

public knowledge, but the implication behind governmental secrecy was that the passenger warrant rate plus the governmental subsidy to the carrier was less than the general conference rate. In view of the tolerance of monopoly practices which prevailed throughout the period of the passenger warrant system, it can be inferred that the greatest proportion of the concession in immigrant fares was made possible by governmental subsidy rather than by downward adjustment on the part of the North Atlantic steamship conference. Figures made public indicated sums spent annually by the Dominion government for passenger warrants and brokers' commissions, combined. These sums varied widely with a fluctuating immigration, varying from $67,000 in each of the years 1874 and 1875 to $10,000 in 1878.[28] In 1874 and 1875 there were 11,000 and 12,000 immigrants, respectively, who were aided by passenger warrants. In 1885 less than 8,000 were so aided out of total Canadian immigration of 79,000, and the cost of their passenger warrants was $24,400 out of total immigration expenditure of $310,000.[29]

Efforts put forward by the Canadian government to promote immigration to Canada must be related to the competitive elements involved. From the eighteen-fifties until the latter part of the century the British American colonies, particularly Canada the province, and later Canada the Dominion, were up against the most intensive competition in the immigrant markets from the United States, the Australian colonies, and to a lesser extent from Brazil and the Argentine.[30] Of 2,500,000 migrants between 1853 and 1870, 61 per cent went to the United States, 18 per cent to Australia, and a mere trickle to Canada. This was the background of Dominion activities, particularly of the passenger warrant system inaugurated in 1872. Basically the disparity in percentages related to comparative economic, and to a lesser extent political and social, attractions. The magnitude of the gold strikes in Australian colonies served to meliorate the tremendous distance handicap placed upon those areas

[28]Reports of Committees on Immigration and Colonization, Canada House of Commons, *Journal,* 1875, App. no. 4; 1876, App. no. 8; 1879, App. no. 1.

[29]Report of the Minister of Agriculture, Canada, *Sessional Papers,* 1886, no. 10, p. xxviii.

[30]In 1890 the Winnipeg Immigration Agent' commented on the falling off in British entries to the Canadian West since the Argentine Republic had so successfully commenced to attract British tenant farmers. See Report of the Minister of Agriculture, Canada, *Sessional Papers,* 1890, no. 6, p. 86.

as compared with Canada and the United States. But in each area special incentives were added in order to secure advantage in the competitive race.

The federal government of the United States gave no direct assistance to immigrants, but indirectly made great generosity possible.[31] Railway and land companies had been granted vast tracts of land which could only be rendered valuable by waves of immigrant settlers. These companies therefore carried on immigrant promotion campaigns which dwarfed the best efforts of the Dominion government by comparison. Their foreign agencies were well financed and well stocked with persuasive literature. Their agents, or "passenger brokers," were well paid for immigrants secured. Ocean passages were assisted and railway transportation was either assisted or free. Lands were provided under long-term contracts and capital advances were not uncommon.[32] As for American governments, if they gave little or no direct assistance to immigrants, they did give direct encouragement. In 1887 Lowe, Deputy Minister of Agriculture for Canada, pointed out that in the American picture there must also be considered "the amount spent by the United States in its consular service . . . which is very largely an immigration agency. . . . [It] would correspond with our High Commissioner's Office and the offices in the United Kingdom and Europe."[33] Lowe pointed out that the whole consular service cost over a million and a quarter dollars yearly, of which the federal government paid $445,000 in salaries.

[31]Report of the Select Standing Committee on Immigration and Colonization (Lowe's evidence), Canada House of Commons, *Journal*, 1880, App. no. 3, pp. 6 ff.

[32]In 1880 Mr. Dyke, Canadian agent at Liverpool, reported that tenant farmers with capital often left his district headed for Canada, only to be intercepted and diverted to the United States, so intense was the competition. To make at least a visit to Winnipeg necessary he persuaded some emigrants to take their funds in the form of drafts on Winnipeg. Some emigrants were even followed there and persuaded to return to the United States (Report of the Minister of Agriculture, Canada, *Sessional Papers*, 1880, no. 10, p. 123).

[33]Report of the Select Standing Committee on Agriculture and Colonization, Canada House of Commons, *Journal*, 1887, App. no. 4, p. 30. At this time the whole Canadian immigration service was under fire. The Department of Agriculture sought to defend it, and Lowe concluded that by comparison with the United States "it would appear that the efforts or expenses which are being paid by the Dominion of Canada for the services of immigration are very small indeed."

Castle Garden, the immigration reception establishment maintained at New York, cost $150,000 to $200,000 per year.

The Australian colonies were under a great distance handicap as compared with either the United States or Canada, and after the gold rushes of Australia and New Zealand had passed their peaks in the eighteen-sixties the continuance of immigration required other incentives. Early in the eighteen-seventies the Canadian immigration authorities took increasing note of the competitive efforts of these southern colonies. In 1875 the Canadian Minister of Agriculture attributed the decline in Canadian immigration partly to the commercial depression, and partly to "the very active exertions made by the Australian Colonies, particularly New Zealand, and the very large expenditure of money made by them in granting free passages."[34] In 1876 Mr. Lowe stated that in 1874 and 1875 the Australian and New Zealand colonies were paying total transportation costs for intending settlers, about $100 per capita in Canadian funds, and were paying large per capita agency commissions as well.[35] In 1878 the Minister of Agriculture reported that "The Australian and New Zealand colonies have continued to make very great exertions in the emigration market of the United Kingdom and the continent, offering at an expenditure of millions of dollars, free passage and free kits to those distant colonies."[36] In 1883 all the Australian colonies spent $2,446,000 for immigration, of which sum Queensland spent $1,202,000.[37] In 1884 there was a great reduction, chiefly by Queensland, to a total of $1,490,000 for all Australian colonies.[38] Much of this went for passenger warrants towards which the following per capita contributions were made: by Queensland, $135.53; by South Australia, $111.75; by West Australia, $38.00; by Tasmania,

[34]Report of the Minister of Agriculture, Canada, *Sessional Papers*, 1875, no. 40, pp. vi-vii.

[35]Report of the Select Committee on Immigration and Colonization, Canada House of Commons, *Journal*, 1876, App. no. 8, p. 14. At the same time agricultural labourers were getting to Canada transportation free, due to the combination of a Canadian passenger warrant of £2.5s., plus a $6.00 bonus provided by Ontario, plus assistance from agricultural unions in Britain.

[36]Report of the Minister of Agriculture, Canada, *Sessional Papers*, 1878, no. 9, p. xxv.

[37]Report of the Select Standing Committee on Agriculture and Colonization (Lowe's evidence), Canada House of Commons, *Journal*, 1887, App. no. 4, p. 80.

[38]*Ibid.*

$51.00.[39] From 1879 to 1884, inclusive, Australian colonies reported immigration totalling 1,117,403, with emigration estimated at 750,000.[40] From 1879 to 1890, inclusive, their total immigration was 2,563,000.[41] During these twelve years their total expenditure for immigration was over $25,000,000, while Canada spent $3,119,000.[42]

As Canadian immigration recovered somewhat from the depths of the middle eighteen-seventies it was noted that the proportion of newcomers possessing capital was increasing. British tenant farmers, under increasing pressure at home from the agricultural products of the new frontiers in the Americas and Australia, turned to migration for relief. The trade in Canadian live cattle which grew rapidly in the eighteen-seventies served as an excellent advertisement of Canadian prospects. The Canadian government seized the opportunity to press its advantage regarding these highly desirable prospective settlers, and instituted a programme of expense-paid tours of Canada by selected delegations of tenant farmers. The first delegation came in 1879, comprising sixteen delegates from England, Ireland, and Scotland, the invitation requiring "that the delegates should be selected at a meeting of farmers of good standing, who might think it well to consider with seriousness the question of emigration in connection with the wide-spread agricultural depression."[43] The delegates reported back to their local communities and the Canadian Department of Agriculture printed their statements and circulated them widely. From time to time the venture was repeated. In 1880 thirteen delegates came from England, Ireland, Scotland, and France. In 1881 four delegates came from Germany and one from Switzerland. In 1890 a dozen came from Britain, and two in 1891. In 1884 the British Association for the Advancement of Science met in Montreal, and the C.P.R. arranged a special excursion to Manitoba and the Rocky Mountains.

Confederation and all the ensuing efforts to promote settlement and agriculture on the prairies were unable to make any of the

39*Ibid.*   40*Ibid.*
41Report of the Select Standing Committee on Agriculture and Colonization, Canada House of Commons, *Journal*, 1892, App. no. 2, p. 141.
42*Ibid.*, p. 143.
43Report of the Minister of Agriculture, Canada, *Sessional Papers*, 1880, no. 10, p. xxv.

remaining part of the nineteenth century Canada's. From 1867 to 1899 one million and a half immigrants entered Canada compared with two and one half million in the period 1900-13. During the decade 1881-90 Canadian immigration totalled 885,000 as compared with immigration to the United States totalling 5,570,000, and with Australian immigration during the twelve-year period 1879-90 of 2,563,000.[44] Immigration must be distinguished from settlement. For the twelve-year Australian period mentioned, Australia recorded emigration of 1,845,000, equal to more than two-thirds of the entrants.[45] For the decade 1881-90 estimates for the United States were that immigration plus natural increase should have swelled the population by 23,818,000, but the census-recorded increase was only 12,466,500.[46] From 1871 to 1891 the estimated immigration to Manitoba totalled 330,000 while the census indicated a population increase of only 200,000, a loss of 130,000 with no account taken of natural increase. From 1871 to 1901 the Manitoba population increased from 73,000 to 420,000.

Dominion expenditures on "Immigration and Quarantine" varied widely from year to year, from $73,400 in 1870 to $507,000 in 1884. Annual immigration also fluctuated widely, but not in proportion to Dominion expenditures thereon. Basically significant was the state of employment opportunities within Canada, this in turn dependent on the extent of current investment processes. McGee had analysed the relationship between immigration and public works before Confederation,[47] and experience since Confederation has clearly substantiated his case. Accompanying the steady climb of immigration figures to a peak of 50,000 in 1873 there was great investment in railways, canals, and miscellaneous works, and with the collapse of these expenditures immigration fell to levels approximately half the peak figure. The first Canadian immigration figures surpassing 100,000 yearly occurred in 1882, 1883, and 1884, coinciding with the phenomenal construction drive of the Canadian Pacific Railway. During the depressed nineties Canadian immigration sank to mere annual dribbles of less than 20,000.

[44]Report of the Select Standing Committee on Agriculture and Colonization, Canada House of Commons, *Journal*, 1892, App. no. 2, pp. 141, 144.

[45]*Ibid.*, p. 141.   [46]*Ibid.*, p. 144.

[47]*Minutes of the Executive Council*, Public Archives of Canada, Series E, State Book Y, May 9, 1863. See above, p. 136.

3. *Western Colonization and Its Significance*

Settlement in western Canada before 1900, however, was important beyond that to be expected from its numbers. Much of this earlier settlement was in the form of colonies of a variety of British and European groups, and these acted as nuclei for later settlement of much more substantial proportions. The colony was a compact and typically homogeneous group which retained its identity over a considerable period of time, and thus constituted a particularly effective device for rallying and attracting additional migrants. Mr. Dyke, Canadian immigrant agent at Liverpool, argued the importance of colonies as follows: "I respectfully urge the vast importance of offering special inducements for the establishing of new detached colonies in different parts of the Dominion. Each of these would act as a nucleus of attraction and interest with the old country for many years to come. From an emigration point of view here, I should attach more value to such a colony of some half a dozen or dozen farmers from any one district or county here, than to four or five times that number going out to join friends already established, or scattering themselves indiscriminately over the country."[48]

From the standpoint of competition for immigrants, with Australia and the United States, the cumulative nature of immigration is significant. Persons contemplating emigration were persuaded to follow friends or relatives who had formerly migrated, not only by ties of friendship but also by monetary considerations. Emigrants ordinarily needed assistance to travel, and a great proportion of the total assistance granted towards "assisted passages" was rendered by former emigrants already established in a new land. The Canadian Minister of Agriculture explained this point in 1873:

A very large proportion of all the Immigrants who come to this Continent are aided in some way or other. Very few of the poor labouring classes who have come, for many years past have been able to pay the cost of passage from their own means. They have been aided by individuals, by charitable societies who collected funds from the public, by poor law guardians, and to the largest extent by remittances from friends who had emigrated before them. The amount of these ascertained remittances in 1871 from North America as reported by H. M. Emigration Commissioners, was about five million dollars; over half of which was in the form of prepaid passages. In some years the amount of these

---

[48]Report of the Minister of Agriculture, Canada, *Sessional Papers*, 1880, no. 10, p. 123.

ascertained remittances (many were not ascertained) was more than double those in 1871. The ascertained amount from 1848 to 1871 was £17,036,799 sterling.

The greater part of this large sum was sent from the United States, the stream of immigration having, in the first place, more decidedly set there; and this, coupled with the large aid in the form of advances from companies of various kinds, to be repaid from wages, is the cause of the large continued immigration to that country. . . . The class of Immigrants of whom Canada is most in need is agricultural and other labourers; and the Department of Agriculture is in possession of information which establishes the fact that unlimited numbers of these are both anxious and willing to come, but are wholly without means to enable them to do so. The wages earned by agricultural labourers in the United Kingdom being from 12*s.* to 16*s.* per week. . . .[49]

In 1881 Sir A. T. Galt, Canadian High Commissioner in London, discussed the distress in Ireland as conducive to emigration, but added that he was unable to influence the destination of the migrants since three-quarters of the passages were paid by friends already in new countries.[50] Mr. Lowe, Deputy Minister of Agriculture, pointed out in 1892 that 60 per cent of United States immigrants came on tickets "which had been prepaid for them almost wholly by their friends in the United States."[51] But proportions varied with nationality. The Liverpool passenger agent for the Allan Line estimated that of the emigrants going to Canada "about 10 per cent of the English are prepaid, and that from 30 to 40 per cent of the Irish are prepaid; but when they came to Germans and Scandinavians, from 70 to 80 per cent of those who came are prepaid."[52] Mr. Lowe concluded: "Nothing can show more clearly the importance of establishing the beginning of colonies and settlements which always go on annually growing from that influence."[53]

The Dominion government employed the colonization method in the West from the very first. Orders-in-Council of 1872 reserved 100,000 acres of land for a Swiss colony, a block of land for a colony to be organized by the German Society of Montreal, and one for a Scottish settlement.[54] Little came of these early attempts. The

[49]*Ibid.*, 1873, no. 26, p. 6. He thus sought to justify the introduction of the passenger warrant system, and the passage of an act providing for immigrant societies (35 Vic., c. 29, 1872).

[50]Canada, *Sessional Papers*, 1880-1, no. 12, p. 85.

[51]Report of the Select Standing Committee on Agriculture and Colonization, Canada House of Commons, *Journal*, 1892, App. no. 2, p. 140.

[52]*Ibid.*   [53]*Ibid.*

[54]Morton and Martin, *History of Prairie Settlement*, p. 54.

first successful colonies came unsolicited. In 1872 the German Mennonites of the Province of Berdiansk, Russia, appealed to the Colonial Office to learn the possibilities of moving to Canada, for the Russian government was by this time retracting a former pledge not to require military service.[55] Mr. Hespeler, Canadian immigration agent in Germany, went to Berdiansk and induced delegations to travel to Canada in 1872 and 1873. The Canadian government promised the 1873 delegation that the group should be exempt from military service, should have its own schools and the privilege of affirming in court; and that the Canadian government would grant free lands in the West, and adult passenger warrants from Hamburg to Fort Garry for $30.00, with provisions from Liverpool to Collingwood. This constituted a Canadian bonus of about $20.00 per head. Lands were set aside for the Mennonites, nine and one-third townships in one area and seventeen in another, and by 1877 there were 6,150 Mennonites in the Manitoba settlements.[56] In 1874 the first reservation was made for French Canadians repatriated from the New England States. In a period of ten years, 1876-85, 4,800 of these migrated to the Canadian West, forming themselves into "ten new settlements in Manitoba and have added a good number of permanent settlers to sixteen other settlements."[57] In 1875 and 1876 an Icelandic colony was formed on the west shore of Lake Winnipeg.

The attempt in 1881 and subsequent years to introduce the system of company colonization to the West was unsuccessful.[58] Considerable spontaneous settlement occurred in Manitoba, and more particularly in the North West Territories beyond, in the decades 1881-1901. Most significant, however, were the settlements of a variety of foreign groups in the form of reservations and "nominal reserves."[59] Numbers were disappointing, but among the groups represented were English, Scottish, Hungarians, Scandina-

---

[55]Report of the Minister of Agriculture, Canada, *Sessional Papers,* 1874, no. 9, pp. xi ff.

[56]*Ibid.,* 1877, no. 8, p. xvi.

[57]*Ibid.,* 1885, no. 8, p. 85.

[58]Morton and Martin, *History of Prairie Settlement,* pp. 74 ff. Morton points out that nearly thirty contracts were made under the scheme, but that "Probably nobody got anything out of the scheme but the directors of the companies" (*ibid.,* p. 75).

[59]*Ibid.,* pp. 80 ff., and map, pp. 62-3. Nominal reserves did not bar homesteading by outsiders.

vians, Germans, Roumanians, Icelanders, Mennonites, Danes, Finns, Russians, Ukrainians, Belgians, and Jews. Of some groups there were several settlements, some quite widely diffused. Maps of western Canadian settlement in 1901 are shaded to show population in the south of Manitoba, the south-east of Saskatchewan, a thread along the Canadian Pacific Railway to the foothills, a band from Edmonton through Calgary to the boundary, and a cluster around the forks of the Saskatchewan River.[60]

4. The Period 1896-1914

It is well known that the hopes built around the Canadian West at the time of Confederation were realized only after 1900. Between 1900 and 1913 Canadian immigration totalled 2,500,000 as compared with 1,500,000 in the period 1867-99. Immigration was at a standstill throughout the period of the first World War, but after 1920 there was considerable recovery in the movement, so that by the middle nineteen-thirties it could be said that "Since the war, Canada has admitted over half a million British, nearly a quarter million from the United States, and over·four hundred thousand from Continental Europe."[61] These newcomers had served by 1930 to round out the agricultural structure of the western provinces; they had at the same time enjoyed and contributed to the era of western expansion which ended in 1929. So much has been written about the migration and settlement of the period 1900-30 that little need be said about it here.[62] The significant features of the period were immigration and

[60]*Ibid.*, p. 102.

[61]England, *Colonization of Western Canada,* p. 81.

[62]See Mackintosh and Joerg (general eds.), Canadian Frontiers of Settlement series. See also Carrothers, *Emigration from the British Isles;* Dafoe, *Clifford Sifton;* England, *Central European Immigrant in Canada; Colonization of Western Canada;* Hedges, *Federal Railway Land Subsidy Policy of Canada; Building the Canadian West;* Johnston, *History of Emigration from the United Kingdom to North America.* See also the following articles: Ashton, "Soldier Land Settlement in Canada" (*Quarterly Journal of Economics,* May, 1925); Carrothers, "Immigration Problem in Canada" (*Queen's Quarterly,* summer, 1929); England, "Emergent West" (*Queen's Quarterly,* autumn, 1934); "Land Settlement in Northern Areas of Western Canada" (*Canadian Journal of Economics and Political Science,* November, 1935); Murray, "Continental Europeans in Western Canada" (*Queen's Quarterly,* winter, 1931); Oliver, "Coming of the Barr Colonists" (Canadian Historical Association, *Report,* 1926); "Settlement of Saskatchewan to 1914" (Royal Society of Canada, *Transactions,* 1926, sec. ii; Riddell, "Cycle in the Development

settlement, and not the assistance deliberately extended thereto. Though the Liberal government after 1896, and particularly Mr. Sifton and Mr. Oliver in the Department of the Interior, undoubtedly made the most of the favourable situation, the remarkable turning of the immigration tide towards Canada with the turn of the century was due to factors more fundamental than anything comprised within the possibilities of a change of government or of an intensification of efforts directed towards the promotion of immigration.[63]

Basic elements in the immigration promotion programme after 1897 were those already of long standing: the immigration agency in foreign countries, immigration literature of all sorts, the head-bonus to booking agents, and, for the immigrants themselves, the promise of free and fertile land either in or out of reservations. All such instruments were used more intensively than before, yet much of the inspiration came from the responsiveness of the migrating hordes. With the curtailment of economic opportunity in the United States, the relative advantages of the Canadian plains became evident. The educational work of Canadian immigration authorities over the preceding thirty years combined with the drawing power of a multitude of racial or religious colonies to tilt the balance in favour of Canada. The century was Canada's, with or without imagination and driving force in Canadian immigration offices.

A number of governmental aids which were extended to immigration and agricultural settlement on the Canadian prairies after 1896 may be noted. In 1894 the system of railway land grants was given up and, of equal importance, the railways were pressed to select the lands which they had "earned" by mileage construction. Railways had earned 24,000,000 acres of land in the West by 1896 but had patented only 1,825,000 acres.[64] They had held off because once they accepted title to a given block of land it became subject to provincial and municipal taxation; and there may also have been

of the Canadian West" (*Canadian Historical Review*, September, 1940); Wilson, "Migration Movements in Canada" (*Canadian Historical Review*, June, 1932).

[63]Mackintosh, *Economic Background of Dominion-Provincial Relations*, pp. 22-3.

[64]Dafoe, *Clifford Sifton*, p. 133.

the desire to wait and see where productive prospects appeared the greatest. During Mr. Sifton's term of office as Minister of the Interior 22,500,000 acres of land were patented by the railways, and only odds and ends of earned railway lands remained.[65] With these selections made, the Department of the Interior could go ahead freely with its homestead and settlement policy.

Along with the discontinuance of the railway land grant and with success in the policy of pressing the railway companies to make their selection of earned lands, Mr. Sifton set about simplifying departmental organization and procedure in relation to homestead and land-grant matters.[66] More important than any change in administrative detail, however, was a firmer conviction on the part of government officials that there were profits to be made in giving lands away. Canadian officials had paid lip service to this thesis for at least half a century, but they had never made it a part of their working philosophy. Free grants were made much of, as an element of land policy during the eighteen-fifties, but free grants in practice were intended merely to facilitate the construction of developmental roads, roads through new territory, which would serve to give value to the crown lands behind the free grants within these territories. The Dominion adopted a homestead policy in 1872, but the Orders-in-Council and the administration of these Orders reveal nothing of a homestead philosophy. Again the free-grant elements of land policy were nominal. Land was still thought to owe government so much per acre as an alienation fee. Homesteads were to be available twenty miles from proposed railroads, but closer than that the lands were to be sold to build the railroad and to assist in governmental financing. Under pressure from the Canadian Pacific Railway syndicate, a decade later, the government was induced to give, with obvious reluctance, a more generous interpretation to the homestead elements in its policy. The syndicate could readily encourage the government to institute a genuine and unrestricted free-grant policy, for such a policy would provide the traffic for which the railway was being built, and would furthermore give value to the syndicate's land. The continuance of the railway land-grant system until the middle eighteen-nineties, and the parallel hesitancy on the part of government to urge railways to select their earned

[65]*Ibid.*, note.
[66]*Ibid.*, pp. 133-7.

lands, indicate clearly the absence of any genuine homestead philosophy: homesteads, free grants, might be made provided they did not interfere with land sales by railways, by the Hudson's Bay Company, and by the government itself.

Protestations are a poor indication of land-grant philosophy, for, ostensibly, free grants had been a substantial element of Canadian land policy as far back as 1841, and had been constantly extolled in public by public leaders. Yet, late in the century the working principles were as outlined above. Superficially Sifton's and Oliver's philosophy of land grants was little if any different from that of their predecessors in the Department of the Interior, for at the most they said nothing which in effect had not been said before, though they did say it more vigorously. Indicative of their point of view is the following statement made by Oliver:

> . . . the interest of the Dominion in the lands is in the revenue which it can derive from the settler who makes that land productive. This Dominion of Canada can make millions out of the lands of the Northwest and never sell an acre; it has made millions out of these lands without selling an acre. The increase in our customs returns, the increase in our trade and commerce, the increase in our manufactures, is to a very large extent due to the increase in settlement on the free lands of the Northwest Territories. . . . The interest of the Dominion is to secure the settlement of the lands, and whether with a price or without a price makes little or no difference. It is worth the while of the Dominion to spend hundreds of thousands of dollars in promoting immigration . . . in surveying and administering these lands, and then to give them away.[67]

Sifton's and Oliver's activities in the Department of the Interior suggest that they made these ideas a part of their working philosophy.

Even with the new administration after 1896, and with the new attitude towards land policies, the homestead system was, of course, regarded as a means to an end, rather than an end in itself. Settlement was the object, and whatever contributed towards that object was worth consideration. Thus Sifton and his successors were not opposed to dealing with land companies simply because they were land companies. In contrast with the experience with such companies in the eighteen-eighties,[68] there were some notable successes among

---

[67]Canada, *House of Commons Debates*, 1905, vol. II, pp. 3157 ff., as quoted in Morton and Martin, *History of Prairie Settlement*, p. 402.

[68]See above, p. 176.

the companies organized after 1900.[69] The Saskatchewan Valley
Land Company was the most outstanding success.[70] By 1890 the
territory between Regina and what is now Saskatoon was surveyed
and traversed by a north-south railroad. By 1900 settlement extended
north from Regina for thirty miles, then skipped completely for
sixty-five miles. The Qu'Appelle, Long Lake, and Saskatchewan
Railroad Company refused to choose lands in this area, where they
were entitled to a million acres. In 1902 a syndicate of American
and Canadian real-estate operators contracted to buy 450,000 acres
of this land from the railway company and got an agreement with
the government whereunder they might buy government land in a
township at $1.00 per acre after having placed thirty-two settlers
on lands within the township, twenty of the settlers to be on free
homesteads. The syndicate might buy up to 250,000 acres of
government land under this agreement. Incorporating as the Saskatchewan Valley Land Company the group opened two thousand
selling agencies in the western states and conducted an unprecedented
advertising campaign. Tremendous settlement and improvement
results speedily followed. Sifton later said: "The coming of this
company was the beginning of the great success of our immigration
work in the West."[71]

Among the devices more formally thought of for immigration
promotion was the head bonus to booking agents. Sifton granted
bonuses to booking agents both as a means of assuring immigration
and as a means towards its selection. Salaried agents were placed in
strategic centres, but sub-agents and agents of transportation companies were induced to encourage migration to Canada by means of
the payment of per capita bonuses somewhat of the order of £1 for
adults and 10s. for minors, or, as in the United States, $3.00, $2.00,
and $1.00 for male and female adults and persons under eighteen,
respectively.[72] To encourage settlers from particular areas, bonuses
were made especially attractive. Sifton later recalled that while he

[69]There was a variety of land companies, not all dealing directly with the
government, for railways typically organized subsidiary companies to administer their grants.
[70]Dafoe, *Clifford Sifton*, pp. 306 ff.; Morton and Martin, *History of
Prairie Settlement*, pp. 120, 296 ff.
[71]Dafoe, *Clifford Sifton*, p. 308.
[72]*Ibid.*, pp. 319-20; Report of the Minister of the Interior, Canada, *Sessional Papers*, 1898, no. 13, p. 27.

was Minister of the Interior the bonuses were doubled for steamship agents in the north of England and Scotland, and were cut very low for agents in the south of England.[73] Similarly, bonuses were applied selectively to types of migrants, at times being paid only for farmers, farm labourers, and female domestic servants.[74]

The bonus arrangements which the Canadian government made during the Sifton period with the North Atlantic Trading Company are reasonable enough in retrospect, but were the object of severe political attack before their cancellation.[75] Individual booking agents encountered difficulty in working in European countries where governments tried to prevent emigration for military purposes. In 1899 an exclusive arrangement was made with a group of agents and employees of booking houses, incorporated as the North Atlantic Trading Company, whereby immigration promotion and selection throughout Europe were to be conducted exclusively by the group in return for bonuses of $5.00 for a farmer and $2.00 for each member of his household. The port of embarkation was Hamburg, and acting on advices of local agencies the Company selected agriculturists only, so far as possible. The arrangements were kept secret, presumably so that European governments which were hostile to emigration, and even had laws against its solicitation, might not take action against the agents. The secrecy, however justifiable, was sufficient to incite attack by political enemies in Canada, and after several years the agreement had to be cancelled.

Special attention was paid to the United States. Sifton's attention in this field coincided with intensive promotion efforts put forward by the Canadian Pacific Railway,[76] and the latter company co-operated closely with the government's plans by acting as transportation host to the endless delegations and group tours organized throughout the middle western states. Government and the C.P.R. agreed in their recognition of the growing importance of the American press, with more and more widespread literacy in the United States. Delegations of American newspaper men, particularly of rural editors, were organized year after year, were transported to and through western Canada, expenses paid, and were entertained

73Dafoe, Clifford Sifton, pp. 139-40.
74Ibid., pp. 319-20.
75Ibid., pp. 319 ff.
76Hedges, Building the Canadian West, chap. v.

with the utmost hospitality. The publicity afforded the Canadian West as a settlement field was not universally favourable, for a considerable element of the American press was sympathetic to the interests of American land and railway companies; but well-directed Canadian hospitality went far towards counteracting this influence.

The Department of the Interior established and maintained an elaborate system of immigration agencies throughout the western states. In 1898 there were nine "State Agents" maintained by means of salaries plus expenses, and a considerable number of sub-agents who were rewarded for immigrants secured, on a per capita basis.[77] A "press agent" had been appointed to supervise Canadian publicity efforts in the United States. In 1906 there were seventeen agents in the United States. Each agency was amply stocked with printed materials, with maps and agricultural prospectuses, and with persuasive exhibits indicative of Canadian agricultural resources. The Canadian exhibit became a standard feature at American agricultural exhibitions and farm rallies.

5. The Inter-War Years

The war, 1914-18, completely halted British and European migration to Canada, though the migration from Britain had already slackened by 1914. British immigration was halted from 1915 to 1920; continental immigration from 1915 to 1921; immigration from the United States declined from 1914 to 1918 and then substantially recovered.[78] Towards the end of the war the Canadian government returned to the consideration of settlement possibilities, primarily thinking of soldier re-establishment, and later considering settlement as connected with the restoration of the flow of immigration from Britain and the continent. In view of the unexampled prosperity experienced by the Canadian wheat farmer throughout the war years, it seemed clear that further expansion must surely be in order, if on a cautious and selective scale. Americans entered largely on their own resources, attracted by the existing cost-price relationship in the Canadian wheat economy, and bought lands for the most part at considerably inflated values. Europeans and Britishers came

[77]Report of the Minister of the Interior, Canada, *Sessional Papers*, 1898, no. 13, p. 27. Per capita payments were $3.00 for males over eighteen years; $2.00 for females over eighteen years; and $1.00 for persons under eighteen.

[78]England, *Colonization of Western Canada*, p. 75.

throughout the nineteen-twenties under varying degrees of private initiative and finance, and governmental encouragement and assistance. Expansion of western Canadian settlement continued till 1930, with immigration between 1920 and 1929 totalling a million and a quarter.

First consideration for the post-war years was the reabsorption of soldiers into civilian pursuits. The Canadian Soldier Settlement Acts of 1917 and 1919[79] established the Soldier Settlement Board and empowered it to assist eligible returned soldiers to settle upon agricultural lands. Dominion lands within fifteen miles of any railroad were reserved for quarter-section grants to returned soldiers, besides which any soldier might exercise the civilian rights to an additional quarter-section homestead. Financial assistance was given for the purchase of livestock and equipment, and for the purchase of land where desired. Loans to a maximum of $7,500 were extended covering up to $4,500 for land purchase, up to $2,000 for stock and equipment, and up to $1,000 for permanent improvements. Loans were amortized at 5 per cent interest, those for stock and equipment over six years,[80] and those for land and buildings, over twenty-five years. If the settler already owned land, a maximum of $5,000 might be loaned to remove encumbrances, and to provide stock and equipment.

In 1924 the Soldier Settlement Board was transferred from the Department of the Interior and became the Land Settlement Branch of the Department of Immigration and Colonization. In its new role it broadened its activities to give settlement guidance and assistance to others than soldiers, notably assisting in the British Family Settlement schemes and, after 1930, in the Back-to-the-Land Movement.[81] The financial aspects of these activities have been summed up as follows: "As at March, 1935, there were in all 18,733 active settlers with loans, 1,980 properties under lease, and 535 farms on hand for resale, representing a total of 21,248 properties under administration or a net investment of $54,674,525. Of the settlers,

[79]*Statutes of Canada*, 7-8 Geo. V, c. 21, and 9 Geo. V, c. 71. See Easterbrook, *Farm Credit in Canada*, p. 131; England, *Colonization of Western Canada*, pp. 76 ff.

[80]Later extended to twenty-five years (England, *Colonization of Western Canada*, p. 80).

[81]Easterbrook, *Farm Credit in Canada*.

10,828 were soldiers, 5,844 civilians, and 2,061 British family settlers. The sum of $54,429,973 has been paid to the Treasury in principal and interest, and $39,013,737 granted to settlers through remedial legislation. Losses sustained on the resale of land and chattels have amounted to $16,087,172."[82]

The British Family Settlement projects involved Canadian assistance for a British-initiated programme. Emigration and Empire settlement offered a likely measure of relief for Britain's demobilization problems. Following a reorganization of British emigration services in 1918, the Free Passage Scheme was instituted, providing free transportation for ex-service men and women who had employment assured them, or who proposed settling on land under settlement schemes of any of the Empire countries.[83] A substantial proportion of the 39,500 ex-service men assisted under this scheme before its discontinuance in 1922 came to Canada. The Empire Settlement Act of 1922 provided that the British government might co-operate with governmental or private authorities in the Dominions in assisting persons to migrate to, and settle in, any Dominion.[84] Schemes acceptable under the act might provide for land settlement, or for assisted passages. The British government might advance up to half the costs of any scheme with a total grant not exceeding £3,000,000 per year.

The optimism associated with the passage of the Empire Settlement Act was unwarranted, as over a ten-year period less than one-fifth of the annual grants had been utilized.[85] A variety of arrangements was made, those with various Dominions for assisted passages, and with private associations for the assisted migration of women and children. Best known, perhaps, was the "3,000 Family Settlement" scheme arranged with the Canadian government. The British government agreed to advance up to £300 per family for the purchase of stock and equipment. The Canadian government provided lands under bill of sale from reverted soldier-settlement lands, supervised settlement and the purchase of equipment, and collected the payments, amortized at 5 per cent over a twenty-five-year period. At the end of 1929, 3,349 families had applied for consideration

[82]Ibid.
[83]England, Colonization of Western Canada, p. 92.
[84]Ibid., pp. 93-4.
[85]Ibid.

under the scheme; 175 had withdrawn before receiving aid, and
1,165 after receiving loans; 1,981 families were operating farms
under the scheme.[86] Current loans as at March, 1935, totalled
$8,302,021.[87] Under the "500 New Brunswick Family Settlement"
scheme, resting on an agreement between the British and the New
Brunswick governments, 248 settlers had been placed by 1935, with
current loans totalling just over $1,000,000.[88] From 1926 to 1928
the Dominion government contributed towards a system of passenger
warrants which reduced the ocean fare to a level within reach of
accepted migrants.[89] The Dominion contributed, and steamship
companies reduced the total fare so that the migrant paid £3 during
1926, and those travelling after January, 1927, paid £2. The
recruiting of 8,500 Britishers, mostly miners, to form a Canadian
harvest excursion in 1928 was admittedly an unhappy incident for
nearly all concerned. The Canadian government extended no assistance to continental emigrants after the war, 1914-18.[90] By 1930
assistance to Britishers was practically withdrawn, and entry even
without assistance became increasingly selective.

6. Summary

The federal government's first and most persistent form of aid
to Canadian agriculture comprised the encouragement of immigration and of agricultural settlement on the prairies. Land-grant
policy, the subsidization of the Pacific railway, the maintenance of
immigration agencies and the preparation of immigration literature,
the establishment of the passenger warrant system, and the institution
of agents' commissions were all a part of the effort expended in this
direction. The institution of the National Policy of tariffs and the
insistence that the Pacific railway be an all-Canadian railway are
clear indications that the central provinces claimed exclusive entrée
to the profitable developmental processes of the Canadian West.
Land policy remained confused long after the nominal adoption of
the free-homestead policy in 1872, for Canadian leaders found it
hard to believe that land could profitably be given away.

86Ibid., p. 95.
87Easterbrook, Farm Credit in Canada, p. 132.
88Ibid.
89England, Colonization of Western Canada, p. 95.
90Ibid., p. 98.

As late as 1900 the results of federal encouragement of immigration were a great disappointment. The trade in migrants was subject to severe international competition in this period, the leading competitors including the Australian and New Zealand colonies, Argentina and Brazil, and American railway and land companies. Settlement in the Canadian prairie West during this period, however, was of more significance than its numbers would suggest, for it comprised many colonies of widely diffused cultural and geographic origins. These acted as nuclei for later and more substantial accretions of population. With the turn of the century a conjuncture of circumstances assured Canada of an unprecedented influx of settlers, and between 1900 and 1914 the long-suspended hopes for western development were amply realized. From 1920 to 1930 considerable settlement in Canada occurred under schemes for soldier re-establishment and Empire settlement, and much settlement occurred unassisted. In terms of the agricultural plans associated with Confederation, the period 1900-30 should be regarded as a unit, the period during which Canadian immigration and settlement made possible the establishment of the wheat economy, a frontier of investment opportunities without precedent in Canadian experience.

CHAPTER VIII

THE LIVESTOCK AND DAIRY INDUSTRIES

GOVERNMENTS of North American colonies had long if irregular histories of assistance to animal husbandry before Confederation. In animal as in cereal husbandry, establishment and improvement in a new country necessitate the importation of seed stock and cultural methods, and the adaptation of both to local environment. With animals, however, seed-stock units are not divisible as with grains. Individual farmers can readily import one bushel or ten bushels or half a bushel of a particular variety of wheat or oats, for example, at slight expense, and multiplication of seed is but a matter of a few seasons; but to establish, say, a herd of any particular variety of cattle requires the importation of a minimum of two animals at very considerable cost. Perishability in transit is typically greater for animal than for cereal breeding stock.

In the light of these considerations the French very early brought livestock to North America with public funds, so that cereal husbandry might be effectively complemented by animal husbandry. Acadian livestock throve with a minimum of governmental assistance, and from 1713 to 1783, with New England in British hands, it was a matter of indifference to the British whether Acadian livestock prospered or not, for New England's agriculture was more than ample to provision the West Indies sugar plantations and the fisheries of New England, Nova Scotia, and Newfoundland. Hence the wanton liquidation of Acadian herds in 1755.[1] With New England beyond the British Empire's pale, however, the situation changed, for Nova Scotia could replace New England only if she could develop adequate provisions sources. Nova Scotian livestock was far from adequate, but her bread-corn shortages were relatively much worse. For many years, therefore, governmental aid to agriculture in Nova Scotia, and in New Brunswick as well, went towards the improvement of cereal rather than animal husbandry. After 1850 the efforts of all the Maritime governments were turned to the encouragement of livestock-raising, for it was gradually recognized as hopeless to strive for self-sufficiency in cereals in the

. [1]See above, p. 31.

face of the floods of grain pouring in from the upper St. Lawrence, from New York State, and eventually from far beyond, from such states as Ohio, Illinois, and Minnesota.

The governments of Upper and Lower Canada and, after 1841, the government of the Province of Canada, did little except by way of exhibitions and prizes in aid of livestock improvement. French holdings were soundly established by 1763. Loyalists and post-Loyalists brought animals with them. More particularly, British. immigrants after 1825 brought stock (notably Ayrshire cattle) and also the knowledge and appreciation of good stock and its management. Around 1850 American railway-building provided markets for Canadian livestock and livestock products, and this incentive hastened the transition in Upper Canada away from wheat-cropping, which was already increasingly hazardous due to the midge, the weevil, rust, and exhaustion of soil fertility. Farm prosperity permitted the importation of good breeding stock, and governmental fairs and exhibitions were of nominal importance. By Confederation, exports of Canadian live cattle, practically all to the United States, had reached striking proportions.

A. The Livestock Industry

With Confederation the provincial governments retained, without question, the support and supervision of agricultural boards, societies, and exhibitions, and continued to sponsor livestock improvement with varying degrees of intensity and vision. However, the first activities engaged in by the federal Department of Agriculture, which had any appearance of being essentially agricultural, had to do with cattle, with cattle quarantine and with the live cattle trade with Britain. In 1884 the Secretary of the Department of Agriculture informed the Gigault Committee that the Department of Agriculture had as yet had no agricultural grant and had performed no agricultural function other than that of the supervision of cattle quarantine.[2]

Here once more we encounter commercial purposes and the commercial interest in agricultural progress. Provincial governments might work strenuously towards the improvement of the livestock within their respective provinces, and there is some evidence

[2]Report of the Gigault Committee, Canada House of Commons, *Journal*, 1884, App. no. 6, p. 102.

that they would continue these efforts even though each farm achieved no more than self-sufficiency in animals and animal products. The commercial interest in farm progress, in contrast, comes forward only when the farm unit achieves something more than a self-sufficiency in a particular product, or when it shows prospects of so doing. Generally speaking, the federal government fell heir to this latter interest in agricultural activities, and its constitutional control over trade and commerce has served to make this interest operative. When the livestock industry had progressed to the point where there was a cattle trade, where there was commerce in a farm product, the Dominion Department of Agriculture was the logical administrative agency to evince interest and to assume sponsorship, not so much because it was an agricultural department but because it was the department primarily interested in the commerce of the farm, whether of farm products or of farmer immigrants.

Encouragement extended by the federal government to the livestock industry over the decades has assumed a variety of forms. The first aspects of the industry to arouse any interest on the part of the Dominion government concerned the live cattle trade with Britain, of rather spectacular origins in the middle eighteen-seventies; and for forty years the trials and vicissitudes of this farm-product commerce constituted one of the major fields of interest for the federal Department of Agriculture. Cattle quarantine had separate origins,[3] but became closely interrelated with the movement of cattle to Britain and with the importation of breeding stock from Britain. British landlords were still powerful enough to secure the exclusion of foreign cattle on the slightest indication that Canadian or other herds were diseased. Canadian breeders and graziers were, of course, anxious to keep their herds free from the cattle plagues which raged sporadically in other countries. Almost simultaneous with the rise and expansion of the cattle trade with Britain was the development of the range cattle industry in the Alberta foothills and on the plains. Encouragement of this development called for such diverse activities as the establishment of the Royal North West Mounted Police, the provision of grazing leases, the maintenance of a border quarantine control, and the governmental importation and sale of breeding stock.

[3] See below, pp. 199-204.

1. The Live Cattle Trade in Relation to British Emigration

The Canadian live cattle trade with Great Britain was closely related to the migration of population from Britain to Canada. It was instituted on the initiative of a Canadian immigration agent in England and was sponsored by the immigration service primarily because of its obvious value as an advertisement of economic prospects in the Dominion. Furthermore, to the extent that foreign foodstuffs crowded into the British market the position of British agriculturists was rendered more precarious, and the prospects of the newer lands came, by comparison, to appear brighter still, though Canadian agents did not sponsor the cattle trade openly in the latter terms. After Confederation there was always ample emigration from Britain and Europe; Canada's problem was to secure any reasonable proportion of this migration in competition chiefly with the United States and Australia. A generation before the wheat-growing possibilities on the prairies had achieved this objective, a Canadian immigration agent stumbled upon the live cattle trade and saw in it great possibilities for the attraction to Canada of British capital and labour, typically those of the British tenant farmer.

Mr. John Dyke, the Canadian immigration agent in Liverpool in 1874, working under direction of the Canadian Department of Agriculture, was a most enthusiastic sales agent, believing fully in Canada's future, given proper publicity. The provision of that publicity he considered to be the function of immigration agents like himself. He lectured, talked, wrote for the press, answered queries, and in every possible way made himself informative about Canada. He was particularly enthusiastic over the Canadian prospects for tenant farmers and farm labourers. In February, 1874, he arranged to have shipped to him in Liverpool a substantial consignment of fresh meat from Canada, which shipment he widely publicized in the press, "the first large shipment ever sent from America."[4] The venture was so satisfactory that dealers in the Old Country took up the business and extended it to include the importation of Canadian live cattle. In 1876 Mr. Dyke reported to the Minister of Agriculture: "You are aware of the success which attended the large shipment of meat sent to me at Liverpool in February 1874. My

[4] Report of the Minister of Agriculture, Canada, *Sessional Papers,* 1877, no. 8, p. 136.

connection with this led to many enquiries from parties interested in the meat supply of Great Britain, and I am happy to inform you that several of the leading butchers of Liverpool and Glasgow have been induced to import live cattle from Canada, and I understand they are well satisfied with the experiment."[5] Canadians did not follow up the meat trade, probably because of refrigeration difficulties,[6] but Americans did. Canadians expanded the live cattle trade. By 1877 Canada exported 4,000 head of cattle to Britain and 13,850 to the United States; by 1879, 20,600 to Britain and 21,300 to the United States; by 1880, 32,680 to Britain and 16,044 to the United States.[7] The exports to Britain continued to increase, first exceeding 100,000 in 1891, and after 1900 running at 150,000 to 160,000 annually till they were drastically cut by 1912 with a curtailment of western ranching.[8] The trade was wiped out for the duration of the War of 1914-18 but in particular years in the middle nineteen-twenties Great Britain was again the leading importer of Canadian cattle.

Officials of the Canadian Department of Agriculture long considered the live cattle trade primarily as a means of boosting the immigration of particularly desirable classes of settlers, the British tenant farmer and farm labourer. Speaking in 1876 of the factors in the migration situation, Mr. Dyke said, "The importation of cattle and meat from Canada to this country is doing us much good."[9] In 1877 it was reported: "Her Majesty the Queen, ever taking a kindly interest in the social and economic problems of the day, has been graciously pleased to send a letter to one of the principal importers, expressing her satisfaction with the condition and flavour of the [Canadian] beef, a sample joint of which had been sent to

---

[5]*Ibid.*, 1876, no. 8, p. 100. In 1877 the London agent, Mr. F. J. Doré, said of the live cattle trade: "The trade began in Glasgow three years ago, when a firm of salesmen in that city imported, as an experiment, a few head of fat cattle. Finding that the animals stood the voyage well and without in any way deteriorating, the same firm extended its operations, exporting [*sic*] each month cattle from America in large numbers" (*ibid.*, 1877, no. 8, p. 129).

[6]By 1877 "The steamers of the leading lines plying between New York and Liverpool and Glasgow, are fitted with refrigerators of several hundred tons capacity to convey meat" (*ibid.*, p. 136).

[7]Abbott, "Marketing of Live Stock in Canada."

[8]*Ibid.*

[9]Canada, *Sessional Papers*, 1876, no. 8, p. 99.

her."[10]   But for the London agent, who reported this incident, the significance of the successful entrée of Canadian cattle to Britain was the proof thus afforded that "Canadian farmers can send to market meat that will sell side by side with the best Scotch beef, with good profit to themselves, and at 25 per cent less cost to the English consumer. This fact when generally known, will certainly have an important effect upon our tenant farmer emigration in the future."[11] To point the moral the London agent in 1877, Mr. Annand, published a paper on *Canada as a Farming and Stock Raising Country,* addressed it "To capitalists, retired army and navy officers, farmers, and all those who wish to engage in profitable agriculture," and distributed six thousand copies at the Smithfield Club Cattle Show in December.[12]   In 1877 it was reported that: "Fat cattle sent over from Canada took the first prize at the Dublin Christmas Fat Cattle Show of 1876, against the whole of Ireland, and at the Highland Show at Glasgow, in July, 1875, Messrs. Bell & Sons also took four silver medals. Again, five thoroughbred shorthorns bred and sent to this country by the Hon. M. H. Cochrane, realized the highest average price at any sale in Great Britain in the year 1876, viz. £203 14s. 0d. each."[13] These facts Mr. Dyke reported, "feeling confident that emigration to Canada will be materially increased through it."[14]

Affairs soon indicated that the Canadian government would have to do more for the cattle trade than publicize it as an attraction for tenant farmers. If Canadian prospects in the eighteen-seventies and later years looked bright to Britishers, it was by comparison with the gloom of agricultural prospects in the United Kingdom. Improvements in transportation, the application of steel and steam to land and ocean traffic, and the interrelated opening of newer agricultural lands in the United States, Australia, New Zealand, and Canada, had brought an increasing flood of food importations which threatened to undermine completely the British landlords' position.

10*Ibid.,* 1877, no. 8, p. 129.
11*Ibid.*
12*Ibid.,* 1878, no. 9, p. 134. See also Lowe's evidence before the Select Standing Committee on Immigration and Colonization, Canada House of Commons, *Journal,* 1877, App. no. 6, pp. 13 ff.
13Report of the Minister of Agriculture, Canada, *Sessional Papers,* 1877, no. 8, p. 136.
14*Ibid.*

By 1850 the Corn Laws were gone and the last protective barricade had fallen before the golden flood of New World cereals. English agriculturists were told by a leading agricultural authority and tenant farmers' representative in the House of Commons "that owing to the great importation of foreign bread stuffs it did not pay to grow wheat in England, and that farmers must in future depend upon the production of *horn instead of corn.*"[15] By the middle eighteen-seventies this analysis was inadequate, for clearly the British market for horn (cattle) was seriously menaced, as well as that for corn. It was evident that live cattle and fresh frozen meats could be sent profitably from Canada and the United States, as some claimed, "at 25 per cent less cost to the English consumer."

Mr. Dyke submitted the following table of British imports as a striking indication of the pressure on the British agriculturist.[16]

		VALUE OF IMPORTS			
Year	Population of the United Kingdom	Live cattle, sheep and pigs	Corn, grain and flour	Dead meat and provisions*	Total	Per head of population
1858 ...	28,389,770	£1,390,086	£20,164,811	£ 4,343,592	£25,898,471	£ 18.3
1868 ...	30,617,718	£2,698,496	£39,432,624	£13,277,683	£55,408,803	£1.16.2
1878 ...	33,444,419	£6,012,564	£63,536,322	£30,144,013	£99,692,899	£2.19.7

*Beef; meat (salt and fresh); meat preserved, other than by salting; pork; bacon and hams; butter; cheese; eggs; and potatoes.

2. *The Richmond Bill*

British consumers, allied with commercial interest on the issue of cheap food versus protection, had defeated the Corn Laws by 1850, but the landlords were still strong, particularly the graziers. They rallied promptly to meet the rising threat to their remaining position, and the issue was joined when in January, 1878, the Duke of Richmond introduced a bill in the imperial House purporting to exclude from Britain live cattle from countries where specified diseases existed, and to require all foreign cattle to be slaughtered at the port of debarkation. As introduced the bill included Canada and the United States among the "scheduled" countries; i.e., among

15*Ibid.*
16*Ibid.*, 1879, no. 9, p. 100.

the countries from which live cattle could still enter Britain, but which cattle would have to be slaughtered at the port of debarkation within ten days of arrival, or immediately on arrival if disease was found in the shipment.

Canadian and American exporters and shippers, their governments, and Canadian immigration agents, all claimed that the bill was purely an exclusion measure, though ostensibly a thoroughly legitimate quarantine measure.[17] Canadians claimed that, if enacted, the measure would be fatal to the Canadian trade in live cattle, that it would obviously put an end to the British business in Canadian stockers, just beginning, and that it would place Canadian fat cattle in the position of a distressed commodity, unable to move from debarkation ports to inland markets and unable to be sufficiently rested and fed up after the Atlantic crossing. The British House of Commons select committee to whom the bill was referred took evidence of witnesses from the various countries interested in the cattle trade with Great Britain, "Canada excepted."[18] The Canadian government protested by Order-in-Council to the imperial authorities that none of the diseases listed in the bill had ever existed in Canada. Sir John Rose and Mr. Dyke, with the backing of the steamship companies interested in the trade, finally secured permission to lay the Canadian case before a select committee of the House of Lords.[19] As a result of these vigorous representations, when the bill was enacted as the Imperial Contagious Diseases (Animals) Act, effective

[17]Thomas Cramp of Montreal, Director of the Dominion Steamship Lines, in evidence before the 1878 Committee on Immigration and Colonization, said concerning the Richmond Bill, then under consideration: "The proposed action must be taken for different objects than those which are shown to the public; it must be in the interest of the land-owners and farmers of Great Britain, and I need not tell you that the interest of the consumer is in another direction." He added that the farming and landed interests of England were extremely well organized. "Q. You think that antagonism to the trade is at the bottom of it [the Richmond bill]?—Yes, I do." J. McShane, Jr., a Montreal merchant, before the same committee gave his opinion that the graziers, "who are wealthy men," were responsible for the Bill (Canada House of Commons, *Journal*, 1878, App. no. 2, pp. 70-6, 83-9).

[18]Report of the Minister of Agriculture, Canada, *Sessional Papers*, 1879, no. 9, p. 102.

[19]*Ibid.* Also Report of the Select Standing Committee on Immigration and Colonization, Canada House of Commons, *Journal*, 1878, App. no. 2, pp. 7 ff.

January 1, 1879, Canada and the United States were removed from the "schedule" and were left freely to ship live cattle to the British market. While this continued freedom to enter the British market undoubtedly was beneficial to Canadian and American agriculture, it was clearly the commercial interest which was at stake and for which effective protests were made.

With the passage of the modified Richmond Bill, Canada retained free entry to the British cattle market, but was, of course, liable to scheduling at any time, or even to be made subject to complete embargo, if any of the contagious diseases listed in the act cropped up in Canadian herds. The critical problem, therefore, was to prevent this from happening and to prevent even the suspicion of such an event. This was a job for Canadian quarantine law and quarantine authorities, and the evidence is that it was a job well done. The United States were scheduled almost immediately after the passage of the British quarantine law, and the recorded condition of their herds makes such action appear reasonable. Canada escaped scheduling until 1892, despite repeated British efforts to substantiate charges that contagious disease existed in Canadian shipments. It is not clear that the case was proven in 1892, but scheduling was then imposed on Canada and maintained for thirty years.

3. The "Bovine Scourges"

Though protection of the home market for domestic producers was a prime factor in the passage of the British quarantine law, there was real and urgent need for quarantine restrictions on international trade in farm animals. Of the various types of livestock, cattle were most subject to devastating contagion throughout the later nineteenth century, and of the various diseases to which cattle were liable, three stood out among all as the "bovine scourges," viz., cattle plague (rinderpest), foot and mouth disease, and pleuro-pneumonia (lung plague or lung fever).[20] By comparison with these three, such diseases as Texas fever, anthrax, and tuberculosis were trifles. Of bovine tuberculosis the Dominion veterinary, D. McEachran, said in 1880: "Until recently tuberculosis was not considered as sufficiently important to be included in the class of contagious diseases requiring

[20]See McEachran's report to the Minister of Agriculture, Canada, *Sessional Papers*, 1880, no. 10, App. no. 28, pp. 98-117.

legislation for its suppression."[21] He went on to say, however, that investigations on the continent had now demonstrated it to be infectious to man as well as to animals, and transmissible through milk and meat.

By the eighteen-seventies pleuro-pneumonia was the outstanding menace. It was the most insidious, and was contagious as well as infectious, and had an incubation period of from one to sixteen weeks while rinderpest and the foot and mouth disease developed within a maximum of ten days.[22] Pleuro-pneumonia had swept through Europe since 1800;[23] had invaded Prussia in 1802 and northern Germany shortly after; was first described in Russia in 1824; reached Belgium in 1827, Holland in 1833, Great Britain in 1841, Sweden in 1847, Denmark in 1848, Finland in 1850. From Europe it was carried to new continents by breeding stock: to South Africa in 1854, Brooklyn (U.S.A.) in 1843 and 1850, New Jersey in 1847, Boston in 1859, Melbourne (Australia) in 1858, New South Wales in 1860, and New Zealand in 1864. Losses were appalling. McEachran said in 1880 that losses in Australia since 1860 "could not be less than 30 to 40 per cent of the whole number of cattle, or about 1,404,097 head."[24] For six years ending 1860 "it has been estimated that there perished considerably more than a million cattle in the United Kingdom [from pleuro-pneumonia]." Tables of an English cattle insurance company indicated that from 1863 to 1866 the death-rate from pleuro-pneumonia was 50-63 per cent yearly.[25]

In 1879 McEachran was sent to Washington, D.C., to investigate and determine the correctness of claims that pleuro-pneumonia was prevalent in the dairy herds supplying Washington, Brooklyn, and other American cities. His investigations fully confirmed the charges. In Washington scavengers told him that "it is not uncommon to have several dead cows a day from the Washington dairies; that to have a dozen a week has not been unusual, during certain seasons, and that the supply is constant."[26] After much obstruction on the part of proprietors who wanted no interference

21*Ibid.*, p. 112.
22*Ibid.*, p. 109.
23*Ibid.*, App. no. 36, p. 163.
24*Ibid.*, p. 167.
25*Ibid.*
26*Ibid.*, p. 165.

from "sanitary police," McEachran was able to investigate distillery-fed cattle in Brooklyn. Some of his report follows:

Here we found between 800 and 900 dairy cows, owned by different parties, who pay 77½¢ per week for the use of the shed and supply of swill from the distillery. Of all the pest houses possible to imagine this one is the worst. In low roofed sheds cattle are packed as close as they can stand in double rows, with a passage of about three feet between the rows. Swill nearly boiling hot is run into troughs in front of them, into which hay is placed and remains until it is cool enough for them to drink. They have no bedding . . . it would be strange if the disease were not prevalent.[27]

An American, Professor Leontard, who accompanied McEachran, estimated that there were not fifty healthy cattle in the shed.

Americans had been unable to prevent the introduction of pleuro-pneumonia to the herds of the eastern states. They appeared unable to stamp it out. Certain features of the disease rendered this difficult. As McEachran pointed out regarding cattle suffering from pleuro-pneumonia, "for a time they milk freely, and lay on fat rapidly, consequently before the disease has approached the stage in which they die, they are handed over to the butcher, are killed and dressed and sent to Washington Market, N.Y., where it is sold as prime beef. . . . It was assured by a butcher, who dealt largely in this beef, that it commanded the highest price in the market. . . . Others that are too lean are taken in the early stages, mixed with other stock and sent by railway to Baltimore to be sold as stock cows to farmers."[28]

On the basis of conditions such as these, the United States were scheduled by Britain in 1879. Canada was concerned to avoid the same restrictions and was in grave danger because of the proximity of the American pestilential areas to Ontario herds, and because there was movement of American cattle into and through Canada. Some breeding animals entered Canada from the United

[27]Report of the Minister of Agriculture, Canada, *Sessional Papers*, 1879, no. 9, App., pp. 166 ff.

[28]*Ibid.*, p. 169; Report of the Minister of Agriculture, Canada, *Sessional Papers*, 1880, no. 10, App., p. 165. In 1860 Mr. Barbarie was sent by the New Brunswick government to buy livestock in Britain. He found pleuro-pneumonia widespread, and remarked, "and strange as it may appear, it is nevertheless true, that the moment the disease manifests itself, if the animal is fit for the butcher, thither it is speedily transported" (New Brunswick Assembly, *Journal*, 1861, App. no. 4, p. 71).

States and possibly some stockers and feeders. The substantial contact by the eighteen-seventies, however, came in the movement of western feeder and fat cattle to the eastern American consuming centres by way of the Ontario peninsula, over the Great Western Railway. This was a transit trade only, but sufficient to spread contagion among Canadian herds unless extreme care was exercised. This movement provided a severe test of the effectiveness of Canadian quarantine.

4. Early Canadian Quarantine

Livestock quarantine had been provided for in the Province of Canada by an act of 1865, "to provide against the introduction and spreading of disorders affecting certain animals."[29] This act permitted the Governor-in-Council to prohibit the importation of livestock, to prescribe quarantine for animals, to order animals or fodder destroyed, and to prohibit the movement of animals within the country. Immediately following the passage of this act, Thompson, Secretary of the Upper Canada Board of Agriculture, urged that it be made effective regarding cattle entering from England "where the cattle plague is raging."[30] Weeks later the Deputy Minister of Agriculture, J. C. Taché, advised Thompson that the Minister of Agriculture hardly thought it wise to prohibit the importation of cattle from countries with the cattle plague, as this would interfere with reciprocity with the United States. Should the danger become imminent, however, either by the St. Lawrence or by the inland frontier, the Minister would, he said, immediately recommend that the act be implemented.[31]

The Upper Canada Board of Agriculture continued to apply pressure for exclusion of European stock,[32] and in February, 1866, an Order-in-Council provided that "the importation by sea of cattle, sheep, horses, swine, asses and mules, meat, skins, hides, horns, hoofs, or other part of such animals, hay straw and fodder, be and the same is hereby prohibited," except for exemptions which the

29*Statutes of Canada*, 29 Vic., c. 15, 1865 (Second Session).

30Letter Books of the Bureau of Agriculture, Public Archives of Canada, Taché to Thompson, October 25, 1865.

31*Ibid.*, Taché to Thompson, November 23, 1865.

32Canada, *Sessional Papers*, 1866, no. 29, *passim*.

Governor might specifically make.[33]   In November, 1866, horses
were removed from the prohibited list.[34]   By 1867 the agricultural
interests were again anxious to import breeding stock and the
Honourable David Christie, President of the Upper Canada Board
of Agriculture, sought relaxation of the exclusion law since the
cattle plague had virtually disappeared from England. The Council
could not agree to removal of the prohibitory order, but stated their
willingness to consider each proposed importation on its merits.[35]
This, in fact, had been done from time to time during 1866, and
during the months prior to Confederation a number of shipments of
livestock, sheep, cattle, and hogs, entered Canada with the specific
permission of the Council in each case.[36]

The first threat to Canadian herds after Confederation came
from the United States.   In 1868 the Dominion Department of
Agriculture was concerned over the "Epizooties," Texas Fever, raging in the United States and carrying away "thousands and thousands
of cattle" in the states adjacent to Canada.[37]   American cattle went
to eastern American markets through Canadian territory *via* the
Great Western and Grand Trunk railways, and the Ontario Board
of Agriculture insisted that the danger of contagion was great and
that quarantine should be imposed.   The federal Department of
Agriculture had been assigned the superintendence of public health
and quarantine[38] but as yet there was no federal quarantine law.   On
the advice of the Minister of Customs the government issued an
Order-in-Council, August 13, 1868, prohibiting the importation of
cattle into Ontario and Quebec, from the United States, under
authority of the quarantine act of 1865.

Interests other than agricultural were at stake and in a conflicting direction.   Railroad companies hated to see their traffic impaired.
Only the severity of the danger impelled the government to yield
to the request of agricultural groups and to prohibit the traffic in

33*Minutes of the Executive Council*, Public Archives of Canada, Series E,
State Book AC, February 20, 1866.

34*Ibid.*, State Book AD, November 3, 1866.

35*Ibid.*, State Book AE, April 30, 1867.

36See, e.g., *ibid.*, State Book AC, April 23, 1866; State Book AE, March
22, 1867.

37Report of the Minister of Agriculture, Canada, *Sessional Papers*, 1869,
no. 76, pp. 3-4.

38By the act constituting the Department (31 Vic., c. 53, 1868).

American cattle, which meant immediate loss of revenue to Canadian railways. The Minister of Agriculture explained the situation and the compromise as follows: "The prohibition thus ordered [August 13, 1868], although of paramount importance and even of absolute necessity, was nevertheless entailing on many individuals, and on the Grand Trunk and Great Western Railway Companies very serious losses, in consequence of which it was a question of justice and good policy to allow this prohibitory order not to stand any longer than was rigorously required for the protection of the farming interest of the Country."[39] Consequently, after consultation with the Ontario Board of Agriculture, the prohibition was revoked by Order-in-Council, October 1, 1868.[40] American cattle might then resume their movement through Canada, with the provision that until November 1 (by which time Texas fever was usually ended for the year) the shipments could be inspected at Windsor or Sarnia by officials of the Department of Agriculture. These officials were to supervise the disinfection of cars as well. Here is the first application of quarantine as contrasted with embargo.

The Dominion government enacted livestock quarantine in 1869,[41] copying the Canadian provincial act of 1865(29 Vic., c. 15) and broadening it to apply to the Dominion. This law became important in the middle eighteen-seventies with the constant importation of breeding stock from Britain where livestock plagues followed one another in devastating cycles. By 1875 the Minister of Agriculture was concerned over "the epizootic disease which for some years past had proved to be very destructive in the United Kingdom, and on the Continent of Europe, involving loss in cattle to the value of many millions of dollars."[42] Pleuro-pneumonia and the foot and mouth disease were both rife in Britain at this time, but the officials of the Department of Agriculture were primarily anxious not to cause alarm which might disrupt either the importation or the exportation of cattle. They "carefully and quietly watched the arrivals of imported cattle," inspecting but not quarantining, and the

[39]Report of the Minister of Agriculture, Canada, *Sessional Papers*, 1869, no. 76, pp. 3-4.

[40]Canada, *Sessional Papers*, 1869, no. 67, p. 2.

[41]*Statutes of Canada*, 32-33 Vic., c. 37, An Act respecting Contagious Diseases affecting Animals.

[42]Report of the Minister of Agriculture, Canada, *Sessional Papers*, 1876, no. 8, p. vii.

diseases, oddly enough, were not transmitted to Canadian herds. The Minister of Agriculture stated that "The circumstances were not then [1875] such as to warrant the adopting of quarantine measures, which, of course, always entail great embarrassment and expense, both on individuals and the public."[43]

Early in 1876 it became evident that the policy of avoiding alarm was not enough. The diseases in British herds were reaching such proportions that it was clear that quarantine would have to replace inspection.[44] In time for the opening of navigation an Order-in-Council of April 20, 1876, under authority of the quarantine law of 1869 (32 and 33 Vic., c. 37), prohibited the importation of cattle, sheep, and swine into Canada from Europe except through the ports of Halifax, Saint John, and Quebec. At each of these ports quarantine was established, with an inspector in charge and with facilities for the reception and detention of animals. The principal quarantine establishment was situated at Point Levis (Quebec) "in one of the forts, the vacant space of which was fitted for the reception of animals."[45] Professor D. McEachran, Principal of the Montreal Veterinary College, was appointed Chief Inspector of Stock for the Dominion government,[46] and until his supervisory duties became too heavy he acted as inspector at the Point Levis quarantine.

Vigorous action was taken immediately. Professor McEachran ordered that incoming stock be detained eight days for inspection and disinfection. No stock was entered by Halifax or Saint John, but through Quebec there entered 109 cattle, 320 sheep, and 35 hogs consigned to established breeders in Ontario and Quebec.[47] Mc-Eachran was "happy to be able to report that out of all these animals, only one case of contagious 'Lung Disease' Pleuro-pneumonia was met with . . . and being prevented from passing over the line of

43Ibid., 1877, no. 8, p. vi.

44Ibid., p. vii.

45Ibid., and App. no. 26.

46McEachran's evidence, Report of the Select Standing Committee on Immigration and Colonization, 1880-1, Canada House of Commons, Journal, App. no. 1, p. 91.

47Such as Hon. M. H. Cochrane of Compton, P.Q., Stone of Guelph, the Ontario Agricultural College, and several partnerships.

travel, the possibility of spreading the disease was prevented."[48] In 1877 rinderpest was prevalent in England and Europe, and cattle quarantine regulations "which had been aimed against Foot and Mouth and other like diseases" had to be modified to bar European cattle entirely.[49] This prohibition "entailed a painful case of private hardship, but one which could not be avoided, on account of the immense interest at stake, viz.; the safety of the cattle of the country, and the position to be maintained in England for our cattle trade, which is assuming very large proportions."[50] A valuable shipment of breeding cattle had to be turned back at Quebec. Agriculture and commerce temporarily had common requirements. By 1878 the prohibition was removed and cattle were permitted to enter Canada through quarantine.[51]

The passage of the imperial contagious diseases act in 1878 (the Richmond Bill) took freedom of action concerning quarantine largely out of Canadian hands. Only by the most strenuous representations on the part of Canadian officials and other interested parties were Canadian cattle finally exempted from the slaughtering clause of the British act. To secure this concession Canadian officials had to satisfy British authorities concerning the following three matters:[52] (1) Canadian laws applying to importation of animals, (2) methods employed to prevent the spread of animal diseases, and (3) the health of domestic animals at regular intervals. Until 1892, when the blow finally fell, when Canada was finally "scheduled," the federal government directed its assistance to the Canadian livestock industry, chiefly towards the protection of the cattle trade with Britain, and this by assuring that Canadian herds be kept free from foreign contagion.

Early in 1879 McEachran had visited cities in the eastern states and verified the worst possible rumours regarding the diseased condition of American cattle.[53] In his report to the Minister of

[48]Report of the Minister of Agriculture, Canada, *Sessional Papers*, 1877, no. 8, App. no. 26, p. 86.

[49]*Ibid.*, 1878, no. 9, p. viii.

[50]*Ibid.*

[51]*Ibid.*, 1879, no. 9, p. vii.

[52]*Ibid.*

[53]See above, pp. 197-8.

Agriculture[54] he made plain the menace to Canadian herds failing adequate safeguards, "if the cattle from the infected states are allowed to enter the Dominion, either for breeding, feeding, or shipping." He favoured immediate exclusion while at the same time he pointed out that no pleuro-pneumonia existed in the western states, and consequently western cattle were no threat to Canada provided the Americans took steps to confine the disease to the seaboard. On February 6, 1879, cargoes of American cattle arriving in Liverpool were found to have "a contagious disease" and the United States were scheduled under the British contagious diseases act. On information that Canada would be scheduled as well unless she acted promptly, American cattle were excluded from the five eastern provinces by Order-in-Council.[55] The transit trade through the western peninsula was allowed to resume under bond after April, 1880.[56] The Minister of Agriculture spoke of the reluctance with which they finally placed an embargo on American cattle. A clue to this reluctance is found in the argument put forward by Thomas Cramp, an agent of the Dominion Steamship Lines, that Canada should risk scheduling by Britain rather than exclude American cattle since the American transit trade brought $500,000 annually to Canada.[57] The embargo was relaxed in 1880 to permit the transit trade *via* the western peninsula, but continued to rule out shipments of American cattle to Britain *via* Quebec.

5. Institution of Outbound Inspection

The basic condition for the maintenance of health in Canadian cattle exported to Britain was that Canadian herds be free from disease. So long as none of the "bovine scourges" had appeared in Canada, it was the function of livestock quarantine at points of entry to prevent their introduction. Breeding stock was constantly being imported from Europe, and occasionally from the United States, and American cattle went eastward *via* Canada. These points of contact required constant vigilance. Cases of pleuro-pneumonia and foot and mouth disease were stopped at Canadian quarantine and

54Report of the Minister of Agriculture, Canada, *Sessional Papers*, 1879, no. 9, p. 170.
55*Ibid.*, 1880, no. 10, p. vi.
56*Ibid.*, 1880-1, no. 12, p. vii, and App. no. 35.
57Report of the Select Standing Committee on Immigration and Colonization, Canada House of Commons, *Journal*, 1879, App. no. 1, pp. 145 ff.

their introduction thus prevented. In 1886 pleuro-pneumonia appeared in Canadian quarantine and two hundred head of stock had to be destroyed.[58] But for the meticulous British market, with officials constantly on guard and some almost hopeful that contagion might appear in Canadian shipments, cattle had not only to be free from contagion, they had to *appear* perfectly healthy and they had to arrive in good condition. Certain factors rendered this uncertain and led to the introduction by the Canadian government of a system of outbound port inspection and supervision of animal shipping, as a complement to the inbound quarantine.[59] This was effected under a new quarantine act of 1879[60] which supplanted the act of 1869.

Experience indicated the need for supervision of shipments. The ocean voyage from Canadian ports to Britain was long and trying, and it was added to a train journey of hundreds of miles and the general distress of transfer at the ocean port. Only the best of care at all stages of the journey could make it possible for animals to arrive in Britain in reasonable condition, or even to survive. Such care was lacking. The Committee on Immigration and Colonization reported in 1881 as follows:

> It has been brought prominently to the notice of the Committee, through the evidence of Mr. McEachran, and by communications from shippers, that there is much to be done in the way of absolutely necessary improved accommodation for the proper care of cattle and sheep at ports of shipping and also on board ships, in order to secure sufficient profits and permanency of trade to stock raisers and shippers. It is found that animals, awaiting shipment at Montreal, are penned in spaces entirely too small in area, exposed to the weather and sunk in depths of mud and filth for successive days, and unprovided with feeding troughs and hay cribs. In other instances they are confined in small dirty yards surrounded by a poisonous atmosphere; sometimes animals are confined for a day or more in railway cars on the wharf without food or water; frequently they are put on board ship, crazed and bruised by being driven through crowded thoroughfares of traffic, and hustled in this condition into the hold of a ship the atmosphere of which is densely laden with the dust from grain loading;—a combination of circumstances strongly tending both to rapidly deteriorate the condition of the animals and to induce disease. Also

---

[58]Report of the Minister of Agriculture, Canada, *Sessional Papers*, 1887, no. 12, p. vii.

[59]*Ibid.*, 1880, no. 10, p. vi and App. 27, pp. 99 ff.

[60]*Statutes of Canada*, 42 Vic., c. 23.

better ventilation and more care of the proper preservation of feed on board ships appear to demand increased attention.[61]

For the ocean voyage the custom was for ship-owners to rent space to shippers and to permit the shippers to fill it as they chose. McEachran reported: "The consequence was in many cases a disgraceful state of overcrowding, which in some cases was only held in check by the Insurance Inspectors refusing to accept the risks; competition, however, in many instances rendered them powerless to insist on proper space being allowed."[62] After consultation with persons well acquainted with the trade, McEachran instructed his assistants to require each cow or bullock to have a space two feet nine inches by eight feet, this space to be known as "a bullock space," selling at from £5 to £6.[63] Other animals were placed as follows: unsheared sheep and swine, eight to a bullock space; and sheared sheep, ten. The first year's inspection out of Quebec applied to 110,000 animals. McEachran estimated the mortality rates at sea for the year (1879) as 1 per cent for cattle, $2\frac{1}{2}$ per cent for sheep, and $4\frac{1}{2}$ per cent for hogs, "extremely small" considering all the circumstances. Most of the casualties occurred on the river, though some were washed overboard or jettisoned in storms. From one steamer 186 sheep were washed overboard. Proper attendance was always a problem. A common practice was to entrust the stock to the "tender mercies of discontented emigrants, who wished to work their way to England, or rather, who pretended to do so to get a free passage."[64]

Canadian inspection and quarantine were performed with sufficient success that Americans made considerable use of the St. Lawrence route both for exporting live cattle to Britain and for importing breeding stock from Britain. The time spent on the outward voyage in the quiet waters of the lower St. Lawrence was found to be a helpful preparation for stock for the ocean crossing. In 1880 the Honourable Mr. Leduc, Commissioner of Agriculture in the United States, noting that insurance rates on cattle from Canadian ports ranged from $2\frac{1}{2}$-3 per cent while parallel rates from

[61]Report of the Select Standing Committee on Immigration and Colonization, Canada House of Commons, *Journal,* 1880-1, App. no. 1, p. 6.

[62]Report of the Minister of Agriculture, Canada, *Sessional Papers,* 1880, no. 10, App. no. 28, p. 101.

[63]*Ibid.,* p. 102.

[64]*Ibid.,* p. 104.

American ports ranged from 3-10 per cent (according to season and source of cattle), commented as follows: "Of course these rates are based upon the actual results of experience. . . . What is the cause for this difference in experience between the United States and Canada? To this the unqualified answer is that it is due to a proper veterinary inspection, under proper laws, both of which are maintained by the Canadian Government."[65]

Similarly, Canadian quarantine on incoming livestock, with a ninety-day duration for cattle to cope with the long incubation period of pleuro-pneumonia, interdependently with the Canadian freedom from contagious diseases, led American breeders to import breeding stock by way of the St. Lawrence. The American Atlantic seaboard and eastern states were infested with cattle plagues. In 1882 a deputation of the United States Cattle Commission visited the Quebec quarantine station, and Dr. McEachran, who accompanied them, reported that "though the quarantine station was not perfect, yet none of them had ever visited one more so, and expressed themselves as highly pleased with what they saw, and returned to organize quarantines at Portland, Boston, New York, and Baltimore on nearly similar principles."[66] In Chicago, Dr. McEachran met "most of the Western importers . . . and nearly all of them expressed the hope that no restrictions would be placed on our quarantine that would prevent their importing by the St. Lawrence route, on Canadian steamers, which are so admirably adapted for the safety and comfort of stock at sea, and through a country where no disease existed, and where the cost of quarantine was less than half what it had hitherto cost at United States ports, averaging from $10 to $15 per head, and where they were properly looked after."[67]

6. *Assistance to the Range-Cattle Industry*

The last quarter of the nineteenth century saw the range-cattle industry sweep northward out of Texas to cover large portions of the central American plains and to flow over into the Canadian foothills.[68] The Texas Longhorn had little to commend him but his hardiness, and it soon became evident that exceptional hardiness was

[65]Report of the United States Commissioner of Agriculture, as cited in the Report of the Minister of Agriculture, Canada, *Sessional Papers*, 1882, no. 11, p. vii.

[66]*Ibid.*, 1883, no. 14, App. no. 34, p. 249.

[67]*Ibid.*

[68]Dale, *Range Cattle Industry;* Webb, *Great Plains.*

not required for either American or Canadian ranges. By the eighteen-eighties efforts were being made to improve range cattle in the United States, and two British breeds of beef animals rivalled each other for leadership in this project, viz., Herefords and Polled Angus, with Herefords substantially preferred. Much of the breeding stock entering Canada after 1880 was destined for the United States, and of the cattle a very large proportion consisted of these breeds. Of 6,100 cattle which entered Canada through quarantine in the five-year period 1880-4, 2,650 were Herefords and 1,550 were Polled Angus; 68 per cent of the total were comprised in the two breeds.[69] Holstein, Galloway, and Shorthorn made up practically all the remainder. Nearly two-thirds of all the cattle were billed for the United States. Most of the remaining third went to breeders in Ontario and Quebec, though already specific shipments went to the North West Territories.[70] The cost involved is suggested by Mc-Eachran's estimate that the 323 Polled Angus cattle imported into Canada in 1882 cost "at a low average $400 each."[71]

Federal assistance to the livestock industry in eastern Canada resolved itself into assistance to the commerce in livestock. This commerce was fostered for its own profitable sake, and also because it stimulated migration of labour and capital to Canada. Inspection and quarantine were essential to the survival of the live cattle trade with Britain, and agriculture in the eastern provinces benefited indirectly in the maintenance of a profitable market and in the governmental guardianship over the health of farmers' herds. Shortly after Confederation there appeared the prospect that western Canada might share in the development of the range-cattle industry then moving northward through the United States. The interest of the federal government in any western prospect was certain, for the federal government was constituted largely on the basis of western prospects. Lacking any knowledge of the grazing industry, designers of Confederation in the central and Maritime provinces thought of agriculture and settlement on the western plains in terms of what

[69]Reports of the Minister of Agriculture, Canada, *Sessional Papers,* annually; reports of McEachran as Chief Inspector of Livestock.

[70]In 1881, 136 imported cattle went to the North West Territories; in 1882, twenty-three—both shipments consigned to the Cochrane Ranch, Bow River, the project of Cochrane and McEachran. All cattle were Polled Angus.

[71]Report of the Minister of Agriculture, Canada, *Sessional Papers,* 1883, no. 14, p. 248.

they did know—wheat-growing, and stall-fed livestock. So much the better if other forms of agriculture should prove adaptable to the plains, if wheat and stall-fed cattle could be supplemented by other agricultural products.

In 1866 cattle were first wintered out on the northern ranges of the United States. Horses and cattle were brought to the Canadian foothills in 1870 and 1871, but were not turned loose on the open range.[72] Cattle, if turned loose at that time would have been swallowed up by buffalo herds, or would have been slaughtered by Indians or whiskey traders. Prerequisite to the development of the open-range industry[73] were the establishment of a minimum of law and order, starting with the suppression of the Missouri River whiskey traders, the elimination of the buffalo, and the limitation of Indian claims. The establishment of the North West Mounted Police in 1873 assured the first condition; buffalo disappeared late in the eighteen-seventies; and in 1877 the Blackfoot Indians accepted a treaty limiting their claims and confining them to reservations. In 1877 Fred Kanouse turned one bull and twenty-one cows loose on the open range and has been considered the originator of western Canadian ranching.[74] In 1879 the Dominion government brought a thousand head of breeding stock into the Canadian West from Montana to serve as foundation stock to provide meat supplies for the Indians.[75]

Land regulations necessarily took cognizance of the special requirements of the grazing industry. The first Dominion Lands Act, 1872, authorized grazing leases to bona fide settlers.[76] An act

[72]For the history of the Canadian ranching industry see Booth, "Ranching in the Prairie Provinces" in Murchie et al., Agricultural Progress on the Prairie Frontier, pp. 51-66; Craig, Ranching with Lords and Commons; Kelly, Range Men; MacInnes, In the Shadow of the Rockies; Macoun, Manitoba and the Great North-West; Rutherford, Cattle Trade of Western Canada; Stock, Ranching in the Canadian West; Stock, Confessions of a Tenderfoot; Trotter, Horseman and the West. See also articles, Burton, "Early Development of Cattle Ranching in Alberta" (Economic Annalist, June, 1941); Vrooman, "History of Ranching in British Columbia" (ibid., April, 1941).

[73]The open-range industry involves the raising of stock by pasturing on natural grasses, unenclosed by fences, and without winter feeding.

[74]MacInnes, In the Shadow of the Rockies, p. 194.

[75]Booth, "Ranching in the Prairie Provinces," p. 54.

[76]Morton and Martin, History of Prairie Settlement and "Dominion Lands" Policy, pp. 438-43.

of 1876 (39 Vic., c. 19) authorized grazing leases subject to cancellation on two years' notice where the land might be required for agricultural settlement. An Order-in-Council of 1881 limited these leases to 100,000 acres for twenty-one years, the rental to be one cent per acre and the lessee to stock the range with one head of cattle for every ten acres—much in excess of the grazing capacity of the areas involved.[77] In 1886 and 1887 rentals were increased to two cents per acre; then provision was made that the leaseholds be put up for public tender. At the same time stocking requirements were cut in half, so that one head was required for every twenty acres instead of for every ten. More suggestive of newer trends was the 1887 provision that grazing leaseholds should be terminable for homestead or preemption at any time instead of after two years' notice. With the completion of the Canadian Pacific Railway the great desire was for agricultural settlement, and it was taken for granted that nothing should be allowed to interfere with that object.

Not till after 1900 was any stand taken on the question of excluding the settler from lands obviously or with reasonable certainty suitable only for grazing operations. Railways and eastern interests generally saw surer prospects for abundant traffic and consumption in agricultural settlement than they did in large-scale cattle grazing. By the turn of the century, and especially shortly after 1900, immigration had become so substantial that there was agitation from land seekers to have grazing leases restricted. Ranchers with tens of thousands of acres of leasehold granted at $20.00 per thousand acres for long periods of years were pictured as wealthy and avaricious cattle kings who barred the way to the creation by home-building settlers of a populous and thriving countryside.[78] In spite of pressure of this sort, Sifton, on the point of retiring from the Department of the Interior in 1905, projected the policy of closed grazing leases. That is, in areas declared by the Inspector of Ranches to be unsuited for other agricultural purposes, grazing leases were to be granted without fear that homestead entry might require their cancellation. In other areas open leases survived (i.e., leases subject to termination on two years' notice). Land classification was still given no real weight in directing land utilization.

[77]Burton, "Early Development of Cattle Ranching in Alberta."
[78]Dafoe, *Clifford Sifton*, pp. 312 ff.

Under public pressure whatever elements of exclusiveness attached to the closed lease policy had to be abandoned.[79]

7. Federal Livestock Policy Since 1900

Activities of the federal Department of Agriculture for the encouragement of the livestock industry have assumed increasing complexity since 1900. Yet there is underlying simplicity throughout. Measures introduced and maintained by the federal government bearing on the livestock industry have been commercial-agricultural. Assistance has been given towards the improvement of livestock in order to contribute to farm prosperity and to expand the export trade. Much attention has been paid to the quality of the livestock population. Examples of federal assistance in the improvement of breeding stock are the bull-loaning policy of 1912, the free-freight policy of 1917 for female breeding stock, the sire purchase plan of 1920, and the encouragement given over the years to boys' and girls' stock clubs of various kinds. More distinctly stressing the commercial interest in agriculture are the federal government's hog-grading, and meat inspection and grading programmes, and its attention to stockyard supervision and to market news services. Serious efforts have finally been directed towards the control of bovine tuberculosis in line with the increasing realization of its threat to human health.

B. THE DAIRY INDUSTRY

8. Development of the Canadian Butter and Cheese Industry

Towards the turn of the century the federal government began to interest itself in the dairy industry, and its concern over other aspects of the livestock industry declined relatively if not absolutely. The two principal branches of the dairy processing industry, butter- and cheese-making, have been conducted both on the farm and in factories. Factory production is a comparatively new development in each case, with this difference, that the cheese factory has practically ended the manufacture of cheese on the farm, while the butter factory (commonly called a creamery) has by no means ended the farm manufacture of butter. Dairy butter, that made on the farm, continues to be produced and sold, along with creamery butter. Factory manufacture of cheese in Canada preceded that of butter

[79]*Ibid.*, p. 314.

and became widely established much more quickly. The cheese factory was developed in New York State around 1850 and the first one to be established in Canada was set up in Oxford County, Ontario, in 1864, by a native of New York.[80] So rapid was the spread of cheese factories that by 1867 there were estimated to be 235 in Ontario.[81] Ingersoll, Belleville, and Brockville became widely known as centres of the Ontario cheese industry. The first Canadian creameries were established in the Province of Quebec in 1873 and 1874.[82]

Substantial commerce in Canadian cheese developed only with the development of the factory system. Canadian cheese exports reached a peak of 234,000,000 pounds in the year ending June 30, 1904, with total production approximating 250,000,000 pounds.[83] Since then production has been below half this figure in particular years. Trade in butter, on the other hand, did not await the factory system, nor rely solely on it once it was established. Local trade in butter was an early accompaniment of pioneer development, butter frequently serving as a mainstay in farm purchasing power. Butter was a standard element in the provisions trade. With the expansion of the livestock industry in Ontario after 1840, and with the opening of American markets by railway construction and by reciprocity, butter was one of the products increasingly exported. Britain came to be a substantial market. In the year ending June 30, 1868, Canadian butter exports totalled 10,650,000 pounds; in 1872, 19,000,000; they averaged over 15,000,000 for the next ten years; from 1883 to 1896 they varied from 1.8 million to 8.1 million pounds, as increasing quantities of milk were diverted to cheese manufacture.[84] Before 1897 Canadian butter exports were practically all of farm dairy production. With the establishment of refrigeration on Montreal-United Kingdom vessels in 1897, there was a marked increase in butter exports, particularly of the creamery product, till the record export of 1903 was 34,130,000 pounds.[85] With refrigeration, export interest shifted somewhat from cheese back to butter.

[80]Innis, *Dairy Industry in Canada*, pp. 45-6.

[81]*Ibid.*, p. 47.

[82]*Ibid.*, p. 37.

[83]*Ibid.*, p. 64.

[84]*Ibid.*, p. 42.

[85]*Ibid.*

9. *The Problem of Quality*

Quality was the serious problem in the butter trade. Prior to the establishment of refrigeration facilities, it was difficult at certain seasons of the year to get any butter to market in satisfactory condition, no matter how well made it was to start with. Then, until around 1900, when creamery butter came to be important, there was the more basic fact that the original product, butter made in innumerable farm dairies, was of widely varying degrees of quality from the very start. Farmers' wives, the craftsmen of farm dairies, had wide varieties of skill and standards of cleanliness. Once the butter was made the assembly system was long and destructive of quality.[86] Farmers traded their butter to the country merchant, churning by churning, or at the end of the summer season if they could afford to do so. The merchant packed the butter into casks, sorting it carefully according to colour and quality if he was so inclined, or merely sorting it to put the best on top, if that happened to be his standard of business ethics. This store-packed butter was bought up by exporters' agents or was sent to commission houses in Toronto or Montreal. By the time it reached the consumer it was ordinarily in poor condition.

By Confederation the British market was important for Canadian butter, but there was increasingly keen competition on a quality basis from other countries, from the United States, Denmark, France, and Ireland. By 1879 these countries were making effective use of current experimental knowledge of refrigeration devices.[87] Wisconsin and Minnesota "ladle butter" was arriving in Britain in most attractive condition.[88] Mr. Dyke, the Canadian emigration agent in Britain who so vigorously concerned himself in promoting the Canadian cattle trade, was equally interested in Canadian butter. Canada could not meet the increasing competition in the British butter market, he stated,[89] unless a great improvement was made in her product. In his report to the Minister of Agriculture in 1879 he said:

Of equal, if not even greater importance to the trade in livestock, is the butter trade, which has been sorely neglected in the Dominion. It is admitted

---

[86]See Flavelle's statement (*ibid.*, pp. 34-6).

[87]Report of the Minister of Agriculture, Canada, *Sessional Papers,* 1879, no. 9, App. no. 34, p. 106.

[88]*Ibid.*, 1880, no. 10, App. no. 31, p. 136.

[89]*Ibid.*, 1879, pp. 106-7; 1880, p. 136.

by competent authorities that last year an amount fast approaching a million dollars was lost to Canada through the manufacture of inferior butter. The same tale has to be told again this year. The Canadian butter which has arrived here [Britain], with some few excellent exceptions, has been badly prepared and was unequal and stale in quality . . . the French and "bosh" manufactured butter have nearly driven the Canadian article out of the markets; large quantities of which have been sold for the commonest confectionery purposes, or simply for grease. . . . When it is considered that 13,659,949 pounds of butter were exported from the Dominion to Great Britain in 1877, and that our produce is annually getting into greater disfavour, whilst the price of the superior article is increasing at a corresponding ratio, it must be evident that the question becomes one of national importance.[90]

Dyke added that variation and uncertainty in quality constituted a major handicap for Canadian butter. Lack of refrigeration in Britain complicated the problem, but "little if anything is left to be desired in the means of transport in Canada, or by steamship; a special cheese and butter train provided with refrigerator and ventilating cars is run every Saturday during the season from Stratford, Ontario . . . on to the wharves at Montreal."[91] Vessels as yet were not refrigerated, but had special compartments for butter enabling it to be the last of the cargo loaded and the first unloaded. Dyke felt that "it should be made compulsory for all butter to undergo inspection before being offered for sale, and classed according to quality."[92]

Problems of western settlement and of the cattle trade engaged the exclusive attention of the federal Department of Agriculture at this time and for some years after. In 1889 the Canadian Dairymen's Association was formed, and, on the suggestion of the chairman of the House of Commons Agricultural Committee, a delegation presented its views before that Committee and requested of the Prime Minister a grant of $3,000 for the Association, and also the appointment of a dairy commissioner.[93] Professor James W. Robertson was appointed Dominion Dairy Commissioner beginning February, 1890, and following his enthusiastic guidance the Dominion Department of Agriculture undertook a considerable programme of assistance to the Canadian dairy industry. The essential problem under attack was that of quality, and so important was this factor in relation to the export market that agriculture and commerce had parallel interests in the matter.

90*Ibid.*, 1879, p. 106.   91*Ibid.*, p. 107.   92*Ibid.*, p. 106.
93Innis, *Dairy Industry in Canada*, pp. 98-9.

10. *Types of Aid to the Dairy Industry*

Federal activities concerning the dairy industry involved financial aid, experimentation, education, governmental operation of dairy facilities, and, finally, compulsory grading of butter and cheese destined for export markets. Robertson spent his first year as Dairy Commissioner in travelling throughout the country, addressing meetings and interviewing persons interested in dairying, and, in general, learning the important elements in the Canadian situation. Beyond that, the first step taken was directly into the operation of dairy facilities, the establishment and operation of the first two winter creameries in Canada. The idea was that if butter-making machinery were added to cheese factories, butter could be made from the cream secured between cheese-making seasons. The first two Canadian winter creameries thus opened, in Oxford County, were operated by the Dominion government for three winters. Others were added, but after the winter of 1894-5 the government left the projects in Ontario and Quebec to private enterprise.

The Dominion Dairy Branch also operated a number of dairy stations. In 1892 and 1893 one was operated at Kingsclear in New Brunswick, the purpose being educational. The government charged 3½ and 4½ cents per pound for making the butter in the two years, respectively. A cheese factory in New Brunswick was similarly operated for a short time. The first creamery in Nova Scotia, one established by private enterprise, was taken over by the Dairy Branch in 1893 and operated as a dairy station, producing both butter and cheese, until 1903. In the North West Territories, dairies at Moose Jaw, Indian Head, and Prince Albert were operated for a time as dairy stations. The financial arrangements involved in governmental operation varied according to circumstance. Some plants were established by government. Some were taken over for operation, with or without financial assistance towards building and equipment. The government charged so much per pound to cover operating costs. In 1901 farmers in Pictou County, Nova Scotia, had built and equipped a creamery. The provincial government gave financial assistance and the federal Dairy Branch took the plant over for operation on a commercial basis, so continuing until the end of 1910. In Prince Edward Island the first venture was where farmers had built a cheese factory and sought government aid. The Dominion government equipped the plant and agreed to operate it for a time

till local personnel might be trained. Other groups liked this arrangement, and eleven new cheese factories were established in 1893 on
the same basis. In 1895 twenty-eight cheese factories and two
creameries were operated in this way, after which year the Dominion
withdrew except for continuing supervision. In 1896-7 the Dominion
government formulated a plan for the assistance of dairying in the
North West Territories, where all nine creameries were in difficulties.
The government proposed that all dairies already established or to be
established should receive loans to cover the cost of equipment, that
they should be operated by the Dairy Branch charging 4 cents per
pound for making butter, and that one additional cent per pound
should go towards the repayment of the loans. Seven new creameries
were started in the Territories under this plan, making a total of
sixteen so assisted. With the formation of the provincial governments of Saskatchewan and Alberta in 1905 the Dominion withdrew
from the dairy field within the area of these provinces.

Education was one of the basic ideas in the operation of
Dominion dairy stations. Persons with adequate knowledge of the
factory production of cheese and butter were not common and the
dairy stations served as demonstration institutions or as places of
practical instruction. The Dairy Branch also conducted dairy schools
in various places, offering short courses chiefly for cheese and butter
makers. Bulletins were prepared and distributed. For the western
provinces and territories a "travelling dairy" was used for demonstration purposes. The travelling dairy was sent to Manitoba in
1894 with J. A. Ruddick in charge. It consisted of a churn, a butter-
worker, a cream separator, and a Babcock milk tester, and the
demonstration involved the use of these instruments accompanied by
explanatory talks. The cream separator and the Babcock milk tester
were recent developments at that time and were new to practically
all westerners. The same year another travelling dairy covered
points in Saskatchewan and Alberta. In 1895 the four western
provinces were visited, and in 1896 British Columbia alone.

The extension of factory production for butter and cheese, and
the education of operators for creameries and cheese factories, struck
at the basic cause of Canadian difficulties concerning the quality of
dairy produce. Butter and cheese made in factories could be fairly
uniform in quality provided operators were skilful and conscientious,
though close uniformity awaited federal inspection which came years

later. Good quality in production, however, was not enough, for transportation to Britain and storage at the various marketing stages were long and trying processes, quite sufficient under ordinary conditions to reduce the best of butter and even cheese to barely marketable articles. Part of the problem in the British market after 1870 was the comparative one, that Canada's competitors were adopting refrigerating techniques and were moving far ahead of Canada on a competitive basis. The commercial-agricultural situation concerning Canadian dairy products in the eighteen-nineties was that unless refrigerating devices could be applied to marketing channels, and even to production stages, the Canadian product would be forced out of the export market.

The Dominion Dairy Branch was given supervision over the federal refrigeration-promotion scheme. Plans and specifications for small cold-storage plants were prepared and distributed. In 1896 the government offered $100 to any creamery that would construct an air-circulating cold-storage room according to government specifications. This offer continued until 1931, when nearly all creameries in Canada had qualified for the bonus. Rail transportation to Montreal was the first stage in the long trip to the British market, and much damage was done through lack of refrigeration on local trains. The Dairy Commissioner arranged with the railways for regular ice-car service, at first fortnightly and later weekly, over stated routes to Montreal. Eight routes were opened in 1895 and a few years later sixty cars ran on a weekly schedule. The government guaranteed earnings on the basis of a minimum carload from the starting point on each route and paid a fixed sum towards the cost of icing. The service has been continued since, though on a gradually reduced scale with the development of the motor truck.

By the middle eighteen-nineties there were cold-storage facilities at Montreal wharves, but none on Montreal-to-Britain vessels. In 1895 the federal government constructed ice-cooled and insulated compartments in six steamers running between Montreal and British ports, and in 1896 fitted four more in similar fashion, the purpose being to secure weekly refrigerated service over this route. In 1897 the government offered to pay half the cost of equipping steamers with refrigeration equipment, up to $10,000 per vessel, and in a few years thirty-four vessels were so equipped. In 1900 federal cargo inspectors were appointed for specific Canadian and British ports to supervise the loading and unloading of perishable products in refrigerated compartments.

In 1907 the federal government further attacked the problem of local cold storage by providing[94] for a subsidy up to 30 per cent of the approved cost of new warehouses equipped with mechanical refrigeration, "in places where no cold storage warehouses already exist." Notable installations under this act include the New Brunswick Cold Storage at Saint John, 1908; the fish-freezing warehouse at Prince Rupert, 1909; and the Island Cold Storage at Charlottetown, 1910. In 1920 the Nova Scotia Public Fish and Cold Storage at Halifax, and the Pacific Coast Terminals at New Westminster qualified under the act. By 1937 fifty-nine establishments providing 10,000,000 cubic feet of refrigerated space had received subsidies under the Cold Storage Act.

11. *Summary*

Assistance to the livestock trade was the earliest activity undertaken by the federal government in aid of Canadian agriculture. It was, however, assistance designed to facilitate the commerce in, rather than the production of, cattle. The live cattle trade with Britain was instituted and sponsored as a means of encouraging the migration of tenant farmers and farm labourers to Canada. The trade developed rapidly after the middle eighteen-seventies, and its success aroused British agrarian opposition symbolized by the passage of the imperial Richmond Bill aimed at the exclusion of foreign cattle. Canadian herds would have to continue free from the "bovine scourges," rinderpest, foot and mouth disease, and pleuro-pneumonia, and all cattle shipped from Canada to Britain would have to arrive in good shape, or scheduling would be applied under the Richmond Act. To secure freedom from these and other diseases the Canadian government instituted and maintained cattle quarantine and inspection. The job was effectively performed. Scheduling came in 1892, but the evidence concerning justification therefor is confused. The interest of the federal government in the range-cattle industry involved the importation of breeding stock, the establishment of the Royal North West Mounted Police and their administration of western cattle quarantine, and an hesitant adaptation of land policy.

[94]The Cold Storage Act, *Statutes of Canada*, 6-7 Edw. VII, c. 6 (1907), amended by 8-9 Edw. VII, c. 8 (1909).

During the latter part of the nineteenth century Canadian production of butter and cheese increased markedly on the basis of export prospects. Quality, however, was a major problem particularly in regard to butter, the Canadian product being quite unable to compete with that of Wisconsin and Minnesota, or of Denmark, France, and Ireland. Following the appointment of a Dairy Commissioner in 1890 the federal government entered upon a varied programme of assistance to the Canadian dairy industry. This programme included financial aid, experimentation, education, government operation of dairy facilities, grading—first voluntary and eventually compulsory—of butter and cheese destined for export markets, and the subsidization of refrigeration equipment in warehouses, steamers, and in producers' establishments. The programme involved assistance to the dairy industry from coast to coast. Under its varied attack the quality problem was greatly meliorated.

CHAPTER IX

THE PRODUCTION AND MARKETING OF WHEAT

A. EXPERIMENTAL FARMS

THE experimental farm idea had a long and confused evolution in British North America, but a national emergency was necessary to force its acceptance as essential to the Canadian economy. The emergency was the realization that after nearly twenty years the western territories were not serving their "national" purposes; they were not attracting the great droves of immigrants which, it had been anticipated, would create anew the moving frontier of economic activity so necessary for the support of the developmental overhead already incurred by government, and for the prosperity of commercial, financial, and industrial centres of the Dominion. Much had been done to make it possible for the West to serve its purposes. Territories had been acquired and administrative agencies provided; ungranted lands had been retained by the central government, and the homestead system established; and, finally, a thoroughgoing programme of immigration promotion with cash transportation aids had been followed by the Dominion government.

1. *The Uncertain Western Prospect*

Immigration to Canada had shown promise within a few years of Confederation. In 1873 the Minister of Agriculture reported that "The increase in the number of settlers in Canada appears contemporaneous with the remarkable increase of the prosperity of the Dominion since Confederation."[1] But the slump in annual immigration returns which occurred immediately after this period was not overcome until the early eighteen-eighties when figures for 1882, 1883, and 1884 exceeded 100,000 yearly. In 1885 and 1886 the totals collapsed again. More disturbing, however, was the situation regarding western migration and settlement. From a figure for western migration of a few hundred in 1870 the entries to the West were estimated by the Minister of Agriculture to be 18,000 in 1880, 22,600 in 1881, 57,500 in 1882, and 50,000 in 1883, but the corresponding

[1]Report of the Minister of Agriculture, Canada, *Sessional Papers*, 1873, no. 26, p. 6.

estimate for 1884 was 24,000 and that for 1885 only 7,740.[2] There was some reassurance in the fact that the North West disturbances of 1885 occurred just at the booking season, and so undoubtedly contributed to the collapse of immigration for that year, but there was no similar means of rationalizing the slump in 1883 and 1884. Railway-building had accounted for much of the western boom in the early eighteen-eighties, but railway-building could not be continued merely to provide jobs for potential settlers. Settlers continued to pour into Australia and the United States. Was the whole project of Canadian colonization on the prairies, with all its significance for the commerce, finance, and industry of the central provinces, to fail entirely?

What proof was there that the Canadian West could perform its agricultural-commercial function? Could it produce an agricultural staple in adequate quantities? George Brown and the *Toronto Globe* had ferreted out and publicized all available success stories from both sides of the western Canadian-American boundary. John Macoun had outlined the isothermal theory.[3] Simpson and other officials of the Hudson's Bay Company had denied that the West possessed agricultural possibilities,[4] but their evidence had long since been discounted as emanating from prejudiced and purposeful Cassandras. But in the early eighteen-eighties the evidence was not reassuring. The seventy years' life of the Red River Settlement was not long enough to disprove the evidence of the Hudson's Bay Company officials. Confederation had not moderated the natural crop hazards of the West. Grasshoppers had damaged the Manitoba crops of 1873 and 1874 and had destroyed that of 1875.[5] Relief extended by the Department of Agriculture to the extent of $60,000 was all that averted starvation in many cases.[6] The year 1876 was unusually rainy, and this condition prevailed more or less until 1880.

[2]See Annual Reports of the Minister of Agriculture, Canada, *Sessional Papers*.

[3]Macoun, *Manitoba and the Great North-West*, chaps. IX and X.

[4]Minutes of Evidence, Report of the Select Committee on the Hudson's Bay Company, *British Parliamentary Papers*, 1857, as cited in Mackintosh, *Prairie Settlement*, pp. 28-30.

[5]Morton and Martin, *History of Prairie Settlement and "Dominion Lands" Policy*, p. 57. Report of the Minister of Agriculture, Canada, *Sessional Papers*, 1876, no. 8, App. 9, p. 50.

[6]*Ibid.*

The Gimli settlement of Icelanders on Lake Winnipeg had fences and barns swept away by flood and were determined to move in 1881. Three hundred out of seven hundred families of Mennonites moved from an eastern Manitoba settlement which had become much too wet for cultivation, to a settlement farther west.[7] Quickly the cycle turned and 1883 was a year of "abject failure" because of drought.[8] In 1884 the spring was late and there were frosts in the West.[9] In 1885 the crops were destroyed by frost on August 23.[10] In 1886 there was general drought.

2. The Gigault Committee

The immediate impetus to the establishment of the experimental farm system was the Gigault select-committee report of 1884. Early in the 1884 session at Ottawa, George A. Gigault, Conservative and completely undistinguished member for Rouville, Quebec, voiced discontent over the government's agricultural policies.[11] Speaking in French, and derisively, he moved for copies of all petitions to the Minister of Agriculture asking for prizes for the best essays, and treatises on agricultural industry, and for the circulation of pamphlets and essays.[12] Referring to a French report of 1876 he outlined briefly the experience of France, Germany, Austria, Scotland, and the United States with agricultural academies, experimental and model farms, with agricultural colleges and agricultural boards, and urged that the Dominion government should come to the aid of the provinces in their effort to propagate agricultural knowledge. Auguste Landry (Conservative, Montmagny) supported Gigault and argued that farmers would prefer to receive publications on agricultural matters rather than the reports on trips to the North-West, such as those of the Scottish delegates who saw nothing till they passed the western boundary of Quebec.[13]

[7]*Ibid.*, 1880-1, no. 12, p. 57.

[8]Morton and Martin, *History of Prairie Settlement,* p. 83.

[9]Report of the Minister of Agriculture, Canada, *Sessional Papers,* 1885, no. 8, pp. 45-6, 53-4, 64.

[10]Morton and Martin, *History of Prairie Settlement,* p. 83.

[11]Canada, *House of Commons Debates,* 1884, pp. 33-5.

[12]Sir Hector Langevin, answering for the Minister of Agriculture, said that these, if any, would be tabled, though "he [Gigault] is under the impression there are none" (*ibid.,* p. 35).

[13]Landry stated that the observations of these delegates concerning Quebec had been limited to the remarks of one man who had noted that in rural

A week after Gigault had made his first tentative protest on agricultural matters, he moved "that a Select Committee be appointed to enquire into the best means of encouraging and developing the agricultural· industries of Canada."[14] Replying to Edward Blake who wanted to know the purpose of the proposed committee, "whether it is in the direction of improving and developing the tariff, or in the way of protecting and developing the agricultural industries," Gigault said that it was mainly intended to learn what parts of the experience of foreign countries might well be adapted to the improvement of Canadian conditions. Especially apt seemed the American experience where in 1860 a Board of Agriculture was organized and a commissioner of agriculture appointed, and "a garden or experimental farm is also attached to the Department of Agriculture in Washington."[15] Mr. Foster (Liberal-Conservative, King's, N.B.) seconded Gigault's motion, reasoning that:

> Not only is it [agriculture] a very impoftant interest, but it is more nearly related in the way of supplying a stimulus to all other industries of Canada, than perhaps any other one we might mention. The Dominion of Canada has expended a great deal of money and a great deal of energy in developing those very great interests—the shipping interest, the interest of railways and canals, and the manufacturing interests of the country; and yet it is not too much to say that all these different interests have as their object, and look towards, the development of the agricultural interests of the country as a source of supply and feeder for the trade and traffic which shall pass over them and be carried by them.[16]

Foster's statement is as clear an expression as is available of the functional justification for agricultural assistance. A committee, he argued in effect, should enquire into agricultural improvement because it was the task of agriculture to render profitable the government-sponsored extensions in transportation and manufacturing enterprise. Yet the committee as named by Gigault was not designed to consider the commercial aspects of agriculture, its membership assuring rather that agricultural improvement should be considered in terms of a relatively self-sufficient agricultural community. Five of the ten members of the committee represented Quebec constituencies; six of them were farmers; two of them were

---

Quebec the churches were larger than the houses, and who, at first glance, had mistaken the stumps for inhabitants (*ibid.*).

[14]*Ibid.*, p. 74.   [15]*Ibid.*   [16]*Ibid.*

members of the Quebec Council of Agriculture and presidents of agricultural societies, and a third was president of the Quebec Council of Agriculture.[17] The Quebec membership predominated, the French influence was strong, and much of the work of the committee was carried on with reference to agricultural reports from France introduced by the French-Canadian chairman, Gigault.

The Quebec influence was significant. The experimental farm idea was not new in Canada, and in no province had it a longer currency than in Quebec. As late as 1884 Canadian historical experiments with anything of the nature of an experimental farm could be counted on the fingers of one hand, but no single instrument of agricultural reform had been more often urged in the various Canadian provinces, throughout the preceding decades. Private petitioners, agricultural societies and agricultural boards, parliamentary committees and commissions had long advocated the establishment of farms by the respective provincial governments. Terminology here is confusing and indicates that the advocates of governmental farms had no clear idea of what possible functions might be performed. Names which were used interchangeably included the following: experimental farm, model farm, illustration farm, pattern farm, livestock farm, farm schools, school farms, and agricultural schools. Frequently two or more of these terms appeared synonymously in a single public document.

Terminology on this point may be well sorted out at the present time, but it was not, as late as 1885, when the Canadian "experimental farm" system was being created, and since this confusion of terminology represents confusion of thought on a functional basis, a word of clarification is in order. If the terms listed in the preceding paragraph mean anything, they suggest four distinct functions which might be performed by governmental farms: (1) the experimental function, where the purpose is to establish new frontiers of knowledge in agricultural techniques; (2) the demonstration or illustration function, where the purpose is to demonstrate established knowledge to the farming community; (3) the educational function, which is distinct from the experimental or research function, and may even be conducted without demonstration, though the idea of a "farm school" is that demonstration may

[17]For list of members see *ibid.;* for biography see Gemmill (ed.), *Canadian Parliamentary Companion,* 1885.

be an integral part of education; and (4) the breeding-farm function. Regarding the latter function, governmental stock farms might serve either the experimental, the demonstration, or the educational function, or various combinations of the three; but as advocated and tried in Canada prior to 1886 they had other functions primarily. They were used to improve the quality of livestock in the frontier communities by transferring improved breeds from older communities, rather than by conducting experimental breeding and feeding in the local environment.[18] They either maintained improved sires for breeding on a fee basis, or maintained male and female animals to multiply breeding stock for the farming community. The fact that such farms were called "model farms," "experimental farms," or "model stock farms" gives no clue regarding their purpose.

Special committees, particularly in Lower Canada, casting about for remedies for agricultural distress following the Napoleonic Wars, stressed the need for publicly-supported experimentation after the model provided by the British Board of Agriculture and its secretary, Arthur Young.[19] From then until 1886 similar advocacy recurred constantly. Despite this fact, however, governmental farms were few. Two or three abortive attempts were made to stimulate hemp-growing near Quebec between 1800 and 1810 by means of experimental or "demonstration" farms.[20] In 1852 the Board of Agriculture of Upper Canada started an "experimental" or "illustrative" farm on ground provided by the Senate of the University of Toronto, the intention being that it be operated in connection with the chair of Agriculture at the University; but within three years the venture had proved a failure.[21] In the Maritimes there was

[18]To the extent, of course, that many breeds were imported, and some were found better adapted to local conditions than others, the governmental stock farm might be said to be engaged in experimental work.

[19]See, for example, the Report of the Committee to Enquire into the State of Agriculture in this Province, Lower Canada Assembly, *Journal*, 1816, App. E; Report of the Special Committee to Enquire into the State of Agriculture, *ibid.*, 1817, p. 628; Report of the Special Committee on the Petitions of the Montreal and Quebec Agricultural Societies, *ibid.*, 1818, p. 82.

[20]Gorham, "Development of Agricultural Administration in Upper and Lower Canada." In these efforts the Colonial Office took the initiative and contributed financially.

[21]See *Journal and Transactions of the Board of Agriculture of Upper Canada*, vol. I, *passim*. The Act of 1850 which created the Upper Canada Board of Agriculture (13 and 14 Vic., c. 73) provided in part that it should be "the

much agitation for governmental livestock farms, as part of the
drive towards improved animal husbandry around the middle of the
nineteenth century.[22] By Confederation, Prince Edward Island had
such a farm, with several years of experience in its operation; the
Nova Scotian Legislature had passed an act[23] authorizing the establishment of one, and had voted $8,000 towards this purpose; and
New Brunswick agricultural interests were pressing hard for similar
legislation. In 1881 New Brunswick placed thirty cattle, forty sheep,
and six hogs on a farm as the beginnings of a governmental
project.[24] Experience in the Province of Quebec had centred around
agricultural schools as far back as the School of Saint-Joachim,
1670-1715, organized by Bishop Laval in connection with the Semi-
nary of Quebec.[25] By 1884 fourteen specific agricultural schools
had been projected in Quebec, eight had existed for periods of time
varying from six months to forty-five years, and in 1884 three were
in operation, those of Ste. Anne de la Pocatière, L'Assomption, and
Richmond.[26] The Ontario Agricultural College, organized in 1873,
was of considerable importance to the Gigault committee as the
single noteworthy example of an agricultural enterprise conducted
by a Canadian government.

---

duty of the said Board to prepare as soon as practicable, and present to the
Legislature, a plan for establishing an experimental or illustrative farm in
connection with the Chair of Agriculture in the University of Toronto, or in
connection with the Normal School, or otherwise, as they may deem best."
Simultaneously the Senate of the University of Toronto, establishing a Chair
of Agriculture, provided grounds for an experimental farm to be "placed
under the control of, and supported by, the Board of Agriculture" (*ibid.*, p.
246).

[22]After 1854 Alexander Forrester, Superintendent of Education under
the newly-created Nova Scotian Normal School system, tried hard to get into
operation an "experimental garden and farm" to be used for demonstrating
the practical features of agricultural chemistry to normal-school students. He
secured one hundred acres of land and some buildings in connection with the
Normal School at Truro, but made little progress in developing the property
as a farm. See the annual reports of the Superintendent of Education, Nova
Scotia Assembly, *Journal and Proceedings*, pp. 1856 ff.

[23]*Statutes of Nova Scotia*, 29 Vic., c. 22 (1866).

[24]See Report of the Gigault Committee, Canada House of Commons,
Journal, 1884, App. no. 6, p. 30.

[25]Chapais, *Notes historiques sur les écoles d'agriculture dans Québec.*

[26]*Ibid.*

Mr. Gigault had the possibility of an experimental farm in mind when he moved the appointment of the agricultural committee in 1884.[27] The committee examined fourteen witnesses and submitted a questionnaire to 1,500 agriculturists named by members of the House. By the time four hundred replies were in and the report[28] was being compiled, the committee had concluded that the establishment of an experimental farm, or farms, was the one vital consideration in the agricultural situation. This conclusion was in conformity with a large proportion of the answers to their questionnaires,[29] and was in line with European and American experience. The sole recommendation of the committee was, "That the Government take into earnest and favorable consideration the advisability of establishing a Bureau of Agriculture, and an Experimental Farm in connection therewith . . . in connection with and under the supervision of the present Department of Agriculture."[30]

3. Government Reception of the Gigault Report

The government showed no hesitation in implementing the Gigault recommendation. When, within two weeks of the tabling of the report, Mr. Gigault asked if the government proposed to effect

[27]Speaking of the United States he said, "A garden or experimental farm is also attached to the Department of Agriculture at Washington. . . . It will be the business of this Committee to enquire into the possibility, on the part of the Department of Agriculture in Ottawa, to adopt in part the system followed by Washington" (Canada, *House of Commons Debates*, 1884, p. 74). The Ontario Agricultural Commission, 1880-1, had heard representations favouring "experimental agricultural stations . . . thoroughly practical in their character," but had observed non-committally: "The time may come when these views will receive endorsation from the government and people of the country. They are now merely presented as the suggestions of able and competent men, who are known to take the warmest interest in the subject of agricultural education" (Ontario Agricultural Commission, *Report of the Commissioners*, 3rd edn.: Toronto, 1881, pp. 532-3).

[28]Report of the Gigault Committee, Canada House of Commons, *Journal*, 1884, App. no. 6.

[29]"The question of the establishment of an experimental farm being, in the estimation of the Committee, one of great importance, they have carefully endeavoured, as far as time would permit, to ascertain to what extent such institutions are employed in other countries and how their operations are regarded. In our own country public sentiment appears to be very strongly in favour of the establishment of an experimental farm with branches" (*ibid.*, p. 7).

[30]*Ibid.*, p. 26.

the recommendation regarding a board of agriculture and an experimental farm, Sir Hector Langevin replied that the government had not yet decided "although we have been informed that the report, with the evidence taken, is a valuable one," and that it would be considered during the recess.[31] Early in the 1885 session, a similar query from Gigault drew the reply from Sir John A. Macdonald that the matter was engaging the attention of the government and that they hoped to bring down a measure on the subject during the session.[32] The estimates when introduced contained an item of $20,000 "For the establishment of a Model Farm," and Macdonald himself explained briefly the government's plan, in response to a few desultory comments by less than half a dozen members.[33] Sir Richard Cartwright and Edward Blake thought that the members should hear the plan. The closest approach to a protest came from Mr. Trow who felt that "If the government are to undertake to purchase Berkshire Pigs and Shropshires and Downs, it seems to me it will be travelling out of the record."[34] Early in November the Minister of Agriculture, John Carling of London, Ontario, instructed Professor William Saunders, F.R.S.C.,[35] also of London, to visit as many of the more important agricultural colleges and experimental farms in the United States and Canada as necessary to determine their benefits for agriculture, and to facilitate the establishment of

[31]Canada, *House of Commons Debates,* 1884, p. 1387.

[32]*Ibid.,* 1885, p. 76.

[33]*Ibid.,* p. 3453. See also the Revenue Act, 48-49 Vic., c. 41 (1885). The same year the Dominion government spent $370,000 on immigration and quarantine.

[34]Canada, *House of Commons Debates,* 1885, p. 3453.

[35]William Saunders, 1836-1914, came to Canada from Devonshire when twelve years old. He had little schooling, but taking employment in a pharmacy in London, Ontario, he started in business for himself when eighteen years old. He founded the Ontario School of Pharmacy and was appointed Professor of Materia Medica in the Medical School of the new university at London, Ontario. Meanwhile for health's sake he bought a seventy-acre farm, planted it with fruit trees, and set about improving the varieties by selection and cross breeding. He founded and became president of the Ontario Entomological Society and was president of the Ontario Fruit Growers' Association. In 1883 he published a book on insects injurious to fruits, a work recognized as a standard authority for many years. He became a Fellow of the Royal Society of Canada, and its president in 1906. He was an active member of the American Association for the Advancement of Science. See *Fifty Years of Progress on the Dominion Experimental Farms,* pp. 29-30.

the experimental farm projected by the Gigault report and by the financial vote of 1885.[36] When the "Experimental Farm Stations" Bill[37] was under consideration in the 1886 session the main suggestions of the half-dozen members who commented upon it were: that the Minister of Agriculture should be more specific regarding details of the proposal, that there was something to be said for extending aid to provincial institutions rather than inaugurating a Dominion scheme, and that, in any case, branch farms might be made unnecessary by reliance on co-operative and intelligent farmers for the conduct of supervised experiments.[38]

The government was willing and anxious to effect the Gigault recommendation for a variety of reasons. In the first place, it appeared that the cost would be small. The vote of 1885 was for $20,000, though there was no suggestion that that sum would cover the total outlay.[39] By 1886 Mr. Carling estimated that $240,000 would establish and equip the central farm and the four branch farms proposed by the act, and that the annual cost would not exceed $30,000 or $35,000.[40] Secondly, the Gigault recommendation was essentially a farmers' recommendation, and the farmers of the central and Maritime provinces were doubtful about their share in the new era proclaimed by the National Policy.[41] It was desirable to acquiesce in a specific farmers' request of minor significance in order easily to allay suspicion. Third, and finally, there was the problem of the North-West.

The agricultural problems of the North-West were not the first consideration of the advocates of the Canadian experimental farm system, but they were part of the picture. In the early eighteeneighties there was no clear idea among easterners that wheat would one day be the exclusive western staple, but there was general agreement that whatever the agricultural development of the West there

36See Report of Professor William Saunders to the Minister of Agriculture on the Agricultural Colleges and Experimental Farms of the United States, in Report of the Minister of Agriculture, Canada, *Sessional Papers,* 1886, no. 10, App. no. 54, pp. 211-90.

37Passed as An Act Respecting Experimental Farm Stations, *Statutes of Canada,* 49 Vic., c. 23 (1886).

38Canada, *House of Commons Debates,* 1886, pp. 1146-53.

39*Ibid.,* 1885, p. 3453.

40*Ibid.,* 1886, p. 1146.

41*Ibid ,* 1884, pp. 1003, 1006-9.

would have to be an accompanying development of trees and shrubs suitable to the prairie areas. At the time of the Gigault committee, then, there was much talk of experimentation to learn the kinds of trees which might eventually provide lumber, firewood, shelter, and fruits for western farms. Grasses and cereals for western needs were discussed from the same point of view, but no position of peculiar prominence was given to wheat. Before the Gigault committee, John Lowe, Secretary of the Department of Agriculture at Ottawa, agreed that Canadian agriculture would benefit from the establishment of an entomological department, "and [from] the testing of grains, and the testing of trees, and the adapting of fruit trees to the North-West."[42] When the Minister of Agriculture commissioned Saunders to travel through the United States and learn something of their experimental and educational work concerning agriculture, he mentioned "tree planting in the Western States" as one of the several fields of enquiry.[43] Saunders's plan for the experimental farm system (the plan closely followed by the Dominion government in establishing the system) called for tree-planting reservations in the North West Territories, in addition to the experimental farm projected for that area.[44]

Evident through the deliberations was a note of urgency regarding the West and its agricultural problems. Asked by the Gigault committee whether the Manitoba government was not doing something to solve western difficulties, Lowe replied: "There is nothing being done, and the farmers are too busy to do it. I think these are questions of vast magnitude to the North-West, especially in view of the very large expenditures which are taking place there, the very large numbers of people who are going in, and the still larger numbers that might be attracted to that almost illimitable territory."[45] Saunders proposed the establishment of a central experimental farm at Ottawa and four others, adding, "it is important that the organization of the central station should be begun without delay; also a station in the North-West,"[46] while the others, he thought might be

[42]Report of the Gigault Committee, p. 108.

[43]Saunders Report to the Minister of Agriculture, Report of the Minister of Agriculture, Canada, *Sessional Papers*, 1886, no. 10, p. 211.

[44]*Ibid.*, p. 269.

[45]Report of the Gigault Committee, p. 108.

[46]Saunders Report, p. 271.

added as soon as practicable. It was his opinion that "there is no question that could we obtain for our vast wheat fields in the North-West earlier ripening varieties of good quality the area of wheat culture would be extended, and the benefits resulting difficult to over-estimate. Other field crops could, in all probability, in like manner, be extended."[47] Defending the Experimental Farm Stations Bill in 1886, Carling, Minister of Agriculture, said: "with the exception of Ontario, there are none [agricultural schools and farms] of any importance in the Provinces. In Manitoba there are none, and honourable gentlemen will agree with me that it is very important we should make experiments in the North-West, so that parties going there will have no difficulty in ascertaining what is the best kind of seed to be used, and the best kind of trees and the stock best fitted to stand the climate. To make all these experiments and give the new-comer, and those who desire to become settlers, such valuable information would be advantageous."[48] Sydney Fisher thought that experimental farms could serve both east and west, the latter by discovering trees suitable for wind-breaks and fuel; and, he added, "Another [service] of great importance to the North-West is the discovery of a kind of wheat which will ripen there without any danger of frost."[49]

4. Saunders's Plan for Experimental Farms

Saunders's report to the government, following his tour of American experimental stations and agricultural colleges, outlined the system of experimental farms which was constituted by legis-lation in the 1886 session.[50] Until his plan was adopted, however, the nature of the new enterprise was quite uncertain. The Gigault committee were concise in their recommendation of an "experimental farm," but there was the long tradition in British North America of confusion over the functions to be performed by a governmental farm. There was also the European and American tradition of combined educational and experimental establishments. In Quebec the government-aided farm schools, and in Ontario the recently established Ontario Agricultural College, combined experimental,

---

[47]Ibid., p. 273.
[48]Canada, House of Commons Debates, 1886, p. 1147.
[49]Ibid., p. 1153.
[50]Statutes of Canada, 49 Vic., c. 23 (1886).

educational, and illustrative activities. As late as 1885, while defending a second $20,000 appropriation for the proposed system, whatever its details might be, Sir John Macdonald argued that the money "cannot be better spent than by having a first rate model farm."[51] But he also contemplated "pupil students." His statement, in part, indicates his idea:

> We intend to have a model farm; we will obtain teachers, and the farm is intended to be worked by the pupils. Those pupils will be self-sustaining. The hon. gentleman [Edward Blake] knows there are a great number of young men who are anxious to be educated as farmers, and who pay considerable fees to private teachers at this moment, in various portions of the country. There are gentlemen agriculturists who give handsome fees to be taught farming. No doubt a Government farm, conducted on scientific principles, with competent teachers and a sufficient area to employ students, will be well attended, and the pupils will pay a reasonable amount for their education. There is a very successful model farm conducted by Major Strickland, in Peterboro' district; he has a large number of pupils, and receives very handsome fees.[52]

There is no suggestion here of the experimental function. Edward Blake paraphrased the government's plan as follows: "Besides being a model farm and an exemplar to the farmers, provided by a paternal Government, it is also to be a college of more or less ample character, a school in which to teach the young the art of farming. If that is part of the work of the model farm, and it is not necessarily a part of a model farm at all, we are going into a scheme of an agricultural college."[53] Still no mention of experimentation, but a sharp distinction between the illustrative and the educational functions.

Saunders's plan, as embodied in the Experimental Farm Stations Act, designed an institution specifically and exclusively for experimentation. The structure was to comprise one central station at or near Ottawa, to serve Ontario and Quebec, and one sub-station each for the Maritimes, Manitoba, the North West Territories, and British Columbia. The suggestion regarding prairie farms conformed to the recommendations of Dr. George M. Dawson, Assistant Director of the Geological and Natural History Survey of Canada. In a letter to Saunders, Dawson outlined the experimental problems awaiting solution in the West and indicated that two or more farms would be necessary, one on the Red River plain and one near the

[51]Canada, *House of Commons Debates*, 1885, p. 3453.
[52]*Ibid.*   [53]*Ibid.*

Qu'Appelle valley. He warned that neither farm should be in the valley. All five farms, or stations, were to conduct "research and experiment."

Saunders's advice was that the educational function should be left for later consideration. The size of the outlay should be related to potential benefits, he argued, and certain needs were more urgent than others. He said:

From the facts . . . regarding the expenditure connected with agricultural education in teaching colleges in America, added to the necessary cost of equipping the various institutions, it is evident that the outlay is very large in proportion to the number of persons directly benefitted. Further, it has been shown that agricultural experimental stations have been of very great service in supplying much needed information and stimulating progress in agriculture wherever they have been established, and that these good results have been and are being brought about at comparatively small cost. In Canada agriculture may be said to lie at the foundation of the nation's prosperity . . . but since any very large outlay at the commencement might be injudicious, it would perhaps be better to consider first the most pressing needs, and provide for them as soon as practicable, leaving the important subject of agricultural education in colleges for future consideration.[54]

Saunders outlined the financial aspects of the Ontario Agricultural College, but without comment.

William Saunders was appointed Director of the proposed Dominion experimental farm system and proceeded immediately to effect his plan. Acreage for the central farm was secured near Ottawa in 1886 and clearing commenced. Locations for the branch farms were investigated. The first department opened at Ottawa was a seed-testing laboratory where farmers could have seed grains tested for germination qualities.

5. The Search for Earlier-Maturing Wheat: Marquis

The earliest research problem of any significance which Saunders attacked was that of securing earlier ripening wheats for the prairies, in order that western crops might avoid the common devastation of early frosts. The first approach was to import seed from areas judged to be similar to western Canada in climatic conditions. Certain regions in Russia had attracted attention from this standpoint for a number of years. Saunders linked the problem with the prospect in the following words: "For many years past the importance of obtaining the earliest ripening varieties of grain which the

[54]Saunders Report, p. 268.

world could furnish for test in the Canadian North-West, had impressed itself on the minds of many of those who took an interest in that country. In 1882 when the late Charles Gibb, of Abbotsford, Quebec, visited Russia in company with Professor J. S. Budd, of Iowa, for the purpose of inquiring into the character and hardiness of the fruits grown in the northern parts of the country, he made enquiries also regarding the early ripening varieties of wheat to be found there."[55] In an earlier statement Saunders stated that "Wheat was sought from Northern Russia with the hope of obtaining a hard wheat of good quality, equal if possible to the Red Fife, so much esteemed, with an earlier ripening habit, so as to lessen the loss which early frost sometimes entails on the vast wheat crops of Manitoba and the North-West Territories."[56]

Russia was mentioned in the deliberations surrounding the creation of the experimental farm system. Saunders referred to Russian researches in his report to the Minister of Agriculture, 1886, stating that "Recent researches in Russia, lately published in St. Petersburgh, demonstrate the fact that wheat grown in the northern provinces of that empire ripens in less time than that grown in the southern, the difference being about sixteen days." Speaking on the experimental farm bill Sydney Fisher indicated the importance for the Canadian North-West of "the discovery of a kind of wheat which will ripen there without any danger from frost." Regarding sources, he added, "There is no doubt that in certain parts of Russia such wheats have been found."[57] Saunders talked with Mr. Gibb after the latter's return from Russia and "as soon as the experimental farm system was inaugurated, early in the winter of 1886, under instruction of Hon. John Carling, Minister of Agriculture, correspondence was opened with a noted seed dealer in Riga, Russia, Mr. E. Goegginger, who had made a special study of Russian cereals."[58]

By the time the experimental farm system was inaugurated Red Fife wheat had replaced other varieties on the prairies, after a circuitous migration from Ontario down the Ohio, into Minnesota,

[55]*Experimental Farm Bulletin*, no. 18, February 24, 1893.
[56]*Ibid.*, no. 2, December 15, 1887.
[57]Canada, *House of Commons Debates*, 1886, p. 1153.
[58]*Experimental Farm Bulletin*, no. 3, March 15, 1888.

and back to Canadian territory.[59]   Saunders imported varieties of wheat from widely separated areas and tested them alongside Red Fife on the various experimental farms.   The imported varieties came from far northern Russia, from northern Europe, from the United States, from Australia, from various altitudes in the Himalayas, and from Japan.[60]   Some varieties took longer to mature than Red Fife, some gave poorer yields, some were quite unsuitable for milling and baking.   One variety, Ladoga, secured from the Riga seed merchant, appeared most promising for a number of years. Ladoga was a hard red spring wheat, grown near Lake Ladoga, by latitude six hundred miles north of Winnipeg.   On an average over the various farms and over a period of several years it matured ten days earlier than Red Fife, and yielded well.[61]   By 1892 a carload of this wheat was finally secured, from near Prince Albert, for milling and baking tests in Toronto.   These tests discredited Ladoga as a competitor of Red Fife, for its flour was weak and its bread yellow and coarse.[62]

While Saunders was attempting to secure by selection a variety of foreign wheat to equal Red Fife in yield and milling qualities, and to surpass it in early maturity, he was seeking similar results by means of cross-breeding, by means of combining varieties so as to unite their desirable qualities.   Saunders was experienced in this process from his activities among the fruit trees on his farm at London, Ontario.[63]   He began his crosses at the Ottawa farm in 1888.[64]   Marquis wheat resulted from cross-breeding on the experimental farms.   Since the experimental farm system, and Saunders's name, are more closely associated in the minds of westerners with the discovery of Marquis wheat than with any other single contribution, the steps in this discovery, and its significance, merit consideration.

[59]Morton and Martin, *History of Prairie Settlement*, p. 70.

[60]Buller, *Essays on Wheat*, p. 146.   In 1889, seventeen varieties of wheat were sown at the Brandon experimental farm (Morton and Martin, *History of Prairie Settlement*, p. 71).

[61]Buller, *Essays on Wheat*, p. 146.

[62]*Experimental Farm Bulletin*, no. 18, Feb. 24, 1893.

[63]*Fifty Years Progress on Dominion Experimental Farms*, p. 29.

[64]Buller, *Essays on Wheat*, p. 148.

Red Fife wheat was used in many of the crosses on the experimental farms, because of its admirable qualities. In 1892 Dr. A. P. Saunders, son of the Director, was sent to western farms to conduct cereal crosses.[65] He visited the farms at Brandon, Indian Head, and Agassiz, B.C., and grains resulting from the crosses which he made were sent to Ottawa for selection. For a decade the new varieties, more or less mixed, were grown and regrown at Ottawa, the Director too involved in general duties to undertake the painstaking task of careful selection. In 1903 his son Dr. Charles E. Saunders was appointed Cerealist for the Dominion government, and set to work on the mass of material and data awaiting selection and classification. In 1904 he selected, or "discovered," Marquis wheat.

The records indicated that the original cross was of male Red Fife on female Hard Red Calcutta, made by Dr. A. P. Saunders in 1892. Whether the cross was made at Brandon, Indian Head, or Agassiz is uncertain, but Dr. Charles Saunders considered Agassiz as most likely.[66] Marquis was one of a mixture of types handed on to the new Cerealist as the result of the original cross a decade earlier, and was selected and propagated for comparison with other types over a number of years. Maturity period and yield were qualities to be established in the test plot. Milling and baking qualities were tested by chewing a few kernels, the colour and elasticity of the flour thus being roughly indicated. Marquis wheat appeared hopeful on all counts. By the fall of 1906 there was enough Marquis wheat to permit proper milling and baking tests in model equipment which Saunders had developed, and again the results were encouraging. In 1907, twenty-three pounds of Marquis were planted at the Indian Head farm; in 1908 quantities were planted at Indian Head and Brandon; in 1909 four hundred samples were distributed to farmers widely scattered throughout the Prairie Provinces. By 1911 or 1912 Marquis wheat was available for all who wished to buy it.

It is not part of the present analysis to attempt a measurement of the contribution which Marquis wheat has made towards agricultural, or general, welfare. Its rapid general adoption throughout the Canadian and American West indicate superiority over competing varieties. It, however, contributed little to the conquest of the

65*Ibid.*   66*Ibid.*, p. 152 n.

West, for it was not available until the end of the period of phenomenal western settlement. Nor did it contribute greatly to the solution of the problem which first prompted its search. The first major problem of the Dominion experimental farm system was to secure earlier maturing wheats for the West so that the devastation of early frost might be avoided. But the frost problem was particularly acute in the areas where wheat was grown in the post-Confederation years; that is, in southern Manitoba and in strips and patches north-westerly throughout the Park Belt. The settlement after 1900 was essentially that of Palliser's "triangle," the prairie areas proper; and here the prime problem was not of frost but of drought. Marquis ripened as much as a week earlier than Red Fife,[67] but was not strikingly more drought-resistant. Had Marquis wheat been developed in 1870 instead of forty years later, it would have hastened western settlement only slightly. Had Marquis wheat not been discovered at all, the pattern of western settlement would have been only slightly affected.

6. Significance of Summer-Fallow

The Dominion experimental farm system contributed more significantly to prairie settlement through the popularization of summer-fallowing than through the discovery of Marquis wheat. Summer-fallowing on the plains meant moisture conservation rather than soil restoration. Its capabilities towards this end were reputedly developed by the Mormons in Utah, had spread to the north-western wheat states, contiguous to the Canadian boundary, and were known in western Canada at practically the time of the establishment of the experimental farm system.[68] Among the earliest tests on western experimental farms were those designed to prove the merits of summer-fallowing. Angus Mackay, director of the Indian Head Farm, was convinced of its value from the very first years. In his 1889 report he said:

> Our seasons point to only one way in which we can in all years expect to reap something. It is quite within the bounds of probabilities that some other and perhaps more successful method may be found, but at present I submit that fallowing the land is the best preparation to insure a crop. Fallowing land in this country is not required for the purpose of renovating it, as is the

---

[67]Morton and Martin, *History of Prairie Settlement*, p. 148.
[68]*Ibid.*, p. 85.

case with worn out lands in the east, and it is a question yet unsettled how much or how little the fallows should be worked, but as we have only one wet season during the year,'it is found beyond doubt that the land must be ploughed for the first time before this wet season is over, if we expect to reap a crop the following year.[69]

Because summer-fallowing had traditionally been an instrument for the rejuvenation of failing lands, and because western lands were new and fertile, settlers were not quickly persuaded of the necessity of this somewhat cumbersome cultural practice. Mackay made of its popularization something of a mission. His reports repeated the experimental proof, and on speaking tours and at conversational opportunity he insistently put forward the case as it appeared to him. By the turn of the century, when the tide of substantial immigration was setting towards western Canada, the necessity for summer-fallowing on the semi-arid plains, the region still available for settlement, was generally accepted. American settlers, coming from semi-arid plains to the south, were already familiar with the dry-farming techniques, but for other newcomers the influence of the Indian Head experimental farm was directly and indirectly important.

By the early nineteen-hundreds, then, a decade before Marquis wheat became generally known, the experimental farm system had made its great contribution to the agricultural purposes of the Dominion. It had become clear that wheat was the western staple, that beyond southern Manitoba frost was a minor problem, that drought was the real handicap on the plains, that summer-fallow was a substantial answer to that handicap, and that there was no need to seek for a better variety of wheat for the plains than Red Fife—granted the adoption of summer-fallowing practice. Momentum carried the experimental farm system on to the discovery of Marquis. But already there was the feeling that the system had accomplished its major purpose, that the problem originally set before it was disposed of, and that new problems would have to be found if the system was not to stagnate.

7. The Changing Environment

The search for new problems has induced persistent expansion of the experimental farm system based on the principle that agricultural problems must be studied in their geographic locus. The

69Canada, *Sessional Papers*, 1890, no. 6C, p. 133.

first increases in the experimental farms after the original system was created, were made after 1905. In the years from 1906 to 1911 new stations[70] were established at Lethbridge to specialize in irrigation problems; at Lacombe, a mixed farming area; at Rosthern, Scott, Charlottetown, and Cap Rouge; and a sub-station on the geographic frontier, at-Fort Vermilion in northern Alberta.[71] In 1912 the search for new problems led to the establishment of five sub-stations in northern Alberta and the North West Territories.[72] Other stations pushing into new agricultural areas include those started at La Ferme in northern Quebec, and at Kapuskasing in the northern Ontario clay belt, in 1914; at Normandin in the Lake St. John region of northern Quebec, superseding the farm at La Ferme in 1935; at Melfort, Saskatchewan, in 1935; and sub-station work in the Yukon Territory. Stations and sub-stations have been established in older regions from time to time for the study of new problems or of old problems newly appearing important. The system of illustration stations was started in 1915 as an educational device.

The question has been raised at times whether or not the Dominion government should give up the experimental farm system and leave it to the respective provinces.[73] This is too big a question for argument here, but one or two points may be noted. So far as the Prairie Provinces are concerned the experimental farm system was designed to enable prairie lands to fulfil "the purposes of the Dominion." Prairie lands were retained by the Dominion for these purposes, and the experimental farm system was logically and necessarily administered by the Dominion with the same objects in view. Experimental farms contributed to the grand strategy of Confederation by facilitating the settlement of the West; and this they did by the popularization of the dry-farming technique of summer-fallowing, and to a lesser extent by the discovery of Marquis wheat. By 1900 summer-fallow was generally accepted and by 1910 Marquis wheat was plentiful. If the original purposes of the

[70]The original five units in the system have always been called "farms," while new units of comparable size are called "stations."

[71]*Fifty Years Progress on Dominion Experimental Farms*, p. 22.

[72]*Ibid.*, p. 23.

[73]See, for example, the *Report of the Royal Commission on Dominion-Provincial Relations*, Book II, pp. 175-6.

Dominion in establishing the experimental farm system required continued federal supervision beyond 1900, that requirement was certainly gone by 1910. In any event, the system might well have been turned over to the provinces in 1930, along with what was left of the natural resources.

The restoration of the natural resources to the western provinces in 1930 marked the completion of the original design for western Canada. It recorded the realization that western agriculture had served its original purposes in the national economy, that the great period of capital creation on the prairies was at an end, and that in future the frontier dynamic would have to be sought elsewhere. Meanwhile it was well known where this new dynamic was gathering, in the pulp and paper and mineral areas of the Precambrian Shield, chiefly in Ontario and Quebec. It was a development clearly strengthening already strong provinces and weakening the federal government. Since 1850, even since 1830, the dynamic of the Canadian economy had been sought in immigration and agricultural settlement. The federal government was created as an agency for stimulating and directing these vital forces. From the day of its organization in 1852, the Department of Agriculture—first of the Province of Canada and, after 1867, of the Dominion of Canada —was working at the very heart of this task. The Department of Agriculture and the Department of the Interior were the administrative core of federal vitality dealing as they were with immigration and agricultural settlement. This was before 1930, more particularly before 1914. In 1935 the Director of the experimental farm system was charged temporarily with the administration of the Prairie Farm Rehabilitation Act.[74] This suggests the reversal in federal interest in the prairie economy. Federal concern in the West now is with conservation instead of expansion, with salvage instead of with further capital expansion. If the federal Department of Agriculture and the federal government generally are reduced to the activity of assuring the conservation of relatively static areas within the Canadian economy, to the interpretation and administration of interregional equity, it follows that they will be less significant and less powerful vis-à-vis the provinces than ·they were when administering western expansion.

[74]Under *Statutes of Canada*, 25-26 Geo. V, c. 23.

B. GRAIN TRADE REGULATION

8. Evolution of Canadian Grain Trade Regulation to 1900

In the regulation of the Canadian grain trade it is possible to see a considerable degree of unity of interest between commerce and agriculture. The Canada Grain Act[75] is regarded as an effective legal instrument of control over a commerce of great volume, of great domestic and substantial international importance. The act has evolved gradually over the decades since Confederation, the controls becoming more specific and more exacting, amendment by amendment. Organized farmers' protests, and federal and provincial royal commissions have been constant companions of the amendment process. It is customary to interpret the evolution of Canadian grain trade regulation largely as a response to the political pressure of the western farm group. It is proposed here to analyse this interpretation briefly as it relates to government policy towards Canadian agriculture.

Details of the evolution of Canadian grain-trade regulation have been carefully recorded in a number of studies,[76] and only main points require to be set down here. Earliest federal regulation of grain marketing was provided for as a matter of course in the early years of Confederation when the Dominion government was gradually moulding a legislative structure to conform to the British North America Act. In 1873 a general inspection act[77] gathered together the pre-Confederation inspection legislation of various provinces, particularly that of the Province of Canada, and modified it to suit the new constitutional situation. This act provided for the repeal of a score of provincial inspection acts. It specifically related to the following "Staple Articles of Canadian Produce": flour and meal; wheat and other grains; beef and pork; pot ashes

[75]*Statutes of Canada,* 2 Geo. V, c. 27.

[76]Particularly MacGibbon, "Grain Legislation Affecting Western Canada" (*Journal of Political Economy,* March, 1912); *Canadian Grain Trade;* Mackintosh, *Agricultural Cooperation in Western Canada;* Patton, *Grain Growers' Cooperation in Western Canada;* Swanson and Armstrong, *Wheat;* Wood, *History of Farmers' Movements in Canada.*

[77]*Statutes of Canada,* 36 Vic., c. 49 (1873), An Act to amend and consolidate, and to extend to the whole Dominion of Canada, the Laws respecting the Inspection of certain Staple Articles of Canadian produce. Chief reference was back to a provincial act, *Statutes of Canada,* 26 Vic., c. 3 (1863).

and pearlashes; pickled fish and fish-oil; butter; leather and raw hides; and petroleum. In general it empowered the government to define inspection divisions and appoint inspectors for each product or group of products listed, the inspectors having first satisfied boards of examiners appointed by boards of trade in each of nine specified eastern cities, and by the government in other localities. Grades were established for the various commodities, grades for wheat including half a dozen each for winter wheat and spring wheat, and several for corn, oats, rye, and barley.

The 1874 revision[78] of the 1873 inspection act was unimportant so far as concerns wheat and grains. The grain trade was still exclusively an eastern affair, and winter wheat still preceded spring wheat in importance. The revision of 1885,[79] on the other hand, was especially concerned with the grades of wheat, and gave ample recognition of the beginnings of a western trade. Spring wheat was now dealt with before winter wheat and five of the fifteen spring wheat grades referred specifically to "red Fife wheat grown in Manitoba or the North-West Territories of Canada." The first three grades listed were "extra Manitoba hard wheat," "No. 1 Manitoba hard wheat," and "No. 2 Manitoba hard wheat." Standard samples to serve as a basis for inspection, however, were to be selected annually in Toronto by representatives of the boards of examiners of specified boards of trade. Of the ten boards of trade specified, two were western, those of Port Arthur and of Winnipeg, and the standards were to be chosen and approved by a majority vote.[80]

The regular movement of wheat eastward from western Canada by rail and lake, through Winnipeg and Port Arthur, began in the fall of 1883.[81] In 1886 federal grain inspection was instituted at Winnipeg. In the same year, the general inspection legislation, incorporating the wheat grades outlined in 1885, was embodied in the

[78]*Statutes of Canada*, 37 Vic., c. 45. The impression that this was the first general inspection act passed by the federal government is apparently in error. See MacGibbon, "Grain Legislation Affecting Western Canada," p. 224; Patton, *Grain Growers' Cooperation in Western Canada*, p. 27.

[79]*Statutes of Canada*, 48-49 Vic., c. 66.

[80]*Ibid.*, s. 12.

[81]Sellers, "Early History of the Handling and Transportation of Grain in the District of Thunder Bay" (Thunder Bay Historical Society, *Reports of Officers and Papers of 1909-1910*), pp. 21-7.

Revised Statutes as the General Inspection Act.[82]   Wheat was still just one of the Canadian staples, and its trade and commerce was regulated by the federal government as a matter of course according to the provisions of the British North America Act.

Further differentiation of the western from the eastern grain trade resulted from pressures from western boards of trade, particularly that of Winnipeg.[83]   Following petitions of western grain-trade men, separate standards boards were established in 1889 for the creation of inspection samples for eastern and western grain, respectively, with Port Arthur set as the dividing point.[84]   In 1891 the General Inspection Act was further amended[85] to provide for "commercial" grades; that is, grades to be established by board of trade examiners in cases where "a considerable proportion of the crop" could not be fitted into the statutory grades. Here again the amendment was sought by western boards of trade.[86]   In the same year it was provided by law[87] that grain inspectors might be appointed official weighers within their respective inspection divisions "upon petition from any board of trade within such division."   In 1899 the Winnipeg Grain and Produce Exchange submitted resolutions to the House, among them one that "all grains in Manitoba and the Northwest Territories passing Winnipeg or Fort William or south or east thereof be inspected at Winnipeg and housed at Fort William or other eastern elevator on Winnipeg inspection."[88] Parliament complied by creating the inspection district of Manitoba,

[82]*Revised Statutes of Canada,* 1886, c. 99.

[83]MacGibbon, "Grain Legislation Affecting Western Canada," pp. 224 ff.; Canada, *House of Commons Debates,* 1891, pp. 4299-4307.

[84]*Statutes of Canada,* 52 Vic., c. 16.

[85]*Ibid.,* 54-55 Vic., c. 48.

[86]Canada, *House of Commons Debates,* 1891, pp. 4299-4307. The Hon. Mr. Costigan, Minister of Inland Revenue, sponsoring the bill said that "the boards of trade in all the towns and cities of the North-West desire it." Also, he said, "This bill is entirely in the interest of the agriculturists, and against unscrupulous buyers." He became greatly annoyed when Mr. Landerkin said, "I should like to ask the Minister if they [western farmers] have petitioned in its favour. Farmers understand their business, and if the Bill is in favour of their interests, petitions will have been sent in its favour. Boards of trade do not usually look after the interests of the farmers as much as people imagine" (*ibid.,* pp. 4304, 4306).

[87]*Statutes of Canada,* 54-55 Vic., c. 47.

[88]MacGibbon, "Grain Legislation Affecting Western Canada," p. 226.

defined to include Manitoba, the North West Territories, and Ontario as far east as the head of the Lakes.[89]

So far, the regulations enacted concerning the inspection and marketing of western grain were purely a matter of commercial convenience, and the various modifications were made at the request of boards of trade. Farmers were, of course, interested in questions of grades and inspection, of weights and weighers. Agricultural and commercial interests have harmonized from time to time throughout Canadian history, even from the short-run viewpoint, which commonly serves as the basis for practical governmental policy. Western grain growers could have no quarrel with the establishment of separate grades for western wheat, with the creation of a western grain standards board, or of the Manitoba inspection district. Doubtless they favoured these moves in the interests of western autonomy.

9. *Farmers' Attack on Monopoly Issue*

By 1900, however, western farmers had marketing worries more fundamental than those which western boards of trade had attacked. The outstanding western problem of the day involved the supply of physical facilities for local storage and for the transportation of grain to terminal markets, and concerned the Canadian Pacific Railway and the line elevator companies. "Standard" elevators had been built along the railway under concessions amounting, so far as farmers could see, to monopoly grants. Specifically, where such elevators existed the C.P.R. refused to permit car loading except through the elevators. Farmers had the doubtful alternative of shipping by way of the standard elevator or of selling to a street buyer. They were convinced that in many cases the monopoly position meant lower prices, lower grades, excess dockage, and in certain cases dishonest weight. It seemed clear that some way must be found to permit alternative shipping channels. In some way, they reasoned, the monopoly must be broken.

The successful attack made by western growers upon the monopoly position which existed in local grain markets around 1900 marks the beginning of a quarter of a century during which these growers possessed considerable political power even in the federal field. They secured and retained this power during this period

[89]*Statutes of Canada*, 62-63 Vic., c. 25.

because for the time being they were important to the purposes of the Dominion. The West was finally justifying the expectations which had surrounded it since pre-Confederation days. Settlers were pouring in and farms were being established; villages, towns, and cities were springing up; and the whole process was accompanied by investment on a scale hitherto undreamed of in Canada. Grain-trade regulation, more and more rigid, even to the point where restrictions favouring farmers were irksome to trade and transportation companies, was a small price to pay in comparison to the stakes involved. Besides, the restrictions were upon a trade which was primarily western and, for the most part, upon western traders; and eastern groups—even merchants and financiers—felt themselves as yet more akin to western farmers than they did to western merchants.

The details of the western farmers' political struggle after 1900 have been told often.[90] They need no repetition here. They began in 1898 when James Douglas, member for East Assiniboia, introduced a bill into the federal Parliament "to regulate the shipping of grain by railway companies in Manitoba and the North-West Territories." The main purpose of the bill was to provide farmers with the legal right to load cars through flat warehouses or over loading platforms, and thus to break the monopoly conditions described above existing in local markets. The bill did not survive the committee, but was re-introduced with additions in the following session. The original introduction of the bill was sufficient to cause the C.P.R. to offer cars for platform loading in 1898; it led to the appointment of the first federal royal commission on western grain marketing, with three Manitoba farmer members under an eastern judge; this led in turn to the passage of the Manitoba Grain Act of 1900[91] which placed the western trade under a warehouse commissioner, in this and other respects following with adaptations the usage under the Railroad and Warehouse Commission Act of Minnesota.

[90]E.g., Boyd, *New Breaking;* Mackintosh, *Agricultural Cooperation in Western Canada;* Moorhouse, *Deep Furrows;* Patton, *Grain Growers' Cooperation in Western Canada;* Wood, *History of Farmers' Movements in Canada.*

[91]*Statutes of Canada,* 63-64 Vic., c. 39. Patton states: "The Manitoba Grain Act was hailed by western grain growers as a veritable agrarian Magna Charta" (*Grain Growers' Cooperation in Western Canada,* p. 30). The first Warehouse Commissioner, C. C. Castle, was one of the farmer members of the 1899 Royal Commission.

In broad outline the significant elements shaping grain-trade regulations after 1900 comprised farmers' organization and farmers' demands, governmental investigation, and legislative amendment. Effective farmers' organization in the West stemmed from the Territorial Grain Growers' Association formed in 1901, and evolved by way of the Grain Growers' Grain Company—a terminal commission agency—to co-operative elevator companies operating lines of local and substantial terminal facilities, and finally to the organization of the pools. Farmers' demands concerned the whole range of relationships between farmers and other community groups, relating so far as grain was concerned chiefly to closer supervision of the trade, abolition of mixing in terminal elevators, government operation of local and terminal elevators, and the closing of the Winnipeg Grain Exchange. Federal investigations into grain-marketing conditions were conducted by House committees, and by royal commissions appointed in 1899, 1906, 1923, 1931, and 1937.[92] Amendment of grain-trade legislation took place from year to year but occurred in most sweeping form in the passage of the Canada Grain Act in 1912[93] which consolidated the Manitoba Grain Act and the Manitoba Inspection Act in modified form.

10. Tests of Agrarian Political Power

The passage of the Canada Grain Act of 1912 followed the agrarian "Siege of Ottawa" of December, 1910, and the defeat of the Liberals at the polls on the reciprocity platform in 1911.[94] Borden had declared in election speeches in the West that he was flatly opposed to reciprocity with the United States but that if elected he would grant the farmers' requests concerning grain marketing. He had also promised a measure of federal assistance to the provinces for agricultural education.[95] The Canada Grain Act of 1912 and the Agricultural Instruction Act of 1913[96] mark the high point

---

[92]A royal commission was appointed in 1920 but was halted by an injunction sought by the United Grain Growers and upheld by the Supreme Court of Canada.

[93]Statutes of Canada, 2 Geo. V, c. 27.

[94]For a brief treatment of the tariff issue see Chapter x, below.

[95]See Gettys, Administration of Canadian Conditional Grants, chap. ii; also Maxwell, Federal Subsidies to the Provincial Governments in Canada, chap. xv.

[96]Statutes of Canada, 3-4 Geo. V, c. 5 (1913). In 1912 the preliminary Agricultural Aid Act (2 Geo. V, c. 3) was passed and under it $500,000 was

in the political importance of the western farmer up to that time. The Grain Act provided comparatively rigid regulation of the grain trade, but nationalization of terminal elevators was not secured. The Agricultural Instruction Act with its $10,000,000 grant to the provinces over a ten-year period was but slight compensation to western farmers for the rejection of their demands for reciprocity with the United States.

The next real test of the political strength of western agriculture came in 1920 and succeeding years over the question of the re-establishment of the Wheat Board. Growers had opposed its establishment in 1919, but in the light of its monetary yield and of the collapse of prices following its demise, there grew a determination among western farmers for its re-establishment. Since the Winnipeg Grain Exchange had been closed during the operation of the Board, the growers were newly convinced that the Board should again operate and that the Exchange should not. Thus the political issue was sharply drawn between the farmer and the "grain trade." Joined with the grain trade were the milling interests and eastern consumers generally.[97] That western agriculture was in a position to exercise national power was witnessed by the elections of 1921 which swept out the Conservatives and seated Progressives for thirty-eight of the forty-two Prairie Province seats. This power was evident in legislation in 1922 purporting to permit the creation of a wheat-marketing agency with practically all the powers of the 1919-20 Wheat Board, the legislation to become effective "as soon as two or more of the provinces have conferred upon this agency such powers possessed by the Board of 1919 as come within provincial jurisdiction."[98] The Wheat Board was not reconstituted, despite prompt permissive action on the part of the Saskatchewan and Alberta legislatures, because it was declared to be "impossible to secure a Board combining all necessary elements of experience, ability and public confidence."[99]

---

appropriated for one year to be paid to the provinces for the benefit of agriculture.

[97]Patton, *Grain Growers' Cooperation in Western Canada*, p. 198.

[98]As cited *ibid.*, p. 203.

[99]Statement by the Premiers of Saskatchewan and Alberta, June 22, 1923, as cited *ibid.*, pp. 208-9.

Whether the high-water mark of agrarian success concerning grain-trade regulation occurred in 1912 or in 1921 is a matter of opinion, and of little consequence. More significant is the probability that the decade bounded by these years represents the high point of agrarian political strength in Canadian history. This is not necessarily to say that this decade marks the peak of agricultural assistance by the Canadian government. Western agricultural expansion was essential to the national economy, as it had been since pre-Confederation days, but from 1900 onwards this expansion occurred and continued with little encouragement except in the way of railway construction. Relatively, at least, much more assistance had been rendered in efforts to secure this expansion in the fruitless decades before 1900. After 1900 the western farmers' case for assistance was weakened by the fact that there was nothing the farmers could do either individually or collectively to prevent the West from growing and continuing to grow beyond all previous expectations. By the end of the nineteen-twenties, in contrast, nothing could be done to maintain western expansion at any positive rate, let alone at a rate paralleling that of newsprint and mineral production.

Agrarian pressure secured the passage of the Canada Grain Act of 1912 and, a decade later, secured legislation permissive of the re-establishment of a wheat board. The Canada Grain Act provided for rigorous governmental supervision of the Canadian grain trade. Even so, important items among the farmers' demands were rejected, particularly those relating to the nationalization of the elevator system, the separation of terminal operation from grain merchandising activities, and the prevention of mixing in terminal elevators. Reciprocity with the United States was not achieved, as demanded by the western delegation in 1910. The Winnipeg Grain Exchange remained open. After 1920 merchant interests could not prevent the passage of legislation permitting the re-establishment of a wheat board, but they were able to prevent such legislation from being used. The Campbell amendment to the Grain Act, restoring the grower's right to designate the terminal to which his grain should be sent, passed in 1926 despite strenuous grain-trade opposition, and is proof that western farmers were not without political power as late as the later nineteen-twenties. During the nineteen-thirties western agriculture received financial assistance totalling many millions of dollars, but the claims of agriculture in the national economy had come to rely on the appeal to equity. By the late nineteen-thirties western leaders were reduced to arguing the case for agriculture on the plea of maintaining the *status quo*.

11. *Summary*

The agricultural prospects of the Canadian West were uncertain at the time of Confederation and remained so for a generation. There was required the demonstration that the West could support some staple production. What this product might be was not known, but Red River and American experience pointed tentatively to wheat. The proposal for a federal experimental farm system was accepted by the Dominion government as a measure whereby it might demonstrate some interest in agricultural problems in the various parts of the country, the West included, incurring only limited costs, and at the same time divert attention from consideration of the agricultural implications of the National Policy of tariffs recently imposed. Dr. William Saunders, instrumental in developing the plan for Canadian experimental farms, and first Director of the system, concentrated his chief energies on attempting to make agriculture feasible on the prairies. His first and most persistent activities concerned the search for earlier-maturing wheats, which would thus defeat the major western crop hazard—that of frost—and which would possess milling and baking qualities at least equal to those of Red Fife. Towards this end he imported samples of staple varieties grown in many foreign regions and tested their adaptability. At the same time he conducted experiments in cross-breeding to develop new varieties which might fulfil the requirements of the prairie regions. So far as concerns the development of the West, the importance of Marquis wheat, the internationally famous product of these experiments, has been over-estimated. A contribution made by the experimental farm system, of more significance to the establishment of the prairie wheat economy, lay in the popularization in the eighteen-nineties of the summer-fallowing technique of dry-farming, already well known in the United States. In fulfilling the latter task the experimental farm system facilitated the accomplishment of the "purposes of the Dominion" in the West.

The development of a western grain trade required specially adapted regulations. The Canada Grain Act has evolved over the decades as an instrument of comprehensive and rigorous control over a commerce of substantial proportions. Commercial agitation shaped the basic provisions out of which this act was developed. After 1900 agrarian protest, tempered by recurring royal commissions, contributed to the further elaboration of controls.

After 1900 the western Canadian farmer was more important to the Canadian economy than any Canadian farm group had previously been. From this fact there derived a degree of agrarian political power. The power was modified, however, by the fact that wheat growers, collectively as well as individually, could not withhold their contribution from the rest of the economy; there was no way in which they could "strike." Thus at the peak of their importance in Canadian history the farm group (here the western farm group) were able to dominate a federal election and to secure legislation enabling the re-establishment of a wheat board; they were at the same time unable to secure other measures which they sought such as the nationalization of the elevator system, the separation of terminal operation from grain-merchandising activities, the prevention of mixing in terminals, reciprocity with the United States, and the abolition of the Winnipeg Grain Exchange. They were powerful enough to secure the construction of the Hudson Bay Railway; they were impotent to assure its effective operation. After 1930 western farmers and Canadian agricultural groups generally were reduced to asking for relief instead of reform, and to asking for this aid on the basis of an appeal to equity.

CHAPTER X

CANADIAN TARIFF POLICY AND THE FARMER

1. *Introduction*

Error creeps into interpretation of Canadian agricultural policy through implicit reliance on one or the other of two extreme views: either that agriculture, on the one hand, and industry and commerce on the other, have no interests in common; or that their interests are fundamentally the same. The latter view has abstract validity considering the very long run; the former appears to be closer to the truth in day-to-day situations. Neither extreme view is helpful in understanding Canadian agricultural policy. If the preceding analysis has revealed any uniformity in such policy it is that non-agrarian interest in Canadian agriculture has been essential to a positive, not to say generous, agricultural policy, and that such interest has varied widely from time to time and from place to place.

Previous chapters have for the most part dealt with the positive side of the picture, with assistance extended to agriculture resulting from varying degrees of harmony between agrarian and non-agrarian interests. Consideration of Canadian tariff policy illuminates the negative side. It shows the Canadian farmer for the most part denied the artificial stimulus of protection on his own products, and subjected to the artificial handicap of protection on the products of others.

The farmer is inherently no more of a free trader than he is a protectionist. The history of the British Corn Laws reveals an effective agrarian devotion to protection in Britain for such a span of years as to dwarf by comparison the few decades of agrarian free-trade sentiment in Canada. History of the British North American colonies indicates that free-trade beliefs have not always characterized Canadian farmers.

Nor, on the other hand, are commercial and industrial groups uniformly protectionist. Britain abolished the Corn Laws and adopted substantial free trade in the mid-nineteenth century under pressure from the industrialists. Canadian industrialists uniformly desire free trade in the raw materials and parts required for their specific processes, and commercial groups have frequently been free traders. In fact, on the Canadian tariff question, commercial and transportation groups must be distinguished from industrial groups and from each other, for, as with farmers, so with these, the attitude of each towards protection has swung from pole to pole depending upon the requirements of particular immediate situations.

Though farmers, merchants, transportation interests, and industrialists have all changed their stands on tariff policy from time to time in Canadian history, they have never been on the same side of the argument at the same time. Manufacturers of farm machinery today, for example, would be in agreement with prairie farmers that raw materials and parts for machine production should enter the country duty-free; but beyond that their interests in protection place them in complete opposition to the prairie farmer. Historically it is true to say, with minor exceptions, that when the Canadian farmer has been protectionist the merchant, manufacturer, and transportation interests have favoured free trade, and when the farmer has sought free trade the others have been protectionist.

Previous chapters have given brief attention to pre-Confederation situations where tariff had significance for agricultural policy.[1] It is sufficient here to recall the following facts: that agrarian protectionist sentiment was expressed without avail in the Maritimes against the free-port legislation of 1818 and succeeding years, legislation which was sought and secured by the merchant group; that on the St. Lawrence the farmers, likewise protectionist, rejoiced at the passage of the Huskisson legislation of the eighteen-twenties which imposed barriers against the importation of agricultural provisions to the St. Lawrence, but that their rejoicing was extremely short-lived because of the effective vigour with which the St. Lawrence merchants attacked this legislation; and, finally, that the agricultural duties of the eighteen-forties were of slight interest to the St. Lawrence farmers because farm produce by this time was normally flowing out of instead of into the country, from Canada to the United States instead of from the United States to Canada.

The two decades preceding Confederation saw marked changes in the attitudes of Canadian groups towards protection. Merchants remained free traders, now concerned that Americans should permit free trade in Canadian produce. Farmers, with growing American markets for their produce, no longer cared whether or not there were

[1]See above, pp. 41-2, 90-4, 112.

tariff walls against the possible entry of American farm products. But the most important new element in the situation was the gradual emergence of Canadian industry and the even more gradual realization among industrialists of their community of interest on the basis of protective tariffs. This development will be analysed below.[2] We shall now consider briefly the agricultural implications of Canadian-American reciprocity, 1854-66.

2. Reciprocity, 1854-66

The background of the reciprocity movement, associated with the British repeal of the Corn Laws after 1846, has been thoroughly analysed in other studies.[3] Here only the agrarian aspect need be stressed. The central point is that the Reciprocity Treaty of 1854 exemplifies clearly the case of a governmental policy generally recognized as beneficial to Canadian agriculture, but made effective primarily on the initiative and urging of the commercial group.

It was easy before 1854 to indicate where the Canadian farmer would stand to gain from reciprocity with the United States. In 1842 the Americans had imposed a duty of 25 cents a bushel on wheat and $14.00 a ton on flour.[4] In 1846 they had put a 20 per cent *ad valorem* duty on grain and flour along with an equal rate on logs and boards and 30 per cent on manufactured goods.[5] Though Canadian farm exports to the United States comprised a wide range of products other than breadstuffs, nevertheless the latter were of great relative importance,[6] and the prospect of wiping out the duty thereon was bound to appeal to Canadian farmers.

The active pressure for reciprocity in Canada, however, came from merchants and processors of a agricultural produce. William Hamilton Merritt, a St. Catharines miller, made it his personal mission in life to secure the treaty. Arguing that the alternative to reciprocity was annexation he urged the farmer's interest in the following terms: "Were our products admitted into their markets

[2]See below, pp. 256-8.

[3]See particularly Masters, *Reciprocity Treaty of 1854;* Tucker, *Canadian Commercial Revolution.*

[4]Tucker, *Canadian Commercial Revolution*, pp. 111-12.

[5]*Ibid.*, pp. 136-7.

[6]In 1856 wheat and flour made up more than two-thirds of American imports from Canada (Masters, *Reciprocity Treaty of 1854*, p. 193).

254   CANADIAN AGRICULTURAL POLICY

. . . the Canadian farmer would at all times be placed on an equal footing, in all respects, with the western farmer . . . he would realize the advantages he possessed and resist any political change."[7] Merritt's chief interest in reciprocity, however, was not that it would facilitate exports of Canadian farm produce but that it would tend to bring the grain of the western states down the St. Lawrence.[8] The commercial interest in reciprocity was in the prospect thus offered for the fuller utilization of the St. Lawrence trade route recently endangered by the British abandonment of colonial preference.

The Reciprocity Treaty when finally made effective in 1854 contained an extensive list of agricultural products[9] which were to be admitted duty-free by the United States and the British colonies which ratified the treaty. The Americans had proposed the inclusion of implements and axes to be interchanged duty-free. The proposal was rejected.

It is extremely difficult to assess the effects of the Reciprocity Treaty on Canadian agriculture. Over the years of the treaty the trade figures between Canada and the United States in agricultural and other products increased greatly. Canadian exports of leading agricultural products increased manifold.

Yet other factors were at work. The treaty applied over the years during which occurred the Crimean and the American Civil Wars, a sharp and widespread financial crisis in 1857, a tremendous burst of railway-building in both the United States and Canada, a building up of eastern American cities, and a considerable expansion of agricultural production in the American West and in Canada West—later Ontario. These and other factors affected trade, production, and economic conditions generally to an extent which overshadows the Reciprocity Treaty.

Some Canadian exports of agricultural produce during the reciprocity period were not from Canadian farms. We have noted

[7]A speech made in the Upper Canada Legislature in 1846 as cited in *ibid.*, p. 9.
[8]Cf. Masters, *Reciprocity Treaty of 1854*, pp. 6-7, and Tucker, *Canadian Commercial Revolution*, p. 139.
[9]Grain, flour, and breadstuffs of all kinds; animals of all kinds; fresh, smoked and salted meats; seeds and vegetables; poultry; eggs; butter; cheese; tallow; horns; manures; plants, shrubs, and trees. As cited in Masters, *Reciprocity Treaty of 1854*, p. 87.

how Merritt, the Canadian miller, urged reciprocity as early as 1846, hoping thereby to draw American wheat down the St. Lawrence. Under the treaty there developed what has been called a "convenience trade,"[10] or trade in products common to both countries, which products moved across the boundary in different directions at different places, depending on local convenience.

Of particular significance to the trade in agricultural products was the convenience trade in wheat and flour.[11] Wheat from the American middle west entered Canada and passed down the lake and river system to be re-exported to the American markets by canal or rail through Buffalo, Oswego, Ogdensburg, or Cape Vincent. American wheat became flour in Canadian mills and was re-exported to American and other markets until 1858 when American customs authorities ruled the product not admissible under the Reciprocity Treaty. To the stream of American grain passing through Canada was added, of course, varying quantities of Canadian wheat and flour. In 1856 Canada imported $3,000,000 worth of grain from the United States and exported $8,000,000 worth of wheat and $4,000,000 worth of flour.[12] Americans, on the other hand, re-exported Canadian wheat and flour to the Maritimes and to Europe, through Boston and Portland, thus partially replacing direct exports from Canada thereto.

Saunders has pointed out that the Maritimes achieved very little in the way of taking advantage of the American market for farm produce.[13] The St. Lawrence provinces, however, exported much oats, rye, and barley to the United States. Toronto and Hamilton provided a market for American beef, pork and hams, mutton, butter, cheese, apples, eggs, and vegetables.

It is useless to try to estimate the agricultural benefit from reciprocity, or to suggest the relative proportion of benefit derived by the Canadian merchant, miller, and transportation group on the one hand and the farmer on the other. It is sufficient to suggest again the considerable degree of harmony of interest between the agricultural and commercial groups over reciprocity at this time.

[10]See, e.g., *ibid.*, p. 191.
[11]*Ibid.*, pp. 192 ff.
[12]*Ibid.*, pp. 193-4.
[13]Saunders, "Maritime Provinces and the Reciprocity Treaty" (*Dalhousie Review*, 1934-5), pp. 364-5.

3. Protectionist Views of Canadian Industry

The American abrogation of the Reciprocity Treaty was to a considerable extent due to Canadian protectionist sentiment and protectionist legislation. While Canadian farmers, merchants, and transportation companies were reasonably well agreed as to the benefits of reciprocity with the United States, another group in the community was not. The manufacturers were opposed. This situation illustrates the suggestion earlier made that the members of the trinity of common speech, "Industry, Commerce, and Finance," are not eternally united in opposition to the farmer's interests.

Canadian industry was in its early stages prior to Confederation. Protectionist sentiment among manufacturers took shape only gradually. There is some uncertainty whether the first effective impact of this sentiment on governmental policy occurred before 1858. What has been called "the first public meeting at which protection was advocated [in Canada]"[14] was held in Hamilton in 1847 to hear R. B. Sullivan discuss the tariff. Sullivan set forth the argument well known to Canadians ever since that Canadian farmers suffered from the lack of local urban markets because Canadian manufacturers were not protected against competition from English and American manufacturers.

Fiscal policy for the next ten years carried hints that the Canadian manufacturer was becoming recognized. Tariffs of 1849 and 1850[15] provided for the admission of specific raw materials at lower-than-average rates of duty. In the 1852 session of the Canadian Legislature there were debates[16] on a motion that tariff should serve the dual purpose of revenue and protection, one of the arguments being that every manufactory provided a market for the farmer. In 1853 new regulations concerned valuation for duty purposes and provided for the levy of *ad valorem* duty on the packing cases in which imports were contained. In 1856 Canadian tariff rates were raised from 12½ to 15 per cent and in certain cases, as on leather manufactured goods, to 20 per cent (by 19 Vic., c. 10).

Probably the earliest real triumph of an organized protectionist lobby in Canada was secured in the tariffs of 1858 and 1859. Depressed conditions after 1857 and the fiscal requirements of the

14Porritt, *Sixty Years of Protection*, p. 166.
15*Statutes of Canada*, 12 Vic., c. 1 and 13 Vic., c. 5.
16Porritt, *Sixty Years of Protection*, pp. 174-9.

government were formative factors. Manufacturers organized to offer specific suggestions.

In the spring of 1858 sixty-two manufacturers, merchants, and newspaper men formed in Toronto the Association for the Promotion of Canadian Industry "for the purpose of recommending such a readjustment of the tariff as would place the manufacturers of Canada on a footing of greater equality with those of the United States."[17] This association sent a delegation to the government to ask that the tariff be increased on manufactures of wood, iron, tin, brass, copper, India-rubber, and leather.[18] Cayley and Galt, successive Inspectors-General, raised the tariff rates in 1858 and 1859 partially in line with the manufacturers' suggestions. Rates on iron and hardware, machinery, cotton, and woollens they raised from 15 per cent to 20 per cent; those on clothing and leather advanced to 25 per cent.[19] The Executive Committee of the Association for the Promotion of Canadian Industry urged its members following the 1858 tariff changes to continue the organization "for the purpose of defending the ground which has been gained."[20]

The tariffs of 1858 and 1859 constituted perhaps the greatest single blow against the Reciprocity Treaty. Galt later minimized the protective elements in these tariffs, arguing the revenue needs of the government and admitting only that these schedules provided "incidental protection."[21] Masters, however, makes the point that the Canadian tariff rates of 1858 and 1859, though moderate as compared with American rates, were on a class of goods where they were particularly irritating to the Americans.[22] Galt also combined the former specific and *ad valorem* rates into new *ad valorem* rates to be charged according to the value of the product in the last foreign market through which it passed instead of in the country from which it was originally exported. This change was designed to favour direct importation from Britain by way of the St. Lawrence instead

[17]As cited by Clark in *Canadian Manufacturers' Association*, p. 1.

[18]Masters, *Reciprocity Treaty of 1854*, pp. 115-16.

[19]*Ibid.*

[20]As cited by Clark, *Canadian Manufacturers' Association*, p. 3.

[21]Canada, *Sessional Papers*, 1862, no. 23, as analysed in Innis and Lower (eds.), *Select Documents, 1783-1885*, p. 638.

[22]Masters, *Reciprocity Treaty of 1854*, pp. 116-17; also pp. xxiii, 121 ff., 204-8, 230.

of indirectly by way of New York. These various factors contributed powerful talking points for the Americans who were opposed to reciprocity and their campaign was eventually effective in securing abrogation of the treaty.

Canadian industrial interests were unable to act unitedly for any length of time prior to Confederation. With the passage of the Galt tariff of 1859 the manufacturers' association broke up. Efforts to reconstitute it in 1866 had no success.

The depression of the eighteen-seventies, however, led to the organization in 1875 of the Manufacturers' Association of Ontario with the single purpose of securing higher tariffs for its members. The Association carried on a strong campaign for protection, and after the election presented detailed tariff proposals to the Minister of Finance. Years later the secretary of the Association claimed that their activities had much to do with the triumph of protectionism in the elections of 1878, and, concerning the institution of the National Policy in 1879, he stated: "With very few exceptions the tariff which was proposed by Sir Leonard Tilley in his budget speech that session was the same as that suggested by the Manufacturers' Association."[23]

In 1887 the manufacturers' organization was renamed the Canadian Manufacturers' Association and in 1900 it was reorganized. At least until 1900 the Association was at times weak and disorganized. A common interest in the exploitation of the tremendous new western agricultural market after 1900 tended to unify the industrial group so that in the reciprocity struggle of 1911 it was a most effective force working to defeat the western farmer.

The tariff influence of the industrialist, however, has not depended on the scope or continuity of his formal organization. Tariffs are made up of countless items applying to the products of hundreds of producers and to scores of separate industries. Personal representations to government and the endless, cumulative publicity of the smaller groups or of individuals have had more to do with Canadian fiscal policy over the decades than has the voice of cumbersome official groupings of industrialists.

[23]*Industrial Canada*, November, 1901, p. 82, as cited by Clark, *Canadian Manufacturers' Association*, p. 7.

4. Development of Agrarian Anti-Tariff Views

A fuller understanding of the agricultural policy of Canadian government requires the attempt to trace the evolution of agrarian tariff views. Farmers on the Canadian side of the St. Lawrence were protectionist until the eighteen-forties when the opening American markets for their produce diverted their attention from the lowness of the Canadian tariff wall against American farm produce to the height of the American tariff wall against their own. Reciprocity was acceptable to them because it admitted their produce freely to the United States. Yet they were not confirmed free traders before Confederation.

Since 1911, if not since a considerably earlier date, the Canadian farmer has enjoyed the traditional characterization of champion of free trade. Some place along the way between the eighteen-forties and the early twentieth century the past was forgotten and the farmer turned from protection to free trade. When did this change occur? Had it occurred by 1867, by 1873, or 1879? What were Canadian farmers' views concerning Macdonald's National Policy?

Detailed analysis of the evolution of agrarian tariff sentiment over this period must await a more highly specialized treatment than is possible in this volume. First approximations are possible, however, through observation of the interests and activities of post-Confederation farmers' organizations. The Order of the Patrons of Husbandry, the "Grange," for example, appeared in Canada in 1872, and expanded its membership to a numerical peak in 1879 particularly in Ontario.[24] The activities of this organization suggest at least the attitudes of organized farmers. Tentative conclusions reached in this way follow.

First, middlemen rather than tariffs were the prime concern of the Grange.[25] Direct purchase in bulk from manufacturers, manufacturing in isolated instances, and ventures in colonization, insu-

---

[24]Wood, *History of Farmers' Movements in Canada*, pp. 13, 60. The following information on the activities of the Grange and of the Patrons of Industry is from this source unless otherwise stated.

[25]*Ibid.*, pp. 73-4. Wood says: "The *bête noire* of the Canadian agriculturist during the seventies and eighties of last century was the middleman in trade. Whether he be wholesaler, retail dealer or travelling agent, any one who occupied an intermediate position between manufacturer and final consumer was considered an encumbrance."

rance, and finance occupied their chief attention. Second, Granger reaction to proposals for a national tariff policy was for some years more favourable than unfavourable.

While forming the opposition after 1873 the Conservatives' main appeal to the farming community on the tariff issue was to the effect that a national policy would create and expand a home market for Canadian farm produce. This appeal was strong, but the farmers bettered it. They urged direct agricultural protection, the imposition of protective duties on farm produce to match the increased duties advocated by Conservatives for manufactured goods. The *Monetary Times* noted the harmony of agrarian and industrial interests on this point and suggested unified action.

In the winter of 1875-6 the Dominion Grange circularized the subsidiary granges with forms calling for the signature of members who favoured protection for agriculture. Five thousand signatures were secured, about one-third of the current membership. The Grange committee felt the results too inconclusive to present to the government. One student of the matter concludes from the evidence available that in 1876 the granges were inclined to favour Macdonald's tariff policy and that the majority of Grangers voted for Macdonald and for higher tariffs in 1878.[26]

Only gradually after 1879 did Canadian farmers come to oppose tariffs with any degree of certainty. Agricultural depression in the eighties was neither averted nor cured by national tariff protection. Farmers organized into granges were attentive to the pricing policies of middlemen and producers. They readily observed the effect of tariffs and bounties in the formation of combines and other monopolistic organizations. The Dominion Grange fought specifically for the removal of duties on coal oil and binder twine.

The Order of the Patrons of Industry, a farmers' organization as was the Grange, incorporated in Canada in 1890, gave greater emphasis to tariffs than did the Grange. They drafted a platform advocating, among other things, a tariff policy of tariffs for revenue only, duties on luxuries instead of necessities, and reciprocal trade

[26]*Ibid.*, p. 93. The tariff of 1879 replaced the 17.5 per cent average on manufactured goods by rates varying from 20 to 40 per cent and imposed specific protection on a variety of agricultural products. Wheat duties were set at 15 cents a bushel; rye, 10 cents; wheat and rye flour, 50 cents a barrel; oatmeal, ½ cent a pound; bacon, ham, and smoked meats, 2 cents a pound (*ibid.*, p. 94).

between Canada and other countries. In 1891 the Patrons sponsored a petition of 25,000 names to the government asking for the removal of duties on binder twine, salt, and iron. A 40,000-name Patrons' petition informed the government in the session of 1892-3 that Canadian farmers sought the removal of duties on agricultural implements, coal oil, wire fencing, and corn. At a Patrons' conference in 1895 delegates from Ontario, Quebec, and the West drafted their platform for the coming election, calling for the removal of duties on farm implements, binder twine, wire fencing, coal oil, iron, corn, cottons, tweeds, woollens, and tools.

Yet the farmers only gradually and uncertainly turned against tariffs. Duties of 20 per cent on agricultural implements imposed in 1879 as part of the National Policy were increased to 35 per cent in 1884. Neither the original rates nor the increase caused marked opposition. In 1893 the Dominion Grange petitioned Ottawa asking that "the duties on agricultural implements be reduced to fifteen per cent, as we consider this would leave the Canadian manufacturer a sufficient advantage over the foreign manufacturer."[27]

With agricultural development in Manitoba and the North West Territories the Canadian tariff picture became clearer. Western wheat growers, so obviously dependent on foreign markets, were never affected by the industrialist's home-market argument for tariffs. The western farmer from the very start presented a more united front against tariffs than the eastern farmer ever did.

While western development, therefore, consolidated tariff opposition, it also consolidated tariff support. The industrialist, protectionist from his earliest days on the St. Lawrence, saw added reason for protection in the western prospect. Merchants and transportation interests on the other hand, as pointed out on preceding pages, have frequently been Canada's great free traders. Not so, however, in regard to the trade with western Canada. So far as concerned the commerce with the growing western agricultural community, it was felt that free trade could only mean supply by American merchants, transport by American railroads. Particularly because of the western prospect, Canadian manufacturers, merchants, and the major transportation group of the country, along with the sustaining and interdependent banking houses in Montreal and Toronto were united in support of the National Policy of tariff protection.

[27] As cited *ibid.*, p. 98.

Earliest farmers' organizations in western Canada stressed their members' opposition to the National Policy. Distress and discontent arising out of crop failure and the collapse of the western land boom in the early eighteen-eighties, led to the organization of the Manitoba and North-West Farmers' Protective Union in Winnipeg in 1883. The declaration of rights which they drew up included demands for provincial control of natural resources, railway construction under provincial charters, provincial grain inspectors, construction of the Hudson Bay Railway, the removal of duties on agricultural implements and building materials, and the lowering of duties on articles of common consumption. The Union had three hundred delegates at its annual convention in Winnipeg in 1885, but was extinct by 1887. At one of the earliest western gatherings of the Patrons of Industry, held in Brandon in 1892, it was reported that one hundred sub-associations were in existence in the West, mostly in Manitoba, and that "Invectives were hurled against the tariff by Patron orators."[28] In 1893 D'Alton McCarthy, an independent federal member for North Simcoe who was sympathetic to the Patrons' tariff views, reported in the Commons that he had received 113 communications from western sub-associations of the Patrons of Industry petitioning tariff reforms.

Meanwhile the voice of the Canadian manufacturer, individually and officially, amplified by those of transportation, commerce, and finance, was the only guide effective in the shaping of Canadian fiscal policy. Liberals went to the polls in 1896 in full support, apparently, of their low-tariff platform of 1893. In Winnipeg in 1894 Sir Wilfrid Laurier had said: "I denounce the policy of protection as bondage—yea, bondage; and I refer to bondage in the same manner in which American slavery was bondage."[29] In an 1896 campaign speech in Deloraine, Manitoba, the Honourable Clifford Sifton declared: "Free coal oil, free clothing, and free implements you shall have if the Liberal Party are returned to power."[30] When elected the Liberals repudiated their 1893 tariff platform along with the election pledges given in its support.

28*Ibid.*, p. 125.

29As cited by Porritt, *Sixty Years of Protection*, p. 316. See *ibid.*, pp. 307 ff. for an account of the Liberal platform of 1893, and of speeches made by leading Liberals at that time.

30As cited by Wood, *History of Farmers' Movements in Canada*, p. 226.

Manufacturers and importers comprised the witnesses who appeared before the travelling tariff commission appointed by the new government in 1897. This commission did not go west of Winnipeg. Tariff changes of 1897 and succeeding years involved the introduction of imperial preference and some compromise with agriculture but no fundamental modification of the protective principle of the National Policy.[31] The Honourable Clifford Sifton came openly to avow a tariff policy based on expediency.[32] In 1905 Sir Wilfrid Laurier, speaking before the Canadian Manufacturers' Association in Quebec City said in part: "They [the settlers in western Canada] will require clothes, they will require furniture, they will require implements, they will require shoes—and I hope you can furnish them to them in Quebec—they will require everything that man has to be supplied with. It is your ambition, it is my ambition also, that this scientific tariff of ours will make it possible that every shoe that has to be worn in those prairies shall be a Canadian shoe; that every yard of cloth that can be marketed there shall be a yard of cloth produced in Canada; and so on and so on. . . ."[33] By 1905 tariff had ceased to be even nominally a political issue in Canada. Agrarian opposition to trade barriers was expected from the West but was taken for granted and largely ignored. In 1900 Manitoba and the North West Territories had eleven members at Ottawa; for the elections of 1904 and 1908 their representation was twenty. But western farmers and farmers' organizations had more urgent worries concerning grain-handling facilities, so that the Territorial, and Manitoba, Grain Growers' Associations and the Grain Growers' Grain Company had little time for tariff protest. Eastern farmers remained an uncertain quantity, apparently readily persuaded by the home-market argument for tariff protection. Nothing associated with the appointment of a tariff commission by the Liberal government in 1905 suggests any feeling in government or opposition circles that the tariff might constitute a real issue within the country.

31Features of the 1897 tariff constituting compromise with agricultural claims were the following: twine, barbed wire, and corn for feed were to go on the free list after January 1, 1898: rates on agricultural tools were reduced from 35 to 25 per cent, on portable machines from 30 to 25 per cent, and on coal oil from 6 to 5 cents per gallon (*ibid.*, pp. 230-1).

32See the report of his speech to the Young Liberal Club of Winnipeg in 1903, in *Canadian Annual Review of Public affairs*, 1903, p. 79.

33*Ibid.*, 1905, pp. 149-50.

The Tariff Commission of 1905-6 held hearings at two score places from Victoria to Prince Edward Island, half a dozen in the Prairie Provinces. Manufacturing and processing interests of all kinds presented the case for more protection, in general, and in particular for their respective industries. Such presentations were expected. Nor was there any surprise evinced by presentations by prairie farmers and farm organizations in favour of lower tariffs. The Manitoba Grain Growers' Association, the Manitoba Live Stock Association, the Saskatchewan Grain Growers' Association, the Canadian Society of Equity, and the Farmers' Association of Alberta all made representations before the Commission at its various hearings in favour of lower tariffs and an extension of British preference. Most surprising to contemporaries was the vigour and unanimity with which the farmers of Ontario argued for tariff relief before the Commission.[34] Individual farmers and official representatives of the Ontario Farmers' Association and of the Dominion Grange presented closely-reasoned cases for tariff reductions.

In November, 1906, before the government had announced its new tariff, a delegation representing the Dominion Grange, the Farmers' Association of Ontario, and the Manitoba Grain Growers' Association memorialized the Finance Minister, the Honourable W. S. Fielding, in Ottawa. Their final statement read: "We therefore ask, in the coming revision of the tariff, that the protective principle be wholly eliminated; that the principle of tariff for revenue only, and that revenue based on an honest and economic expenditure of the public funds, be adopted, and as proof of our sincerity, we will, if this position is adopted by the government, gladly assent to the entire abolition of the whole list of duties on agricultural imports."[35]

The Fielding tariff of 1906 showed slight recognition of agrarian political strength. Rates were reduced on agricultural implements; on mowers, harvesters, and reapers, from 20 to 17.5 per cent;

[34]"Perhaps the most outstanding incident of the investigation in Eastern Canada was the strong stand taken by the Farmers' organizations against any increase of duties and, in many cases, in favour of a lower tariff. . . . The great silent mass of the farmers, who have voted protection for so many years, either did not appear before the Commission, or else had changed far more in their opinions than recent elections would indicate" (*ibid.*, pp. 164, 167). See also Wood, *History of Farmers' Movements in Canada*, p. 241.

[35]As cited by Wood, *History of Farmers' Movements in Canada*, p. 248.

on threshers and separators, from 25 to 20 per cent; on specified tools, from 25 to 22.5 per cent. Gasoline was put on the free list as requested by western farmers. Sir Richard Cartwright acknowledged that their substitution of the three-schedule tariff for the minimum-maximum tariff which they had forecast was a concession to agricultural opinion. At the same time, however, preferential rates within the Canadian structure were made subject to specific rather than horizontal reductions below the general level, the implication being that such reductions were to be regulated in line with the "competitive needs" of particular Canadian industries. Rates on cottons and woollens were left practically unaltered despite particular requests from farmers' organizations for their reduction. Tariffs on agricultural produce were raised despite farmers' protests as to the uselessness of such duties.

5. The Reciprocity Issue, 1910-11

Canadian farmers spoke more emphatically and with a more united voice against tariffs in the reciprocity conflict of 1910-11 than at any other time in Canadian history.[36] Laurier heard a variety of requests on his trip to the prairies in 1910—requests for federal construction of terminals and of the Hudson Bay Railway, for example—but no requests were more consistently or forcefully presented than those urging greater imperial preference and reciprocity with the United States.[37] Tariff and reciprocity issues featured the petitions of the farmers' delegation to Ottawa in December, 1910, a delegation comprising five hundred western Grain Growers and three hundred eastern Grangers. The union of the western Grain Growers' Association with the Grange and the Farmers' Association of Ontario in 1909 to form the Canadian Council of Agriculture made possible a unity of thought and expression on the tariff which might otherwise not have been achieved.

[36]Fruit growers of Niagara and of British Columbia petitioned against reciprocity, thus constituting one of the few organized breaks in the farmers' ranks on this particular issue.

[37]See Canadian Annual Review, 1910, pp. 263 ff.; also Ellis, Reciprocity, 1911, pp. 21 ff. Ellis says that at the time of Laurier's western tour, summer, 1910, tariff reform was only one of a number of leading issues, but that by December, when the farm delegation went to Ottawa, the tariff had come to be the most important item on the farmers' list.

The farmers, however, had said much the same thing about tariffs in 1905 as they said in 1910. In the 1907 Fielding tariff they had gained nothing so drastically counter to the interests of Canadian industrialists as would be involved in genuine reciprocity with the United States. Their political strength then had not been great. Had it increased in the interval?

Relatively, agrarian strength had increased over the fourteen years of Liberal administration in the sense that the party was increasingly aware of criticism of its policies and actions. The naval question, for example, was politically disruptive in the extreme. Charges of administrative inefficiency and even of graft had been made from time to time. Nationalism in Quebec was disturbing. In October, 1910, the Nationalist candidate won the by-election in Drummond-Athabaska, a constituency which had been firmly Liberal since 1887. Farmers' demands even if presented with no more vigour than in former years were assured of a more sympathetic hearing.

But farmers' strength had been growing absolutely as well as relatively. The West had achieved recognized political significance. The census of 1911 was to show that the Prairie Provinces had trebled their population since 1901. Where the prairies had 7.8 per cent of Canadian population in 1901, by 1911 they had 18.4. Following the prairie census of 1906 the representation of the Prairie Provinces in the House of Commons at Ottawa had been increased from twenty to twenty-seven. The 1911 census would increase it even more sharply.[38] More particularly, the western farmers' organizations, the provincial Grain Growers' Associations of Manitoba and Saskatchewan, and the United Farmers of Alberta, had demonstrated their determination and resourcefulness over a period of years. In 1910 the three associations claimed thirty thousand members. The official organ, the *Grain Growers' Guide* was an influential instrument of publicity and persuasion. Recording a realization of these factors and commenting on the farmers' delegation to Ottawa in 1910 the *Toronto Globe* said: "The movement of the Western farmers and their alliance with their friends of Ontario and the East, to secure Tariff reductions, cannot be brushed aside lightly. The growth of the West is so rapid that it will certainly hold the

[38]The Representation Act of 1914 increased the prairie representation from 27 to 43 while the five eastern provinces lost representation, from 186 to 177.

balance of power in the next Parliament. At all events, in a dozen years, which is a very short span in the history of a nation, the West will be in a position to dictate the fiscal policy of the Dominion. To ignore it even now would be folly."[39] The appearance of political strength which the farmers were able to display in 1910 persuaded Sir Wilfrid Laurier that the Liberal party should very markedly revise its tariff policy, that it should modify its adherence to the National Policy of protection by seeking reciprocity with the United States. The party was not easily convinced that the farmers had finally acquired strength to enforce the claims which they had for years made unheeded. Some members remained unconvinced; some, like Sifton, broke with the party in disagreement. However, the announcement made by the Minister of Finance early in 1911 of the terms of a reciprocity agreement newly secured with the United States was a recognition of the political strength of Canadian farmers in general and of those of the West in particular at that time.

The reciprocity agreement, however, required concurrent legislation in the American Congress and the Canadian Parliament. Congress eventually enacted it. After months of opposition in the Canadian House, Laurier dissolved Parliament and took the matter to the polls.

The campaign and election of 1911 have been fully analysed in other sources,[40] and require only brief comment here. It is enough to recall that in the election the party-standing in the House was almost exactly reversed, with one hundred and thirty-three Conservatives and eighty-eight Liberals returned. Ontario returned its greatest Conservative majority up to that time, seventy-two to fourteen. British Columbia returned no Liberals. Quebec returned twenty-seven Conservatives and Nationalists to thirty-eight Liberals. The Maritimes returned sixteen Conservatives to nineteen Liberals and the Prairie Provinces ten Conservatives to seventeen Liberals. Saskatchewan and Alberta returned only one Conservative each, Manitoba only one Liberal.

[39]*Toronto Globe*, Dec. 16, 1910, as cited in *Canadian Annual Review*, 1910, pp. 335-6.

[40]See *Canadian Annual Review*, 1911, *passim;* Ellis, *Reciprocity, 1911;* Tansill, *Canadian-American Relations*, chap. xiv; Dafoe, *Clifford Sifton*, chap. xiii.

The reciprocity conflict of 1911 in Canada offers an extremely interesting and informative study in pressure-group organization and tactics. Farmers' organizations with few exceptions fought for reciprocity and for the party which at the time happened to stand for reciprocity. Industrialists, merchants, and transportation interests with equally few exceptions fought against reciprocity as individuals and in organized groups. The long lists of boards of trade, even on the prairies, which went on record as opposed to reciprocity recorded the adoption of the National Policy by the Canadian merchant class, the class which a century before had been as much in favour of free trade as farmers of the day were in favour of protection. Instruments of persuasion were the press, the platform, the pulpit, and undoubtedly endless conversation. Slogans and symbols—the flag and the Empire—were more effective than analysis. The election went to the group best able to employ the instruments and devices of persuasion. In place of reciprocity the Canadian farmer was granted the Canada Grain Act and the Agricultural Instruction Act.[41]

Infrequently mentioned but worthy of consideration is the fact that the reciprocity agreement of 1911 had no provision for free interchange of industrial goods. It was essentially an arrangement providing for free trade in natural products, as had been the agreement of 1854. Schedule B of the agreement provided for lower and identical rates of duty on a considerable list of products including agricultural implements, but no such articles except barbed wire were listed in schedule A, the group of free products. In other words, the concessions which Canadian farmers would have secured under the 1911 reciprocity agreement, had it become effective, would have been those provided by the American people in better markets for Canadian farm produce, rather than by Canadian industrialists in cheaper farm equipment and supplies. Canadian industrialists in 1911 rallied to the defeat of an agreement which in itself asked practically nothing of them. They fought it for what it might lead to, a later agreement which might not leave their position of economic privilege untouched.

6. *Tariffs After 1920*

Re-establishment of the Wheat Board was a more urgent matter than tariff reform for the Progressives elected in 1921. By 1923,

[41]*Statutes of Canada*, 2 Geo. V, c. 27 (1912), and 3-4 Geo. V, c. 5 (1913).

however, further progress in the former matter was clearly not to be secured in Parliament. In the session of 1923 the Progressives and the few western Liberals in the House chafed openly against the insistence of the Minister of Finance, the Right Honourable W. S. Fielding, on a "stabilized" tariff. Registering protest against the continuance of what was essentially the Fielding-Laurier tariff of 1907, the Progressives cut the majority on the budget vote in 1923 to a margin of one.

This served as a warning for the next session. Also the retirement of Sir Lomer Gouin from the Liberal Cabinet and the ill-health of Mr. Fielding appeared to weaken the Liberal insistence on tariff rigidity. In any case the budget of 1924 contained provision for the reduction of duties on farm implements and for the removal of the sales tax therefrom. Corresponding adjustments were made on the raw materials entering into the manufacture of farm implements.

The tariff reductions of 1924 along with those on the cheaper makes of cars in 1926 and of the Dunning budget of 1929 were overshadowed by the upward changes instituted by the Conservative government in 1930 and after. These changes were greater than any instituted since 1879. Dairymen's representations secured a tariff on butter. The new tariff rates constituted an emergency measure designed to avert depression, rather than a new National Policy. Reductions made after 1933 were insufficient to restore the rates to the level of the late nineteen-twenties, except for those on agricultural implements and automobiles.[42]

7. Summary

Canadian farmers have changed views on the tariff question from one extreme to the other. Over the past one hundred and fifty years they have been protectionist longer than they have been free traders. They have had little success either in securing tariff protection when they were protectionist or in securing freedom of trade when they were free traders. Exceptions have occurred when other groups in the community have sought and secured fiscal policies which for the time being were also sought by farmers. The Reciprocity Treaty of 1854 offers the best if not the only example of such an exception.

[42]Mackintosh, *Economic Background of Dominion-Provincial Relations,* p. 95.

The history of the National Policy stands as a measure of the ability of Canadian, and particularly western Canadian, farmers to influence governmental policy. From 1879 to 1930 the National Policy prevailed without significant modification. Agrarian opposition to this policy reached peaks of strength from 1907 to 1911, and again in the early nineteen-twenties. Each time agrarian political strength was insufficient to secure more than alternative satisfaction.

Tariff changes in Canada since 1930, whether up or down, constitute no part of the National Policy instituted in 1879. The National Policy came to an end by 1930. This was so, however, not because of any waxing of agrarian political strength, but because the National Policy had by that time fulfilled its purposes. It was designed, along with the Pacific railroad, the federal immigration and homestead policies, and Dominion lands, to serve "the purposes of the Dominion"; in effect, to establish on the prairies a new agricultural frontier attached economically to the central provinces. While this purpose was being accomplished, after 1900, western farmers were unable to secure any basic modification of the National Policy, while, at the same time, western Legislatures were unable to secure the transfer of their natural resources, of "Dominion lands." The transfer of the natural resources to the western provinces in 1930 signified that the "national" policy out of which Confederation grew in 1867, and of which Macdonald's National Policy of tariffs was but a part, had been fulfilled.

The history of Canadian tariff policy lends support, negatively, to the hypothesis put forward in other chapters of this study, that Canadian farmers have been a factor of any significance in directing government policy only when their interests have clearly coincided with those of some other group in the community, whether merchant, carrier, or manufacturer. This hypothesis appears true despite an unbroken numerical predominance of farmer electors throughout Canadian history.

CHAPTER XI

CONCLUSION

THE conclusions which one may draw from a study of Canadian agricultural policy are given added emphasis when contrasted with common assumptions on the subject. Among these assumptions are the following: that agriculture is the basic Canadian economic activity, and always has been; that down through the centuries, British and Canadian governments have assisted agriculture in British North America at all times and in every imaginable way; that Canadian agriculturists, because of their numbers, their vigour and organizing ability, and their group loyalty, have had a consistently strong voice in the formulation of government policy; that government assistance to agriculture has commonly been extended on the initiative of agricultural groups and in proportion to their political strength. Moreover, regarding farming practice, typical views have always been that Canadian farmers are reactionary, strongly inclined to ancestor worship; that their farm practices fall far short of the best and most modern methods; that they are typically destructive of land, they "mine the land"; that they specialize too highly, putting "all their eggs in one basket"; that they keep too few livestock; that there are "good" agricultural practices and "bad" agricultural practices, a right way and many wrong ways of carrying on each agricultural pursuit; that a major purpose of governmental assistance to agriculture is to make clear the distinction between good and bad practices, but that the fight against apathy is long and arduous. Another perennial belief, contradictory to some of those listed above, has been that Canadian agriculture, with the support and guidance of governmental agencies, is, at each particular point of time, on the verge of a great revival, a renaissance.

The findings arising from this study of Canadian agricultural policy do not contradict all the common beliefs set forth above; they do belie the impression which these beliefs create when taken as a whole and indicate in the majority of the beliefs considered individually a greater degree of error than of truth. In this summary the findings will be sorted out and stated concisely, and then related to the historical context in order to indicate how they have applied in time and space.

In the first place, agriculture was not, by any test, other than that of numbers, Canada's leading economic activity until comparatively recent times. Until perhaps a hundred years ago it was not agricultural prospects which attracted newcomers to venture energies and resources in the New World. The profitable and attractive opportunities were of other sorts, generally commercial, varying with time and place. Agriculture, it might be said, was not indigenous to Canada; it was established and expanded only under conditions of extreme and prolonged difficulty.

Second, though unattractive in itself for over two centuries after the first settlements in territory now Canadian, domestic agriculture was always considered essential to the profitable and safe conduct of those activities which were of prime economic interest. This is not to concur in the neo-physiocratic interpretation of Canadian agriculture, which considers that the situation is made plain when agriculture is described as a "basic" industry, but merely to say that agriculture was held necessary for what it could offer.

Third, as a result of the above factors, efforts have been made, from the earliest days of settlement in North America, to foster agricultural development. Government assistance has been typically extended to agriculture because of what agriculture was expected to do for other dominant economic interests in return for assistance, rather than for what such assistance might do for agriculture.

Fourth, agricultural organization and the pressure of organized farm groups have been, at least until recently, of negligible importance in shaping the agricultural policy of the Canadian government. Canadian farmers have generally been powerless to secure assistance on their own initiative, though they have generally accepted whatever assistance has been extended as better than nothing. During the period covered by this study they have generally been powerless to secure assistance which would benefit them at the expense of other substantial groups within the community. Canadian tariff history offers the clearest proof of this fact.

Fifth, Canadian agricultural policy has ordinarily been designed to encourage uneconomic uses of the factors of production. It has been designed to put people on the land, or to retain those already there, when comparative economic opportunities would have drawn them elsewhere. In this broad sense agricultural policy may or may not be classed as misguided, depending on definitions. In a narrower sense much of the aid and encouragement extended to Canadian agriculture over the centuries can be termed misguided on the basis that it commonly assumed an absolute quality in "good" and "bad" farming practices. Let us assume, for example, that it was desirable to develop agriculture in Nova Scotia or in New Brunswick after 1800, there was still no justification for trying to transplant British methods of "high" cultivation to the frontier farming areas, or to deride the frontier farmer for failing to embrace the latest advances in Old Country cultural practices. Those administering agricultural encouragement have frequently failed to recognize the relativity of good and bad farming techniques. The farmers themselves have been more realistic on this point than have their advisors.

Finally, Canadian agricultural policy can be understood only by reference to the conception of the functions of agriculture which prevailed during particular historical times and in particular places. The detailed form of this concept has varied, as outlined in preceding chapters and as sketched below, but the underlying uniformity is that agriculture in the New World has been held essential to the erection and maintenance of empire, by the French, the British, and eventually by the central Canadian provinces. Agriculture was held essential for the maintenance of empire whether territorial, economic, or ecclesiastical. Imperial interests long were centred in France and England, and so far as territorial ambitions were concerned these were the significant groups. On the economic plane, however, Old Country groups were eventually superseded by groups which established themselves close at hand in Halifax, Montreal, and York (Toronto), groups which originally were mere branches of Old World commercial houses, but which became more and more independent of external control. For territorial empire, agriculture has been considered essential as an instrument of defence, providing arms-bearers, transport, and provisions. The economic interest in agriculture, on the other hand, related first to the universal need for cheap, abundant, and readily available provisions for New World commerce; later to the profitable character of the wheat trade, and of the investment processes associated with immigration and the expansion of agricultural settlement.

These points can be illustrated by a brief concluding reference to the findings of this study as elaborated in preceding chapters.

The fur trade was the leading economic activity on the mainland during the French régime, and agricultural development was fostered in order that the French fur-trade route (the St. Lawrence) might be defended first against the Dutch, and later against the English, with their Indian allies. Assistance to agriculture included subsidies to immigration and settlement, the selection and supervision of settlers, marriage and family bonuses, crop bonuses, livestock importation, and the establishment by local officials of experimental and demonstration gardens and farm yards. Broader French empire expectations saw the fur trade as but one element in the total picture, the broader interests including the cod fisheries and the codfish trade, as well as the production of sugar on West Indies plantations. The mercantile implications of this programme have been outlined in Chapter II. In summary the important point to notice is that, for the whole set of processes, local agriculture was essential, for mainland defence and for provisioning all activities—the fur trade included. Efforts to encourage agriculture in New France had comparatively little success, and the long-protracted retreat of the French in favour of the English is a measure of the failure of the agriculture in New France as compared with that in New England.

Early English settlements in the Maritimes, Halifax, and Lunenburg, were planned and assisted as a defence against the French. Further to embarrass the French, the Acadians were dispossessed and their lands thrown open to settlement in the hope that New England settlers might be attracted. Settlement assistance extended to Loyalists after the Revolutionary War was prompted partially by considerations of compassion and partially by the uncertain hope that remaining British frontiers might be strengthened. As Nova Scotia and New Brunswick developed their respective profitable pursuits—namely, cod fisheries, the codfish trade, the West Indies provisions trade in Nova Scotia, and the timber and ship-building trades in New Brunswick—the necessity for a diversity of agricultural products became evident, and mercantile reasoning made it plain that such products should have local origins. Thus the provincial governments sought over the years to encourage cereal and animal production by means of bread-corn bounties, livestock importation, the organization of agricultural societies and boards, the establishment of livestock farms, the publication of agricultural literature, and by other means of lesser importance. Agriculture became established in Nova Scotia and in New Brunswick, and by Confederation there was a considerable animal husbandry in both colonies. But other activities expanded more than proportionately to agriculture, and at Confederation these colonies were more dependent on foreign sources of agricultural supplies than ever before. Prince Edward Island became an agricultural colony not by virtue of agricultural policy, but in line with the law of comparative costs, agriculture early having come to constitute the industry in which this colony had the greatest comparative advantage or the least comparative disadvantage.

Turning again to the St. Lawrence, upon the fall of New France, General Murray formulated plans for the new British colony envisaging an expansion of its agriculture so as to increase the supply of raw materials for the mother country and to provide expanding markets for her manufactures. Habitant indifference quietly nullified these plans. Between 1775 and 1820 considerable, if sporadic, encouragement offered to settlement on the upper St. Lawrence by the imperial government indicated the defence problems of the region and the expectation that careful agricultural settlement would contribute to their solution. With the defence problem in abeyance after 1820, formal encouragement only was offered to local agriculture till 1850, the instrument being boards and societies and grants thereto, in the British tradition. During this period agricultural settlement expanded phenomenally on the upper St. Lawrence with the spontaneous influx of transatlantic immigration, and the expansion was sufficient to satisfy all external demands upon it. Agriculturists raised some ineffective clamour for assistance, demanding protective tariffs especially, but governmental assistance to St. Lawrence agriculture throughout the period to 1850 was ritualistic and nominal.

Meanwhile agriculture on the St. Lawrence was developing new commercial attributes, new economic significance for the commercial group. By 1850 wheat was well established as an export staple of profitable proportions. Immigration and agricultural settlement called into play profitable investment activities in providing travel and transportation facilities, and in the creation of the capital equipment of the individual farm, of the farm community, and of the commercial centres which grew up to service the expanding farming areas. Adverse alteration in the rate of immigration and settlement seemed to underline, by contrast, the profitable nature of these activities.

With the occupation of the better lands on the upper St. Lawrence by the early eighteen-fifties, the rate of Canadian agricultural expansion was seriously checked. The problem was to restore the inflow of immigration and to continue agricultural settlement. A Bureau of Agriculture was organized in the provincial government, which Bureau from its inception acted almost solely as an immigration and colonization agency. Colonization roads were opened through undeveloped forest lands in the Ottawa-Huron tract. In the hope that the American agricultural frontier might come to be serviced by Canadian transportation agencies, huge sums were expended on a "grand trunk" railway linking the Canadian-American border with the seaboard *via* Canadian territory.

The gradual realization of the failure of all these plans was an important consideration working towards Confederation. American agricultural development had swept steadily westward and was turning northward west of the Great Lakes. There was no proof that the western territories north of the forty-ninth parallel, still in the hands of the Hudson's Bay Company, would ever make an agricultural region, but some were foolhardy enough to urge that they would. American settlement was moving successfully into territory similar to some of that controlled by the Hudson's Bay Company. In any event, there was no other prospect for the expansion desired by the commercial interests of the St. Lawrence. Settlement could not move step by step westward to the north of the Great Lakes in the way it had done in American territory, for athwart such movement lay one thousand miles of the Precambrian Shield, one thousand miles of rock and forest. To surmount this barrier a major bridge would have to be established; a Pacific railway was needed. If the western territories could not promptly be secured as a hinterland for Montreal and Toronto these territories would quickly and naturally become tributary to Minneapolis and Chicago. By 1860 the St. Lawrence needed for its continued prosperity an expanding agricultural hinterland.

By the process of elimination, only the West offered a possibility in this direction. Confederation and the British North America Act of 1867 provided the constitutional framework whereby Canadian government could establish agriculture on the prairies and assure that its commercial processes be tied to the urban centres of the St. Lawrence rather than to those of the middle-western United States. Since American expansion had advanced to the place where *de facto* American occupation of the British North-West was imminent, the plans for a Canadian sponsored agricultural development in this area envisioned definite defensive purposes in such agriculture.

Under the British North America Act the Dominion government shared concurrent jurisdiction with the provinces over agriculture and immigration. The provinces were left in undisputed charge of agricultural societies and boards and bonus policies related thereto. The design was clearly that the Dominion government should administer assistance to Canadian agriculture wherever such agriculture should be found to possess substantial commercial functions. Thus the four eastern provincial governments were left in control of their lands and natural resources, for these offered no immediate prospect for further agricultural expansion. Thus also the federal government took and kept control over the lands and resources of the North West Territories, for in these lay the only possibility for substantial agricultural expansion, with all that such expansion implied for eastern commercial, financial, and manufacturing interests.

Federal agricultural policy from 1867 to 1930 was concerned chiefly with agricultural commerce of various kinds. First and most continuous was the interest in immigration and agricultural settlement. The federal Department of Agriculture continued the interest and activities of the Department of Agriculture of the Province of Canada in these matters. The federal government planned and facilitated the construction of the Pacific railway in order to render accessible the vast western lands acquired from the Hudson's Bay Company in 1870. Immigration agencies were maintained abroad, well stocked with glowing prospectuses of western Canadian opportunities. Agents' commissions and the passenger warrant system were introduced. Western lands policies were gradually and haltingly liberalized, beginning with the nominal institution of the homestead policy in 1872. Until the latter part of the century, competition of other countries in the immigration markets, particularly that of the Australian colonies, of Argentina and Brazil, and of

American land and railway companies, was so keen that the results
of Canadian efforts were thoroughly disappointing. After 1900, however, a favourable conjuncture of circumstances indicated Canada as
the possessor of the "last great West" and turned the tide of migration largely towards her borders. Colonies established in the North-
West prior to 1900 assumed an importance not to be suspected from
their original size, for they acted as centres of attraction to draw
additional family members, friends, and compatriots of the first
colonists. Canadian immigration from 1900 to 1914 totalled 2,500,-
000 as compared with a total of 1,500,000 for the period from 1867
to 1900. Between 1920 and 1930 considerable additions to western
settlement occurred, partly facilitated by soldier re-establishment and
Empire settlement schemes, and partly unassisted.

The federal government became interested in the live cattle trade
with Britain because of its relationship to immigration and settlement. Canadian immigration agents in Britain saw the development
of a profitable export trade in Canadian cattle as the best possible
advertisement of Canadian agricultural opportunities to set before
British tenant farmers and farm labourers. The British agricultural
opposition to this trade, on the other hand, eventuated in the Richmond Bill, ostensibly a quarantine measure but applied clearly as a
protective measure. To escape "scheduling" under this measure,
Canadian cattle exports, and, behind them, Canadian herds, had to be
free from the slightest suspicion that they harboured one or more
of the "bovine scourges"—rinderpest, foot and mouth disease, and
pleuro-pneumonia. To assure the protection of Canadian herds and
of Canadian cattle exports, the Dominion government established
and maintained quarantine and inspection services at the ports of
entry and departure. The job was well done, and though scheduling
was imposed in 1892 the evidence bearing on the question of justification is confused. The range-cattle industry developed in the
foothills of the Canadian Rockies in the latter part of the nineteenth
century and the federal government assisted in this development by
the importation of breeding stock, by the establishment of western
quarantine, and by a faltering series of modifications in land policy.
Completion of the transcontinental railway, the institution of the
Royal North West Mounted Police, and the localization of Indians
on reservations contributed greatly to the range-cattle industry.

An important part of the federal government's agricultural problem after 1870 involved the discovery and demonstration of the agricultural possibilities of the Canadian West. At that time these possibilities were almost completely unknown. Clearly there was needed some staple product adaptable to the western territory and suitable for large-scale commerce. Parallel American experience, as well as that of the Red River Settlement, tentatively suggested wheat for this major role, but there was little proof. The Red River settlers, precariously established since 1812, had always grown wheat, but had dragged through long decades of uncertainty in the face of recurring major hazards such as frost, rust, grasshoppers, flood, drought, as well as many lesser ones. Among the most destructive of the hazards was frost, and earlier-maturing varieties were necessary to combat this menace.

A variety of motives surrounded the establishment of the experimental farm system, but among them was the important prospect of assessing the agricultural capabilities of the West. Dr. William Saunders, first Director of the system, devoted by far the greatest proportion of his energies, as well as the resources of the system, to the search for earlier-maturing wheats adaptable to the Canadian West, which would possess milling and baking qualities at least equal to the high standard set by the Red Fife variety. Foreign varieties imported and tested were not found suitable, but cross-breeding led to the discovery of Marquis wheat. Marquis has not contributed as much to the development of the Canadian West as is commonly supposed, for it became generally available only in 1910, just at the end of the great period of prairie occupation. A more important contribution to the occupation process, made by the experimental farm system, lay in the popularization of the summer-fallowing technique of dry-farming already well known in the United States. The great prairie expansion after 1900 covered territory where drought rather than frost was the chief hazard, and dry-farming methods were consequently of more significance than were early-maturing varieties.

With the development of a wheat trade based on western production, federal regulation evolved to care for it. Representations put forward by commercial groups formed the basis of the legislation out of which grew the Canada Grain Act of 1912. After

1900 agrarian protest, winnowed and deflected by royal commissions, contributed to a lesser extent to the formulation of controls. After 1900 the western agricultural group was more important in the Canadian economy than a farm group had ever been in Canadian history. The political position of this group was weakened, however, because there was no way in which it could withhold its contributions from the remainder of the economy; there was no way in which the farmers could "strike." Thus while the farm group was able to secure the appointment first of a warehouse commissioner and later of a board of grain commissioners, it was unable to secure other changes which it sought, such as the nationalization of the elevator system, the separation of terminal operation from grain merchandising activities, the prevention of mixing in terminal elevators, the closing of the Winnipeg Grain Exchange, reciprocity with the United States, or effective operation of the Hudson Bay Railway. Instead of a major breach in the National Policy of tariff protection, the farm group was given increased governmental supervision of the grain trade and federal assistance to agricultural instruction.

A consideration of the functions of agriculture remains an important aid towards the understanding of governmental policy to agriculture. Canadian agriculture has provided defence, provisions, and investment opportunities. The defence, or military, role is recurrent, as in the periods 1914-18 and 1939-45, and gives agriculture a degree of political strength which tends to survive briefly into post-war years. The provisioning role is continuous but no longer makes for bargaining strength except in mining, fishing, and lumbering regions where agriculture approaches only with difficulty.

As for providing investment opportunities, the frontier role, Canadian agriculture excelled in this capacity from 1900 to 1930 during the opening up of wheat production in the Canadian West. Wheat remains an important staple of Canadian commerce, but there is a great difference between a continuing commerce and an expanding one. The vitalizing influence of the West to the Canadian economy arose from expansion, from immigration and settlement, and from the capital investment necessary for the establishment of the wheat economy. The wheat economy is established; its limits tend to shrink rather than to expand. The vital frontier of Canadian investment in fixed equipment since 1930 has been in the Precambrian Shield instead of in the agricultural West, in newsprint and minerals instead of in wheat. These facts call for a new Canadian philosophy not only of agricultural functions and agricultural policy, but also of the relationship between the federal and provincial governments in regard to agriculture.

BIBLIOGRAPHY OF SOURCES CITED IN THE TEXT

GOVERNMENTAL documents, including those cited specifically in foot-note references, provided the bulk of the detailed information for the study. They are too numerous for enumeration here, but include the following: *Journals of Assembly* and their *Appendices,* and *Statutes,* of each of the British North American colonies from 1800 to 1870; *Sessional Papers* of the Province of Canada from their institution in the middle eighteen-fifties to 1867, and of the Dominion of Canada thereafter; *Statutes* of the Dominion; *Letter Books* of the Bureau of Agriculture of the Province of Canada from 1852, and of the Dominion Department of Agriculture after 1867 (Public Archives of Canada); *Minutes of the Executive Council* (Series E, Public Archives of Canada), 1841-67; Experimental Farm *Bulletins* from 1886; *Fifty Years of Progress on the Dominion Experimental Farms* (Ottawa: King's Printer, 1939); "Report of the State of the Government of Quebec in Canada," by General Murray, June 5, 1762 (Public Archives of Canada); I. D. Andrews, *On the Trade and Commerce of the British North American Colonies and Upon the Trade of the Great Lakes and Rivers* (House Executive Document, 32nd Congress, 2nd session, no. 136, 1852).

BOOKS

ATKINSON, W. C. *Historical and Statistical Account of New Brunswick, B.N.A., with Advice to Emigrants* (ed. 3; Edinburgh: Anderson and Bryce, 1844).

BOYD, HUGH. *New Breaking* (Toronto: Dent, 1938).

BREBNER, J. B. *New England's Outpost: Acadia before the Conquest of Canada* (New York: Columbia University Press, 1927).

BRITNELL, G. E. *The Wheat Economy* (Toronto: University of Toronto Press, 1939).

BULLER, A. R. H. *Essays on Wheat* (New York: Macmillan, 1919).

BURT, A. L. *The Old Province of Quebec* (Minneapolis: University of Minnesota Press, 1933).

CARROTHERS, W. A. *Emigration from the British Isles* (London: P. S. King & Sons, 1929).

CHAPAIS, J. C. *Notes historiques sur les écoles d'agriculture dans Québec* (Montreal: Extrait de la Revue Canadienne, 1916).

CLARK, S. D. *The Canadian Manufacturers' Association* (Toronto: University of Toronto Press, 1939).

CRAIG, J. R. *Ranching with Lords and Commons* (Toronto: Briggs, 1903).

CREIGHTON, D. G. *British North America at Confederation: A Study Prepared for the Royal Commission on Dominion-Provincial Relations* (Appendix 2; Ottawa: King's Printer, 1939).

..............*The Commercial Empire of the St. Lawrence* (New Haven: Yale University Press, 1937).

CRUIKSHANK, E. A. *The Settlement of the United Empire Loyalists on the Upper St. Lawrence and Bay of Quinte* (Toronto: Ontario Historical Society, 1934).

DAFOE, J. W.   *Clifford Sifton in Relation to His Times* (Toronto: Macmillan, 1931).

DALE, E. E.   *The Range Cattle Industry* (Norman: University of Oklahoma Press, 1930).

DAWSON, S. J.   *Report on the Exploration of the Country between Lake Superior and the Red River Settlement . . . the Assiniboine and the Saskatchewan* (Toronto: John Lovell, 1859).

EASTERBROOK, W. T.   *Farm Credit in Canada* (Toronto: University of Toronto Press, 1938).

ELLIS, L. E. *Reciprocity, 1911* (New Haven: Yale University Press, 1939).

ENGLAND, ROBERT.   *The Central European Immigrant in Canada* (Toronto: Macmillan, 1929).

. . . .*The Colonization of Western Canada* (London: P. S. King & Son, 1936).

GEMMILL, J. A. (ed.)   *The Canadian Parliamentary Companion* (Ottawa: J. Durie & Sons, 1885).

GETTYS, LUELLA.   *The Administration of Canadian Conditional Grants* (Chicago: Public Administration Service, 1938).

GLAZEBROOK, G. P. DE T.   *A History of Transportation in Canada* (Toronto: Ryerson, 1938).

GOURLAY, R. F.   *Statistical Account of Upper Canada* (London: Simpkins, 1822).

HALIBURTON, T. C.   *Historical and Statistical Account of Nova Scotia* (Halifax: Howe, 1829).

HANNAY, JAMES.   *History of New Brunswick* (Saint John: John A. Bowes, 1909).

HANSEN, M. L. and BREBNER, J. B.   *The Mingling of the Canadian and American Peoples* (New Haven: Yale University Press, 1940).

HARVEY, D. C.   *The French Regime in Prince Edward Island* (New Haven: Yale University Press, 1926).

HEDGES, J. B.   *Building the Canadian West* (New York: Macmillan, 1939).

. . . .*The Federal Railway Land Subsidy Policy of Canada* (Cambridge: Harvard University Press, 1934).

HIND, H. Y.   *Eighty Years' Progress in British North America* (Toronto: Stebbins, 1863).

. . . .*Essay on Insects and Diseases Injurious to the Wheat Crops* (Toronto: Lovell & Gibson, 1857).

. . . .*Narrative of the Canadian Red River Exploring Expedition and of the Assiniboine and Saskatchewan Expedition of 1858* (London: Longmans, Green, 1860).

. . . .*North-West Territory Reports of Progress* (Toronto: 1859).

INNIS, H. A.   *The Cod Fisheries* (New Haven: Yale University Press, 1940).

. . . .(ed.)   *The Dairy Industry in Canada* (New Haven: Yale University Press, 1937).

. . . .*The Fur Trade in Canada* (New Haven: Yale University Press, 1930).

Innis, H. A. (ed.) *Select Documents in Canadian Economic History, 1497-1783* (Toronto: University of Toronto Press, 1929).
............and Lower, A. R. M. (eds.) *Select Documents in Canadian Economic History, 1783-1885* (Toronto: University of Toronto Press, 1933).

Innis, M. Q. *Economic History of Canada* (Toronto: Ryerson Press, 1935).

Johnston, J. F. W. *Notes on North America: Agricultural, Economical and Social* (Edinburgh: Wm. Blackwood & Sons, 1851).

Johnston, S. C. *A History of Emigration from the United Kingdom to North America, 1763-1912* (London: Geo. Routledge & Sons, 1913).

Kelly, L. V. *The Range Men* (Toronto: Briggs, 1913).

Lower, A. R. M. *The North American Assault on the Canadian Forest* (Toronto: Ryerson, 1938).
............and Innis, H. A. *Settlement and the Forest and Mining Frontiers* (Toronto: Macmillan, 1935).

Macdonald, Norman. *Canada, 1763-1841: Immigration and Settlement* (London, New York: Longmans, Green, 1939).

MacGibbon, D. A. *The Canadian Grain Trade* (Toronto: Macmillan, 1932).

MacGregor, John. *British America* (Edinburgh: Blackwood, 1832).

MacInnes, C. M. *In the Shadow of the Rockies* (London: Rivingtons, 1930).

Mackintosh, W. A. *Agricultural Cooperation in Western Canada* (Kingston: Queen's University Press, 1924).
............*The Economic Background of Dominion-Provincial Relations: A Study Prepared for the Royal Commission on Dominion-Provincial Relations* (Appendix 3; Ottawa: King's Printer, 1939).
............*Prairie Settlement: The Geographical Setting* (Toronto: Macmillan, 1934).

Macoun, John. *Manitoba and the Great North-West* (Guelph: World Publishing Co., 1882).

Masters, D. C. *The Reciprocity Treaty of 1854* (London: Longmans, Green, 1937).

Maxwell, J. A. *Federal Subsidies to the Provincial Governments in Canada* (Cambridge: Harvard University Press, 1937).

Monro, Alexander. *New Brunswick, with a Brief Outline of Nova Scotia and Prince Edward Island* (Halifax: Richard Nugent, 1855).

Moorhouse, Hopkins. *Deep Furrows* (Toronto: McLeod, 1918).

Morton, A. S. and Martin, Chester. *History of Prairie Settlement and "Dominion Lands" Policy* (Toronto: Macmillan, 1938).

Munro, W. B. *Documents Relating to the Seigniorial Tenure System in Canada* (Toronto: Champlain Society, 1908).
............*The Seigniorial System in Canada* (New York: Longmans, 1907).

Murchie, R. W., et al. *Agricultural Progress on the Prairie Frontier* (Toronto: Macmillan, 1936).

Neatby, Hilda. *Administration of Justice under the Quebec Act* (Minneapolis: University of Minnesota Press, 1937).

PATTON, H. S. *Grain Growers' Cooperation in Western Canada* (Cambridge: Harvard University Press, 1928).

POPE, JOSEPH (ed.) *Confederation Documents* (Toronto: Carswell, 1895).

............*Correspondence of Sir John A. Macdonald* (Toronto: Oxford University Press, 1921).

PORRITT, EDWARD *Sixty Years of Protection in Canada, 1846-1912* (Winnipeg: Grain Growers' Guide, 1913).

RUTHERFORD, J. G. *The Cattle Trade of Western Canada* (Ottawa: King's Printer, 1909).

SALONE ÉMILE. *La Colonisation de la Nouvelle-France* (ed. 3; Paris: E. Guilmote, 1906).

STOCK, A. B. *Ranching in the Canadian West* (London: Macmillan, 1912).

STOCK, RALPH. *The Confessions of a Tenderfoot* (London: Holt, 1913).

SWANSON, W. W. and ARMSTRONG, D. C. *Wheat* (Toronto: Macmillan, 1930).

TANSILL, C. C. *Canadian-American Relations, 1875-1911* (New Haven: Yale University Press, 1943).

TROTTER, BEECHAM. *A Horseman and the West* (Toronto: Macmillan, 1925).

TROTTER, R. G. *Canadian Federation, Its Origins and Achievement* (Toronto: Dent, 1924).

TRUEMAN, HOWARD. *Early Agriculture in the Maritime Provinces* (Moncton: Times Printing Co., 1907).

TUCKER, G. N. *The Canadian Commercial Revolution, 1845-51* (New Haven: Yale University Press, 1936).

WEBB, W. P. *The Great Plains* (Boston: Ginn, 1931).

WHITELAW, W. M. *The Maritimes and Canada before Confederation* (Toronto: Oxford University Press, 1934).

WILGUS, W. J. *The Railway Interrelations of the United States and Canada* (New Haven: Yale University Press, 1937).

WOOD, L. A. *A History of Farmers' Movements in Canada* (Toronto: Ryerson, 1924).

YOUNG, JOHN. *Letters of Agricola* (Halifax: Holland & Co., 1822, reprinted 1922).

UNPUBLISHED THESES

ABBOTT, H. J. E. "The Marketing of Live Stock in Canada" (unpublished thesis: University of Toronto, 1923).

GORHAM, R. P. "Development of Agricultural Administration in Upper and Lower Canada in the Period before Confederation" (manuscript in Main Library, Department of Agriculture, Ottawa).

JONES, R. L. "History of Agriculture in the Province of Canada" (unpublished thesis: Harvard University, 1938).

ARTICLES

ASHTON, E. J. "Soldier Land Settlement in Canada" (*Quarterly Journal of Economics*, vol. XXXIX, May, 1925), pp. 488-98.

BURTON, F. W. "The Wheat Supply of New France" (Royal Society of Canada, *Transactions*, vol. XXX, sect. II, 1936), pp. 137-50.

BURTON, G. L. "The Early Development of Cattle Ranching in Alberta" (*Economic Annalist*, vol. XI, June, 1941), pp. 41-6.

CARROTHERS, W. A. "The Immigration Problem in Canada" (*Queen's Quarterly*, vol. XXXVI, summer, 1929), pp. 516-31.

ENGLAND, ROBERT. "The Emergent West" (*Queen's Quarterly*, vol. XLI, autumn, 1934), pp. 405-13.

............"Land Settlement in Northern Areas of Western Canada, 1925-35" (*Canadian Journal of Economics and Political Science*, vol. I, November, 1935), pp. 578-87.

FOWKE, V. C. "An Introduction to Canadian Agricultural History" (*Canadian Journal of Economics and Political Science*, vol. VIII, February, 1942), pp. 56-68; reprinted in *Agricultural History*, vol. XVI, April, 1942, pp. 79-90.

GATES, P. W. "Official Encouragement to Immigration by the Province of Canada" (*Canadian Historical Review*, vol. XV, March, 1934), pp. 24-38.

INNIS, H. A. "Unused Capacity as a Factor in Canadian Economic History" (*Canadian Journal of Economics and Political Science*, vol. II, February, 1936), pp. 1-15.

JAMES, C. C. "History of Farming," in Shortt and Doughty (eds.), *Canada and Its Provinces* (Toronto: Glasgow, Brook & Co., 1914, vol. XVIII), pp. 551-84.

JONES, R. L. "The Canadian Agricultural Tariff of 1843" (*Canadian Journal of Economics and Political Science*, vol. VII, November, 1941), pp. 528-37.

LOWER, A. R. M. "Immigration and Settlement in Canada, 1812-20" (*Canadian Historical Review*, vol. III, March, 1922), pp. 37-47.

LUNN, J. E. "Agriculture and War in Canada, 1740-1760" (*Canadian Historical Review*, vol. XVI, June, 1935), pp. 123-36.

MACGIBBON, D. A. "Grain Legislation Affecting Western Canada" (*Journal of Political Economy*, vol. XX, March, 1912), pp. 224-53.

MACKINTOSH, W. A. "Economic Factors in Canadian History" (*Canadian Historical Review*, vol. IV, March, 1923), pp. 12-25.

MARTELL, J. S. and HARVEY, D. C. "The Achievements of Agricola and the Agricultural Societies, 1818-25" (Public Archives of Nova Scotia, *Bulletin*, vol. II, no. 2; Halifax: Public Archives of Nova Scotia, 1940).

............"From Central Board to Secretary of Agriculture" (Public Archives of Nova Scotia, *Bulletin*, vol. II, no. 3; Halifax: Public Archives of Nova Scotia, 1940).

MORRISON, H. M. "The Principle of Free Grants in the Land Act of 1841" (*Canadian Historical Review*, vol. XIV, December, 1933), pp. 392-407.

288 CANADIAN AGRICULTURAL POLICY

Murray, W. C. "Continental Europeans in Western Canada" (*Queen's Quarterly,* vol. XXXVIII, winter, 1931), pp. 63-75.

Oliver, E. H. "The Coming of the Barr Colonists" (Canadian Historical Association, *Report,* 1926), pp. 65-86.

............"The Settlement of Saskatchewan to 1914" (Royal Society of Canada, *Transactions,* vol. XX, sec. II, 1926), pp. 63-87.

Riddell, R. G. "A Cycle in the Development of the Canadian West" (*Canadian Historical Review,* vol. XXI, September, 1940), pp. 264-84.

Sage, W. N. "Some Aspects of the Frontier in Canadian History" (Canadian Historical Association, *Report,* 1928), pp. 62-72.

Saunders, S. A. "The Maritime Provinces and the Reciprocity Treaty" (*Dalhousie Review,* vol. XIV, 1934-5), pp. 355-71.

............"The Reciprocity Treaty of 1854: A Regional Study" (*Canadian Journal of Economics and Political Science,* vol. II, February, 1936), pp. 41-53.

Sellers, Harry. "The Early History of the Handling and Transportation of Grain in the District of Thunder Bay" (Thunder Bay Historical Society, *Reports of Officers and Papers of 1909-1910*).

Talman, J. J. "Agricultural Societies of Upper Canada" (Ontario Historical Society, *Papers and Records,* vol. XXVII, 1931), pp. 545-52.

Vrooman, C. W. "A History of Ranching in British Columbia" (*Economic Annalist,* vol. XI, April, 1941), pp. 20-5.

Wilson, Roland. "Migration Movements in Canada, 1868-1925" (*Canadian Historical Review,* vol. XIII, June, 1932), pp. 157-82.